"Eck makes a convincing argument that complex prose or attemp
frustrated readers and muddled ideas. He presents practical tech
write clearly and introduces tools that can help us to evaluate our p
of fun along the way."

Kate Bowers, *Head of the Department of Security and Crime Science,*
University College London, UK

"John Eck's *Writing with Sweet Clarity* is an imaginative, comprehensive, and altogether persuasive and practical 'kit of tools' for improving student writing. I enthusiastically recommend the
book for advanced undergraduate, master's, and PhD students. The book can assist students
regardless of their professional aspirations."

Thomas Blumberg, *Dean and Sheldon L. Messinger Professor of Criminology,*
College of Criminology and Criminal Justice, Florida State University, USA

"Eck provides an essential resource for anyone working in the social sciences with this clever,
simple, and useful guide to good writing. He takes you through key principles for each stage of
the writing process, including important tips for creating the tables, graphs, and diagrams. This
book is an exemplar of writing at its best!"

Danielle Reynald, *School of Criminology and Criminal Justice,*
Griffith University, Australia

"In true Eckian fashion, John cuts through the problems of convoluted academic writing and
provides straightforward guidance for us all. This guidebook is a must-have for students and
early academics who want to be educated and entertained about the basics of simple, meaningful, and audience-specific writing."

Cynthia Lum, *Department of Criminology, Law and Society,*
George Mason University, USA; and Co-Editor-In-Chief of the journal
Criminology and Public Policy

"Few academic programs provide systematic training in writing—the major form of scholarly
and professional communication. *Writing with Sweet Clarity* fills this gap. John Eck develops
the insight that the measure of a text is its success in communicating with its readers. His
treatment is comprehensive and systematic. And he followed his own good advice, writing a
text that will hold the attention of undergraduates and professionals alike."

Paul DiMaggio, *New York University, Department of Sociology, USA; and*
A. Barton Hepburn Professor Emeritus of Sociology and Public Affairs,
and Senior Scholar, Sociology Department, Princeton University, USA

"Finally, a contemporary work full of tips and exercises to improve writing process. Eck's practical guide infuses humor and kindness as he explains everything from the basics, to writing with co-authors, to editing and reviews. *Writing with Sweet Clarity* is now required reading for my graduate and honours students and strongly recommended in my other classes. A must read for anyone seeking to improve their written communication or wanting to help others improve theirs."

Sheri Fabian, *School of Criminology, Simon Fraser University, Canada; and Winner of the 2019 3M National Teaching Fellowship awarded by the Society for Teaching and Learning in Higher Education*

"The role of policing is changing, and our writing must be clear, concise, and convincing. Eck's ten simple commandments will entertain you and improve your writing skills. I found his book witty and easy to read. Every police officer needs this book."

Maris Herold, *Chief of Police, Boulder (Colorado) Police Department, USA*

"Writing in English is challenging for non-native English speakers like myself. We tend to write long sentences to appear sophisticated but create sentences that are hard to comprehend. I could not agree with John more on writing short sentences using active voice to alleviate this problem. I highly recommend this book to anyone in geography, planning, sociology, criminology, or related fields."

Lin Liu, *Department of Geography and GIS, University of Cincinnati, USA*

"In a world where we increasingly communicate by tweets and emojis, John Eck has published this marvelous book as a public service. Clarity of expression is vital in the arena of crime and policing decision-making. Students of this book will improve not just their grade, but also their connection to readers and policy makers."

Jerry Ratcliff, *Department of Criminal Justice, Temple University, USA; Retired London Metropolitan Police officer; and host of the popular Reducing Crime podcast*

"John Eck's *Writing with Sweet Clarity* is a tour de force on the craft and joy of academic writing in the social sciences. Brilliantly written and chalk full of great advice, with a touch of humor, this book is essential reading for current and aspiring academics."

Brandon C. Welsh, *Northeastern University, USA; and Director, Cambridge-Somerville Youth Study*

WRITING WITH SWEET CLARITY

In this book, criminologist and experienced educator John E. Eck draws on decades of academic and professional writing experience to provide an analytical toolkit for clear professional writing. The book focuses on the essential objective of clarity, and addresses topics seldom addressed in other books, such as ethics beyond plagiarism; writing with co-authors; organizing complex ideas; using analytics to improve writing; crafting strong beginnings and endings; using examples and metaphors; and integrating tables, charts, and diagrams.

As universities continue to demand writing-intensive courses in the social sciences, this book is indispensable in university settings and throughout a professional career. The reader will use the practical advice, examples, and exercises in this book to master a method for clear writing unimpaired by stereotypical academic jargon. The book will help both new and seasoned researchers seeking to translate their work into a clear and accessible presentation for both professional and lay audiences.

Designed for and field-tested with graduate and advanced undergraduate students, this lively and easy-to-read book will work for courses taught in criminology, sociology, geography, and other social sciences, and will enable scholars to extend and broaden the impact of their research.

John E. Eck is Professor of Criminal Justice at the University of Cincinnati. There he teaches courses in policing, crime prevention, and writing. He also studies and writes about ways to reduce crime at extreme crime places. John received his master's of public policy from the University of Michigan and his PhD in criminology at the University of Maryland. Before joining academia, John led the research operations at the Police Executive Research Forum in Washington, DC. He then headed the evaluation unit in the Washington/Baltimore High Intensity Drug Trafficking Area. His writing appears in over 150 books, chapters, journal articles, and prescriptive guides for the police, public, and researchers around the globe. In 2001, John assisted the United States District Court, Southern District of Ohio, in developing the Cincinnati Collaborative Agreement. This agreement is a blueprint to reduce police–community conflict and violence. He and his wife live in Ohio and Maine, where he enjoys stone sculpting.

WRITING WITH SWEET CLARITY

John E. Eck

Routledge
Taylor & Francis Group

NEW YORK AND LONDON

First published 2022
by Routledge
605 Third Avenue, New York, NY 10158

and by Routledge
2 Park Square, Milton Park, Abingdon, Oxon, OX14 4RN

Routledge is an imprint of the Taylor & Francis Group, an Informa business

Library of Congress Cataloging-in-Publication Data
Names: Eck, John E., author.
Title: Writing with sweet clarity / John E. Eck.
Description: New York, NY: Routledge, 2022. |
Includes bibliographical references and index.
Identifiers: LCCN 2021036726 (print) | LCCN 2021036727 (ebook) |
ISBN 9780367765620 (hardback) | ISBN 9780367746605 (paperback) |
ISBN 9781003167532 (ebook)
Subjects: LCSH: Social sciences-Authorship. |
Communication in the social sciences. | Social science literature-Publishing.
Classification: LCC H61.8 .E25 2022 (print) |
LCC H61.8 (ebook) | DDC 808.06/3-dc23
LC record available at https://lccn.loc.gov/2021036726
LC ebook record available at https://lccn.loc.gov/2021036727

ISBN: 978-0-367-76562-0 (hbk)
ISBN: 978-0-367-74660-5 (pbk)
ISBN: 978-1-003-16753-2 (ebk)

DOI: 10.4324/9781003167532

Typeset in Interstate
by Newgen Publishing UK

I dedicate this book to the *original* Tom Brady, a true friend, a good writer, and a lifelong mentor.

It is not often that someone comes along who is a true friend and a good writer. Charlotte was both.

E.B. White, the last line of *Charlotte's Web*

CONTENTS

Acknowledgments   xi
List of Figures   xii
List of Tables   xiii

Part I   Thinking about Writing   1

1   Introduction   3

2   The Ethics of Useful Writing   14

3   A Writing Process   23

Part II   Preparing to Write   31

4   Writing with Others   33

5   Getting Started   39

Part III   Writing   47

6   Order   49

7   Words   67

8   Sentences   85

9   Paragraphs and Longer Passages   97

10   Examples, Analogies, and Related Matters   108

11   Beginnings   123

12   Endings   139

Part IV   When Words Are Not Enough   **151**

13   Tables   153

14   Graphs   166

15   Diagrams   184

Part V   Rewriting and Revising   **199**

16   Editing   201

17   Reviews and Reviewers   208

Part VI   The End and Beginning   **217**

18   Future   219

     Further Reading   224
     References   230
     Index   236

ACKNOWLEDGMENTS

Many people helped teach me to write clearly once I left college. Unfortunately, I have forgotten the names of some of them. I apologize. I do recall Tom Brady, Gary Hayes, Bill Spelman, Darrell Stephens, Martha Plotkin, John Stedman, Cliff Karchmer, Karin Schmerler, Rana Sampson, and my other daily lunch companions at the Police Executive Research Forum. Within policing, I must single out for thanks Tom Carr, Maris Herold, Andy Mills, Howard Rahtz, and Jon Shane.

At the University of Cincinnati, Ed Latessa, Frank Cullen, J.C. Barns, and Michael Benson reminded me that some academics value clarity. I have been ridiculously fortunate in the graduate students who have taken my classes, hung out with me in my office and in coffee shops, and who are serious about writing: Tamara Herold, Shannon Linning, YongJei Lee, SooHyun O, and Troy Payne in particular. You inspire me and made teaching fun.

In the final stages of completing this book, and in the midst of the COVID-19 pandemic, I had the good fortune to teach a graduate course on writing. I could not have asked for a more engaged, funny, and supportive group. So I thank you Caroline Allen, Jamie Argueta, Hei Chio, Stacey Clouse, Xin Gu, Rachel Kail, Dylan Kearney, Katelyn King, Minxuan Lan, Feiyang Li, Bradley O'Guinn, Hyunjung Shim, Amanda Shoulberg, Destinee Starcher, Diana Sun, Poppy Theocharidou, Rushar Varlioglu, and Michelle Wojcik.

My lovely wife, Jennifer Stucker, encouraged me more than I can express. She put up with my incessant rants and months of work on this book. She provided solutions to knotty problems. Because of her eagle eye, this book has far fewer errors than it would without her. Many passages are clearer because of her suggestions. She pushed me to rearrange several chapters. And she drafted the index. But most of all, she gave me the confidence to believe I had something worth saying.

At Routledge, I thank Ellen Boyne for her championing my proposal to create this book. Her enthusiasm made a huge difference. I also must thank Kate Taylor and others on the Routledge team for their fast and friendly suggestions, answers to my questions, and help taking this book from an idea to reality.

Despite all the help and support, I fear I have left errors behind, which is mighty embarrassing in a book on writing. These are my mistakes.

FIGURES

3.1	The Writing Process Begins before Writing and Includes Revisions	24
4.1	Deciding Who Will Be the First Author	35
6.1	A Hierarchical Organization of Crime Places	60
6.2	A Problem-Solving Flow Chart	61
10.1	Examples and Analogies	110
14.1	The Three Layers of Graphs	167
14.2	Four Basic Graphs	170
14.3	Pie Chart: Calls to the Police from Eight Bars	172
14.4	Bar Chart: Calls to the Police from Eight Bars	172
14.5	3D Bar Chart: Calls to the Police from Eight Bars	173
14.6	A Terrible Graph: Calls to the Police from Eight Bars	174
14.7	Arbitrary Order: Calls to the Police from Eight Bars	174
14.8	Useful Order: Calls to the Police from Eight Bars	175
14.9	A Bar Chart with Three Variables	176
14.10	A Bar Chart that Would Look Better on End	178
14.11	A Bar Chart Flipped to Make Labels Easier to Read	179
14.12	A Terrible Time Series Graph	179
14.13	An Improved Time Series Graph	180
14.14	A Time Series Graph Showing a Policy Switch	181
14.15	Economic Recessions Do Not Seem to Influence Violence	182
15.1	Routine Activity Theory Imagined as a Triangle	187
15.2	Unbalanced Crime Triangle	188
15.3	Revised Routine Activity Theory Accounting for Place Managers	188
15.4	A Path Diagram of Broken Windows Theory	189
15.5	Word Length Impedes Comprehension	190
15.6	Four Versions of the Same Flow Chart	191
15.7	A General Problem-Solving Flow Chart	192
15.8	A Process Model of Gatherings	192
15.9	An Organization Chart Describing a Set of Definitions	193
15.10	A Diagram Summarizing Multiple Studies	194
15.11	Sherman's Police Crackdown Theory	194
15.12	An Example of the Last Stage in Layering	195
15.13	Exchange Is the Core of Social Science, Mostly	197

TABLES

8.1	Comparison of the Two Flesch Scales	87
8.2	Examples of Active and Passive Voices	91
9.1	Readability Changes	100
9.2	Original Paragraph's Summary Statistics	102
10.1	Using Multiple Examples to Clarify Ideas	112
11.1	The Beginning	138
12.1	Summary of Recommendations	141
13.1	Tables Have Advantages over Writing	154
13.2	Percent Predicted Cleared versus Percent Actually Cleared	155
13.3	Percent Predicted Cleared versus Percent Actually Cleared	156
13.4	Percent Predicted Cleared versus Percent Actually Cleared	156
13.5	Burglary Investigation Outcome Prediction Is 85.9 Percent Accurate	157
13.6	Percent of Places with Repeat Crimes by Neighborhood	158
13.7	Most Places Have No Crime, But a Few Places Have a Lot	159
13.8	Crime Is Concentrated in a Few Facilities, Regardless of Neighborhood	160
13.9	Crime Is Slightly More Concentrated in Neighborhood B	160
13.10	Prediction Accuracy and Errors	161
13.11	Classification of Police Problems	162
14.1	Calls for Police from Bars in Mt. Fog	171
17.1	Tracking Reviewers' Comments	214
18.1	The Art of Writing with Sweet Clarity	221

Part I   Thinking about Writing

1 Introduction

Becoming a Writer

Smoke cleared up my writing. If not for cigar smoke, I would write the way my college professors taught me. My professors, like yours, taught me to write truthfully. My professors, like yours, encouraged me to be useful. But my professors, probably like yours, did not teach me to express my ideas clearly. I had to learn clear writing on the job. I wrote this book so you can write clearly *before* you start your job. Or, if you already have a job requiring writing, to make you a better writer. As for the cigar smoke, I'll come back to that.

My job is to influence people. On your job, you too may need to influence people. As community workers, we want to assist residents and local businesses. As justice advocates, we want to create change. As government policy analysts, we want to improve government services. As consultants, we want our clients to do better. As teachers, we want to guide our students. As researchers, we want others to use our ideas. In these, and many more cases, we want our

DOI: 10.4324/9781003167532-2

writing to help improve the safety and well-being of others. There are numerous ways we exert influence. This book is about one of them: writing.

Writing is one of the most powerful ways to communicate, be it on paper or on a tiny screen. One reason is that it lasts. Speeches and conversations get forgotten. If remembered, they may be misremembered. Writing is stable. People can recall, retrieve, and spread written ideas.

When I left school in 1977, I knew how to be truthful and wanted to be useful. I thought I knew how to write. The University of Michigan's Master's in Public Policy program was superb. My professors were smart, rigorous, demanding, and funny. They had an immense influence on my life. My courses in economics, policy, decision-making, and political science gave me the sharp tools that I have wielded since. Almost everything I write uses these tools. But as I discovered later, I had not learned to write clearly.

You might not consider yourself a writer, but it is likely you will become one. Your choice will not be whether to write or not because most professional jobs require writing. Your choice is to write clearly or unclearly. If you want to be successful, you will choose clarity. By successful, I mean creating beneficial changes to some bit of the world.

Purpose of This Book

If you are like me, you have discovered that much of what you are reading is frustrating. I dislike reading articles and books written by academic researchers. Most of them make exciting topics boring. Many make simple ideas convoluted. When I was younger, I thought I was stupid because I had so much difficulty reading academic articles and books. Years after I left student life I had a revelation; I am not the brightest pebble on the beach, but I am not a dimwit. The problem is the authors of tortured academic texts. They produce muddles.

You have probably read many muddled narratives. Your professors have assigned unclear books and articles, and you read them. I did. You might have suspected your professor was feeding you bullshit, but you read it. I did. In time, you may have even developed a taste for it. I did. You probably became successful at reproducing it. I did. You may have received high grades by imitating the murky prose of the things assigned in your classes. Me too.

In a far tiny corner of philosophy, there is a debate about bullshit. One side of this debate asserts that bullshit is the intentional lack of interest in the difference between truth and falsity. Harry Frankfurt (2005), in his short book, *On Bullshit*, claims that the bullshitter does not care if what he says is true or false. He only cares about getting his way. In contrast, a liar knows the difference but chooses the falsehood. G.A. Cohen (2002), asserts that bullshit is writing that a reader cannot translate into something understandable. The writer might think her statements are true, but the reader cannot interpret what the writer had in mind. If a reader can translate the gobbledygook into a clear message, then the writing is not bullshit.

Much bad professional writing seems to be gobbledygook. But not all. Later, I rewrite examples of obfucationalized academic discourse. If my translations are valid, then the examples are not bullshit, of Cohen's sort. Much academic writing is not bullshit of the Cohen *or* Frankfurt varieties. It is just tortured writing. This book shows you how to avoid writing like a standard academic, even if you become an academic, standard or otherwise. By the time you complete this book, you will have the tools to write with *sweet clarity*.

But make no mistake, this book is a start, not an end. You will have to practice the techniques I discuss to make clarity a habit. Once it is a habit, then you are ready to consider style and art, but let's put off that discussion until the last chapter.

Is This Book for You?

Any person studying any social science should find this book useful. I teach doctoral students, master's students, and advanced undergraduates, so these are the people I have foremost in mind as my readers. A few of my students want to become academics. Others want to go into some policing or correctional agency. A good number of these want to work for a federal law enforcement agency. Some students want to work for a business. Others aspire to work with community groups, treatment organizations, or victim support groups. And others have no strong sense of where they want to work. If you are like any of these students, then I am writing for you.

Clear Writing and a Police Career

A friend told me this story of how writing influenced the direction of his career.

> Make writing a central theme of your life. Others will come to know you through your writing more than fleeting personal interactions; writing is permanent. From my early days in the Newark Police Department, I gained recognition from peers, supervisors, and executives through my writing. When I went through the police academy, instructors demanded we write reports in the first-person, active voice. You'd be amazed how many cops write in the passive voice and in the third-person ("The officer listed above was dispatched to ..." Good grief). First-person, active voice set me apart from my colleagues and launched my career. My style was soooo different from the others. Within six years the department promoted me to sergeant and assigned me to the Police Director's Office of Research, Analysis, and Planning, the highest level of the organization. I wrote policy and worked with legal affairs. Over time, I developed an intense passion to convey my thoughts, opinions, and arguments so others would care to read them.
>
> (Jon M. Shane, Newark Police Captain, retired.
> Associate Professor, John Jay College of Criminal Justice)

I assume that someday you will have a job that requires you to write. I assume that you will be asked to write about something that will have serious consequences for people in your organization and the people your organization serves. That is, if someone reads your work and follows your advice, then others may benefit. Taxpayers may get more for their tax money. Governments may treat their citizens more fairly or less harshly. People may not become victims of crime. Businesses may be better able to thrive. Those who have suffered may have a greater chance of leading safe, productive, and meaningful lives. If your writing contributes to any of these or other tangible outcomes, then you are a success.

You will not be a success if your readers struggle to understand your writing. If you cannot make your ideas clear, then even if you have a great idea it is unlikely anyone will pay attention. Worse, if your writing is not clear, and someone misinterprets it, then you can harm people.

Clear writing is clear writing. The principles of clear academic writing are not any different from the principles of clear police writing, clear community group writing, clear business writing, or clear policymaker writing.

What This Book Is *Not* About

No book on a topic can address all of it unless the topic is tiny or trivial. Writing is neither, so I imposed boundaries. If the topics that come next are what you want, then stop reading and find a book that addresses them.

It's Not about How to Conduct Research

I assume you have taken, or will take, a course in research. By research, I mean anything related to improving your understanding of your topic. This can include: bibliographic inquiries and literature reviews; data gathering and analysis; interviews and observations; legal and procedural inquiries; and consulting with experts and practitioners. I assume you know something about your topic or you are prepared to learn what you need before writing about it.

Writing nonfiction is entangled with research. I experience this entanglement daily. The process of writing reveals facts I need to pin down, so my writing pushes my research just as much as my research pushes my writing. Drawing a line between research and writing is artificial but necessary. I will touch upon research from time to time, but if you want solid advice on research, you need to read something else.

It's Not about How to Form Logical Arguments

Much writing involves putting things in a logical order, without gaps. I have an entire chapter devoted to ordering ideas. Nevertheless, I assume you have a reasonably good foundation in ordering your thoughts. I do not cover deductive logic: statements of the form, "If A and B then C; Here is A and B; Therefore, we have C." Nor do I address invalid arguments due to faulty premises or misapplied principles of logic. This too is a practical, although artificial, distinction. In this book, I assume that many of your mistakes of logic are due to forgetfulness more than they are due to ignorance. If this is true, then clear writing is the best way for you to prevent logic errors. Complex writing hides logical errors from you and your reader. If you write in a clear way, you will detect and correct most of your errors before your readers see them.

It's Not about How to Use Correct Grammar, Punctuation, or Spelling

There are many grammar books. I am not adding to that list. I assume your teachers have taught you basic English grammar. If you know you are weak in this area, or if you have a problem that troubles you (e.g., when should I use a semicolon), look it up. If you cannot spell a word, look it up. If you cannot tell the difference between a past participle and a subatomic particle, you are in good company, but look it up. I have included a list of useful books on writing at the back of this book. Some deal with grammar. The internet has numerous sites devoted to grammar.

The easiest way to avoid grammar mistakes is to write simple sentences that do not require a great deal of punctuation. Simple sentences also help you detect obvious mistakes early. Simple, clear words reduce the number of spelling mistakes you will make, and help eliminate your using the wrong word.

It's Not about Formatting Citations

As I explain in the next chapter, you have a moral obligation to acknowledge where you found ideas and facts that you did not invent or discover. There are many ways to do this, and there are many books to show you how. Mercifully, citation and bibliographic software automate much of the tedium. Further, the organization you work for, or the journal you write for, may demand you follow a style sheet. Follow it.

It's Not about How to Market Your Ideas

I assume that aside from term papers, your goal in writing is to help someone else make better decisions. For that, someone must read your stuff. But how do these someones find your stuff so they can benefit from reading it? The answer to this question is marketing. I do touch on it from time to time, but mostly, I do not. You will have to find out how to market your writing elsewhere. Several of the books I recommend in *Further Reading* address marketing your writing.

It's Not about How to Write Term Papers

You can use this book to help you write your university courses' assignments. I hope you do. Still, that is not my primary goal. Although I assume you are a student, I wrote this book to assist you in your future (or present) role as a professional something or other. I assume in your role as a professional something or other, you will have to write. In your job, you will have the opportunity to use your writing to help people. You will also have the ability to harm people, too. You will help few people if you cannot be clear. You may harm people with bad writing. In short, this book is to help prepare you for writing that has consequences.

Clarity from Cigar Smoke and Numbers

Learning to write clearly began on my first job. The person who had the most influence on my writing was Tom Brady, the communications director of the Police Foundation and a former reporter. I conducted research on policing and had to tell police what I found. My first major effort was a 100-page report on investigations. With little mercy, an abundance of acerbic wit, and clouds of cigar smoke, Tom and my boss dissected that report with me, line-by-line: *every single line*. Tom did not edit my writing in another room and hand me a marked-up draft. We examined each line together. At the end of the day, I returned home deflated and smelling of cigars. My wife was unimpressed by my mood and the cloud that followed me home. I liked neither Tom's cigars nor the ego whoopin'. That is when I learned I did not know how to write clearly. Decades later, I very much appreciate the attention Tom put into correcting my murky academic writing. But I still hate cigars (Tom gave them up in 1988).

To keep my clothing from reeking and to defend my sensitive ego, I decided to learn how to write clearly. I read books on writing. The book that made the biggest difference was Rudolf Flesch's, *How to Write Plain English: A Book for Lawyers and Consumers* (1979). The advice Flesch gave was similar to other writing advice: write simply. What set Flesch's book apart from the others was his formula for a "readability" score. The Flesch score told me the minimum grade level readers needed to understand my writing (I describe Flesch's formula in Chapter 8). I could not assume my readers had a college education, though many did. Therefore, I set my objective to write every passage so someone who had completed high school would understand it.

I liked that Flesch's score measured clarity and did not require artistic judgments that were wooly like a description of an expensive wine. I understood it intuitively and it made sense logically. It emphasized short words and short sentences. It gave me private nonjudgmental advice, and did not smoke. I could experiment with a sentence, get feedback, make revisions, get feedback, and make more revisions.

This is how I revised each paragraph. I counted its sentences, words, and syllables. With a programmable calculator I calculated its Flesch score. If the score was too high, I broke up long sentences into shorter ones. I removed all words I did not need. I discarded all unessential adjectives and adverbs. I then looked at the words left. I inspected words longer than two syllables and sought shorter replacements that were at least as good. The dictionary was my favorite book. (Now I use software to count things and calculate the score. Instead of 10 minutes to analyze a paragraph, it takes seconds. I still have to revise the paragraph by hand, but after 40 years, I am a little quicker.)

All this taught me four things:

1.   Writing is largely technical. The art comes after you get the technical bits right.
2.   Short words and short sentences make things clear.
3.   Paying close attention to item 2 instills a habit of using short words and sentences in the first draft.
4.   Any idea, regardless of complexity, can be expressed simply and clearly.

As much as Flesch's approach helped me write, the thing that sold me on his scoring system was the reaction of my readers. They liked how I wrote, even if they disagreed with what I wrote. Many thanked me for not writing like an academic. When I went back to school and became an academic, I remembered their thanks.

Writing and Thinking

Many people believe that simple writing dumbs-down ideas. This belief is dumb. It is particularly dumb in the social sciences. Social sciences contain very few inherently complex good and useful ideas. Researchers and theoreticians can express almost all of their useful ideas with simple words and sentences, if they choose. Rather than dumbing-down useful complex truths, simple writing makes them understandable. In fact, the more complex the idea, the more important it is for you to write simply and directly.

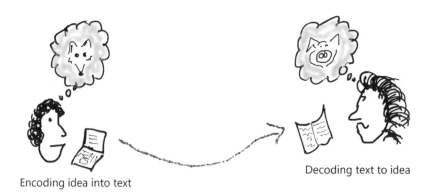

Encoding idea into text   Decoding text to idea

I can explain this with an analogy I lifted from communications theory (Shannon & Weaver, 1949). Every piece of writing has two parts: ideas and code (think Morse code). The ideas are the message you have in your head. They may be simple or complex. Words, grammar, and style are elements of a coding system. When writing, you encode your ideas with your word choices and sentence construction. Your reader must decode your writing to understand your ideas. When they decode your ideas, they should form in their minds the same ideas that you had in yours. If you are trying to hide your ideas from readers, then make your code difficult for readers to break. However, if you feel you have an obligation to communicate to everyone, then make it easy for your reader to decode your ideas with accuracy.

If you have a simple idea, why give it a complex code? That is pretentious and confusing. Your readers will misinterpret your idea. If you have a complex idea, why make your readers struggle with a complex code while they struggle with your complex idea? Make the code simple so their only struggle is with your ideas.

You might assume that writing is only about your readers. This is true, as long as you remember that you are one of those readers. You are the first reader. When you write your first draft, you learn from what you wrote. Instructors often say that writing reflects a student's thinking process. Bad writing suggests that the author is in a muddle. Conversely, good writing suggests the author has a clear idea of what she is writing. She might be wrong, but she has thought things out.

It is not just that muddled ideas create bad writing; the reverse is just as true. Bad writers create muddled ideas. Bad writing gets in the way of clarifying poorly formed thoughts. Few ideas are great when they pop into your head. They need work, usually a great deal of work. And one of the best ways to work on your ideas is to write them down so you can inspect them. However, if you write them down and declare yourself done, then your idea stays a muddle. By thoroughly inspecting and changing your first drafts, you can improve your ideas, correct mistakes of fact or logic, or discover that it's not all that good an idea after all.

Sweet Clarity: Focus on Clear, Not Artful Writing

I downplay writing as an art. There is a well-known and respected academic author on urban life. After reading his second book, I realized that he had little important to say; he could have said it in a blog post. Being a slow learner, I tested my conclusion on another of his books. Sadly, I was not wrong. I did discover that if I luxuriated in his sentences, alliteration, historical anecdotes, literary metaphors, and philosophical wanderings, his books were quite pleasurable. I decided that reading his books is like quaffing a bottle of inexpensive champagne: an unproductive but pleasurable evening followed by a slight hangover and a regret that I had not found something better to do with my time. This author is more interested in art than communicating facts. Clarity was not his goal and so his ideas remain indistinct and unmemorable.

If you set aside artistic pretensions, you can use writing to clarify your thoughts. When I write something (like this book), my first drafts are a mess. I bang out my first thoughts quickly. Best-selling author Anne Lamott (1995: 5), calls this the "shitty first draft." Another writer, Stephen King, calls this the draft with the door shut, or "the story undressed, standing up in nothing but its socks and undershorts" (King, 2000: 271). I will use Lamott's phrase. It is compact, dramatic, and her meaning is absolutely clear. You should embrace your shitty first draft and then clean it up to the point of sweet clarity. Do not stall over its messiness or, worse, pretend it smells sweet and pass it on to others.

My awful first drafts are less crappy than they used to be. Still, they are bad. I do not share them with anyone. I spend far more time revising and editing than I do in writing a first draft. By the time I complete the second (or third or fourth) draft, my ideas are clearer in my head and on paper. I am my first reader. Unlike my future readers, I can talk to myself. If my reading self compares notes with my writing self, I can detect coding problems and fix them. Once I hit the sweet spot, decoding the meaning I intended, my work is ready to share. When I show a draft to someone, I might tell them it's my first draft, but it never is.

If you strive to write with sweet clarity you will improve your thinking. You will not deceive yourself with rococo phraseology and ponderous vocabulary. Do not think of writing as an art. For now.

Rules and Defaults

How do you strive for sweet clarity? Is it by exercising creativity in your style? Or is it by following rules?

Imagine you are 16 and taking a driver's education course so you can get a license to operate a vehicle. Your instructor says:

> When driving, if you see a red octagonal sign, you should stop just before it. That is the rule. HOWEVER, driving is a complex task in complicated environments. Therefore, you can break the rule in numerous circumstances.

The instructor continues the lecture with details of when you can ignore stop signs.

You are confused. You glance at the classroom's clock and realize that she stated the rule in the 30 seconds, but has spent 45 minutes discussing exceptions. You timidly raise your hand, and blurt out:

> How often do these exceptions arise, you know, out of a 100 stop signs? Sorry for the interruption, but what percent are these exceptions? Should I be looking for these all the time? I am just a beginning driver.

Your instructor says:

> Good question. I should have addressed this in the beginning. So thank you for reminding me. I have made a study of these exceptions, so I sometimes get carried away with them. But to answer your question. You, and everyone in this room, will seldom encounter these exceptions. I cannot answer your question precisely, but it may be about one stop sign in a thousand, perhaps fewer.

You say:

> So, I should probably stop at all stop signs?

To which your kindly instructor says:

> Yes, particularly when you have limited experience with driving.

In short, follow rules, particularly when starting out.

But are there rules for writing? Pick up any of the writing books I have listed in *Further Reading*. These writers give numerous rules. Then they break them. Other experts chastise these rule givers then give their own rules. Writing experts frequently declare there are many exceptions and it is impossible to find rules that will work in all situations. Perhaps writing is too complex for rules.

Yes, writing is complex. Yes, there are many ways to form a sentence and express any idea. For every rule, there are three or more exceptions. Yes, there is art involved. Yes, writing circumstances are many and varied. Nevertheless, to get started and produce truthful, useful, and clear text you need to follow some rules.

Do not think of these instructions as "rules" in the sense that the Ten Commandments are rules. Instead, think of them as "defaults." Defaults are like the factory settings in a software package or a smartphone app. Defaults are useful because they cover the typical circumstance. You can change them as you get more proficient. Throughout this book, I will give you defaults. When I say, "Do this," "Don't do that," "I recommend this," "Avoid that," I am giving you advice that should work most of the time.

I am applying one of my favorite truths: most things are produced by a few. You may know this as the 80-20 rule, though sometimes it is 99-5, or 70-20 or some other large-small combination. A small proportion of offenders commit most crimes. A small proportion of earthquakes cause most of the earthquake damage. A small proportion of writers sell most of the books.

A small number of defaults will address most of your writing needs, at least in the beginning. They will keep you from making many writing mistakes. If you get in the habit of applying these defaults, your writing will improve. These defaults will help you produce clear text for your readers. Once you have made clear writing a habit you can look for ways that improve on the default in a very particular circumstance.

Examples

I use a lot of examples of writing. If we learn by our own mistakes, we should be able to learn from the mistakes of others. That is why I use many bad examples. Many come from the writings of well-known smart and productive researchers. I choose their writing for two reasons. First, I am familiar with their writing. Second, choosing poorly written passages by obscure poor thinkers would be of little value to you. You would have difficulty distinguishing between a dumb idea and a poorly written expression of that idea.

Bureaucracies are an amazing source of terrible writing. I use examples from university administrators. Most of these are examples of bad writing. There is nothing special about my university in that regard. As you are likely to join a bureaucracy, there is a high risk you will produce the sort of nonsense in the examples I show. I hope, like a vaccine, once exposed to poor bureaucratic writing, I can inoculate you against this disease. Vaccines vary in their efficacy, however.

I also use myself as an example. In part, this is because I am convenient. I also use my writing as examples because I can describe what I was thinking: why I chose to write this way instead of that way. I cannot explain why other writers made their choices. Finally, I describe my experiences to show that writing involves a great deal of bumbling about, making mistakes, rewriting, correcting new mistakes, and removing even more errors: whatever it takes to get to sweet clarity.

What Is Coming?

Since I am not writing a mystery novel, I can reveal what you will learn. Here are my ten commandments (aka, defaults) of sweet clarity:

1. *Write a true story, credit your sources, and do both clearly.* These are ethical obligations.
2. *It's a craft, not an art.* When my teachers first taught me how to write, they implied writing is an art. Unless you want to write poetry or fiction, abandon artistic notions now. We want to get our points across to our readers and to have our readers recall these points accurately. Achieving this goal requires craft, mostly. Once you master the craft of writing, then consider art, as long as art does not obscure clarity.
3. *Write for your reader.* You are trying to assist your readers, not show off your skills. Your readers are diverse, so consider their range of interests, background knowledge, skills, and abilities.
4. *Keep your ideas in order.* The order might be time, space, process, or something else, but there is an order and your job is to find that order. If you cannot find order, impose order.
5. *Use short common words.* Eschew discursive obfuscation in every textualizing opportunity through application of diminutive vocabulary elements. In brief, to avoid muddling your ideas use short words.
6. *Use short sentences.* Like long words, long sentences confuse writers and readers.
7. *Use the active voice.* "You should use the active voice" is active voice. "The active voice should be used" is the passive voice. The active voice puts the person or thing doing the acting (you, in this example) at the front. Passive voice diminishes the actor. There is a role for passive sentences, but this role is a minor character, not the star performer.
8. *Use examples and exhibits.* They help you to make yourself clear and to express ideas that your reader might find difficult to understand if you only used abstract concepts.
9. *Revise, revise, and revise.* Almost nothing in your first draft is precious, and much may be awful. You will need to rework your drafts several times to hit your spot of sweet clarity.
10. *Embrace the messiness of writing.* Your final draft should be orderly, but the process that you use to produce it can be disjointed and unpredictable.

I communicate these commands in 18 chapters I have grouped into six parts.

Part I covers things you should consider before you have a topic to write about. You are reading the first chapter, so I do not need to explain it. In Chapter 2, I state the ethics of writing. Ethics are not just about plagiarism. There is a great deal more to being ethical in professional writing than whether you cite your sources. The kind of writing that is the subject of this book creates obligations on authors that many people neglect. You can do better. Chapter 3 deals with the process of writing. It's a high altitude overview that shows you how it all fits together. This is important because decisions you make early in your writing influence later decisions, and later decisions often cause you to change earlier ones.

Part II considers the things you will have to confront once you have a topic, but before you have a sense of how you will write about it. I address writing with co-authors in Chapter 4. Most writing books assume you write alone. In professional settings, you are likely to be part of a team. This raises some issues you should think about before getting started. Chapter 5 examines the questions you need to answer before you put your fingers on your keyboard. You should have a sound idea of what it is you are trying to produce, why you want to produce it, and how you plan to produce it.

Part III is the largest part of the book and contains the bits you need to write with sweet clarity. I cover the organization of your ideas in Chapter 6. Your teachers probably taught you to make an outline. There is much more to the organization than that. And there are many ways to organize your writing. Writing is made up of words, the subject of Chapter 7. Clear writing uses short words. I give examples of words that muddle things and advice on how to sort out the useful words from the pretentious words that bloat writing. Naturally, a chapter on sentences comes next. Chapter 8 explains why short sentences are better than long ones and why active voice is better than passive voice. Chapter 9 covers paragraphs and longer passages. Organizing sentences is critical here.

Examples and analogies are vital, so I devote Chapter 10 to this topic. This includes real and hypothetical examples, similes, metaphors, and related ways to create images in your readers' minds. Chapter 11 describes ways to begin your writing so that readers will want to read it. And Chapter 12 examines how to end your writing so your readers leave with your message firmly installed in their brains. Beginnings and endings should be written last and with each other. So, in some respects, these two chapters are really two parts of a single set of ideas.

Part IV describes how to incorporate tables and figures into your work. Chapter 13 describes how to make clear tables. Chapter 14 discusses the use of graphs to display data. And Chapter 15 examines diagrams of ideas. Although numbers and images are the main subjects of these chapters, the principle of simplicity applies to these exhibits.

Part V contains two chapters on revisions. Chapter 16 deals with your rewriting, revising, and editing. This is what you do before you show it to anyone. Chapter 17 deals with how you should deal with reviews by strangers, supervisors, and others. I call these people external reviewers. I emphasize two sorts of external reviewers. Supervisors are the first sort. They are often the people who gave you the task to write something. Peer reviewers for journals and book publishers are the second sort. Those of you considering an academic career will be most concerned with these folk.

Part VI finishes my book with a single short chapter. In it I give advice on how to continue learning how to write with sweet clarity.

Throughout the book I provide exercises. I designed these to help you become more aware of how other writers write, and to look carefully at your writings. Treat these exercises like you might treat physical exercise. Do them repeatedly, regularly, and with friends. If you are in school, you can apply many of these exercises to readings in your classes.

At the end, I provide a list of writing books. They are either companions to this book, advanced books on writing, or reference books. I hope this is not the last book on writing you read, because there is much more to writing than I can say here.

2 The Ethics of Useful Writing

> **Comments on Ethics in Writing**
>
> The truth is rarely pure, and never simple.
>
> Oscar Wilde
>
> Don't worry about people stealing an idea. If it's original, you will have to ram it down their throats.
>
> Howard Aiken
>
> What can be said at all can be said clearly.
>
> Ludwig Wittgenstein
>
> Lack of clarity is the number-one time-waster.
>
> Frank Lloyd Wright

A Command

Let's skip the ethical mumbo-jumbo. Here is my single ethical command: *Write a true story, credit your sources, and do both clearly.*

That is it. If you understand this command, print it in large letters and paste it above your desk as a reminder. And if you do not want more explanation, skip to the next chapter. If you want the reasons for the command, read this chapter.

I organized this chapter around the three principles contained in this command. The first section deals with telling the truth. You are writing nonfiction, so tell the readers the truest story you can create out of the facts. The second section deals with your sources of information. Your writing builds on the works of others, so you must tell your readers how you came to your story. The third section explains the ethics of clarity. You are asking your readers to spend time and effort on your writings, so you should not waste their time or confuse them with muck.

Write a True Story

Telling the truth is the most basic of your ethical obligations, and the most obvious. This is nonfiction, after all. You already know that lying to your readers is a bad thing. So why mention it? For two reasons: first, I needed to say it because we sometimes overlook the obvious; second,

DOI: 10.4324/9781003167532-3

sometimes the truth is hard to discern. In such cases, which are common, describe the ambiguity and uncertainty in your argument. If there is a dispute over a fact you use in your story, tell the story with both versions of that fact. You can side with one version, but you have an obligation to tell your reader of the alternative. This is why, in academic writing, it is standard to describe the limitations and caveats to your findings.

When writing for public agencies and private organizations, acknowledging ambiguity is difficult. If you are writing a policy brief for a law enforcement leader or elected official, you better give the pros and cons. However, your bosses may not like this. Here are two common reasons. The leader may not want to hear the news that contradicts their preset views. Here, you are in a jam. How you cope with this will depend on many details of your circumstances. Alternatively, your boss may want to hear the contradictory positions but does not want you to write them in a document that may become public. Your solution is obvious: present the positions in an oral briefing.

The third reason to remind you of your truth-telling obligation is more complex than the first two. Even nonfiction involves making things up. You are creating a story out of a set of facts. There may be no disputing some of these facts. But for others, there is considerable uncertainty. There are also places where you want facts, but none exist. You have to make reasonable assumptions. Finally, you need to be creative in connecting these facts and assumptions. In this sense, nonfiction writing resembles fiction writing.

If you are original in your writing, then you must say something others have not said, or have not said in the way you are saying it. If you do not provide something new, then there is no point in writing: someone beat you to it. Even when you are summarizing someone's work—perhaps translating a poorly written piece of academic research—you must add something original. You have to come up with a way of saying what the source study's author found difficult to express. To do this, you must interpret the author's text. You are being original, and therefore you are making things up.

My mother was a professional translator for a large pharmaceutical company. She explained that when translating often it is impossible to make a word-for-word substitution. She had to imagine how to compose a set of words in English that conveyed the meaning of a German phrase that had no exact English equivalent. If the German author wrote poorly (as my mom often complained), she still had to find a way of expressing his poorly expressed ideas in clear English. She was keenly aware that readers of her translations would use her work to make decisions that had large monetary and health consequences. For that reason, she consulted numerous medical dictionaries and experts. Because, in the end it was my mom who interpreted the original research.

Consider a literature review. You are going over a well-plowed topic, so in what way are you being original? Here is an example.

Several years ago, one of my students, a colleague, and I undertook a review of the studies of police force size and crime. There were many such studies and they seemed to be contradictory. Some claimed that adding more cops reduced crime and others claimed it did not. We based our review on studies conducted since 1970. Many authors over several decades had done this work. In addition, we found two published review articles that attempted to answer the same question we were trying to answer. Truth-telling would seem rather simple in this situation. It would seem to involve summarizing what everyone else had said.

In fact, truth-telling was complex. First, we needed to look at all the research available. If we did not, then we might overlook an important study that contradicted the others. We did not want to cherry-pick: select a few prominent studies that made our case while ignoring many opposing studies. That is why we used a systematic review designed to identify and incorporate all relevant studies. We could not be certain we found every single relevant study. So, to be truthful, we described how we undertook our search for studies, listed the studies we found, and then acknowledged the potential limitations of our search.

Second, we needed to analyze the results of all the relevant studies we found. We found over 60. Few readers would tolerate the tedium of reading 60 concise summaries. Even if they would, we needed to do more than summarize a bunch of studies. We needed to synthesize them. Synthesis involves identifying patterns across studies. When authors conduct a standard litera-ture review, authors identify patterns they sense. However, they use considerable intuition so their conclusions are very subjective. A different reviewer might find other patterns. We wanted to reduce this subjectivity. Therefore, we used standard meta-analysis procedures to detect patterns in research results. Meta-analysis involves using statistical tools transparently. We described our analysis procedures in our paper and acknowledged the limitations of these procedures.

Third, even by following established analytical procedures, we could not escape the need to make some educated guesses about the patterns we found. To get as close to the truth as we could, we developed counter-arguments to these guesses. Much of this we did in meetings before writing our results. Our discussions went something like this. "These results seem to show A." "That is true, but it is also possible to interpret them as showing Z." "If Z is more likely than A, then we should be able to determine this by running this new set of analyses." "Let's do that." Then later, "I ran the analyses we discussed, and a couple of other versions of it, and they show that Z is unlikely." Or, "I ran the analyses we discussed, and Z is possible. So I reexamined our original finding using a new technique. I think A is probably wrong." We had many of these sorts of discussions. When we wrote our paper, we summarized these discussions in our paper so readers could judge for themselves.

We wrote an article that described why adding police was unlikely to reduce crime. We explained why this finding made sense, given the behavior of police agencies. That is the con-clusion that made the most sense, given the facts we had. Even though we felt confident in this finding, we also noted some limitations to our findings.

There are two morals to this story. First, even when reviewing the works of others, your conclusions are a conjecture. Make up a story consistent with your facts and with the gaps in your facts. Second, finding the truth is mostly eliminating potential errors in your judgments of the evidence. It is a process of explicitly describing your best guess and then challenging your guess.

The conclusion that you put in your final draft should be a conclusion that has survived your many attempts to show it is wrong. When working with my graduate students, I ask that they come up with a good story. Then I demand they try to "break" their story. Only if their story survives destructive testing should they accept it. That does not guarantee the story is true; it only shows the story survived deliberate destructive testing. That is the best we can ever do.

This is especially true of writing a policy brief: a paper that suggests policy or practice. Here too you must be consistent with the facts as they are and with the many gaps in those facts, while fitting them to policy alternatives.

So, to tell the truth as best you can, you should do five things:

- Be comprehensive in your search for facts.
- Use established procedures to assess these facts when such procedures are available.
- Describe what you did to find and assess those facts, and why you did these things.
- Make conjectures based on the facts and gaps and then try to break those conjectures.
- Acknowledge your limitations.

Doing these things does not guarantee you are right. It helps your readers determine if you are close enough to being right. No matter how scrupulously you follow accepted protocols in your analysis, in the end you must tell a story.

In short, if you do not strive to tell the truth while making up a story, then you are being unethical. If you strive to tell the truth you are being ethical. Later, if someone discovers new facts, or better ways of examining the facts you had, and shows that your story is wrong, this does not mean you suffered an ethical lapse.

Credit Your Sources

I suspect that when you saw this book had a section on ethics you thought of plagiarism. Plagiarism is copying someone else's writing and passing it off as your own. It is the theft of credit for the writing.

There are three reasons for crediting your sources. You have a moral obligation to the writers who helped you. You have a moral obligation to your readers. You have a moral obligation to the community of people interested in the topic about which you are writing.

Obligation to Writers

When someone puts their time and effort into creating an understandable sentence, paragraph, or paper, they deserve the credit for it. We should acknowledge the writer. Writing is hard work. By citing someone's work you are crediting their work. Using someone's work without giving him or her credit is fraud. It is like someone who never served in combat claiming he is a combat veteran. It is like pirating music from someone and claiming it is you who made that music. You are not dignifying the work of others who have helped you. You are implying you produced it through your efforts when in fact someone else produced it through their efforts.

Obligation to Readers

Some, but far from all of your readers, will want to dig into the ideas you have brought to their attention. Crediting your sources gives them the ability to do this. Without citations, a reader excited about your ideas hits a dead-end. I have wandered through the footnotes and reference sections of many books and articles. In doing so, I have found many books and articles that help me in my work. Occasionally, I read an interesting statement, want to know more, and then discover the author does not show where her facts come from. This not only undermines my trust in the author, but it also frustrates my ability to do my work. You have a moral responsibility to assist your readers through your work and this extends to helping them locate and read the works of others.

Obligation to Community

I have studied crime long enough to believe that we cannot rely on people to tell the truth if we cannot verify their claims. A few souls will always be as truthful as they possibly can. A few will always lie or bullshit. Most of us are in between. We will be more truthful if we know that our readers can detect falsehood. This is one of the reasons we demand authors credit their sources: we want the ability to check the authors and we want them to know we can check them.

Your citations signal your readers that you have legitimate reasons for the points you made and that you are open to readers checking your story. President Ronald Reagan's adage, "Trust but verify," applies to writing as well as to nuclear treaties. Our readers will trust us if they have the ability to verify what we say. Most never will check, but a few might. That is enough.

You can make two types of mistakes when drawing upon someone else's ideas. The first mistake is not citing them and denying them due credit. This is plagiarism. It is usually the worst of the mistakes. The second mistake is giving them credit when they do not deserve it. This is foolishness. Sometimes it is minor, and sometimes it is major. Here is an example of a minor bit of foolishness. You cite an author, but this person did not come up with the idea. Rather, they were drawing upon some earlier author's ideas. This often occurs when a student cites a textbook when describing a theory. This is not plagiarism because the student is not taking undue credit. Nevertheless, it is poor scholarship.

In contrast, you are writing a memo summarizing research. Your readers may use your memo to develop criminal justice policy. Instead of citing the original research, you cite a summary of that research by someone else. Here the mistake is more serious. It is serious because you prevent your readers from checking your work. It is serious because your readers are relying on your third-hand interpretation.

It is like the game of telephone. As children, we would line up and the first in line whispers something in her neighbor's ear. He then whispers this message to the third kid. This goes on until the last child. That kid then states to the group the message she heard. Inevitably, what she heard is a major distortion of what the first child said. This is the fun. When you cite someone's summary of another person's work, you risk passing on a distorted version of the original. That is serious.

Giving undeserved credit may result from excess humility. You think you learned about an idea from someone else, so you cite her. In fact, the person you cite did not describe this idea.

You created this idea. Someone reading your paper might go to the source and discover the author did not say what you claim they said. Is this a big mistake? It is not a serious error like plagiarism. It is just too much humility and caution, but it's still confusing.

Here is an example based on several pieces of writing. Researcher X describes a decision he made in his study. He cites an earlier well-known researcher (E) as the reason for the decision. I read the study by E and discover that she did not give the justifications claimed by X. X is not trying to take credit that is not his to take. However, he is justifying his actions inappropriately. If there was no earlier study that justifies X's decision he should admit this. If he had, then he would have had to admit that his decision had no precedent.

In this example, X is puffing up his story by asserting a famous person told the story. By inappropriately citing E, researcher X is inflating his decision's credibility. This is an ethical lapse that could have serious consequences. If I read X's story, accepted it as true because X cited the well-respected E, and enacted dangerous policies as a result, then X shares moral responsibility.

My rule of thumb is to over-cite. I would rather make the mistake of providing the wrong citation than not citing. I try to determine if the work I am citing fits the ideas I am writing about. This often means going back to some old study and checking. Later in this book, I discuss the Flesch-Kincaid scale. I have used it for years, but I have never looked at its origins. So I located Rudolf Flesch's original 1948 article and read it. Then I conducted an internet search for Kincaid's 1975 study, a 40 plus-year-old Navy report. I then read that. Is this excessive? No. It helps assure that the story I tell is accurate.

Keep your readers' interests in mind and give the most appropriate citations possible.

Do These Clearly

Unclear writing is unethical. It is not just style, taste, and aesthetics. Does this mean that many of the authors you have read for your courses have behaved unethically? Possibly. Here are four reasons for my harsh judgment.

Unclear Writing Shows Disdain for Readers

Unclear writing suggests you do not care enough to make your readers' lives easier. Most of your readers are not reading your stuff for pleasure: they have to read it. It is part of their work. Your bad writing causes other people to work harder.

When readers confront long words, they spend more time on these words than they do for shorter words that mean the same thing (Hyönä & Olsen, 1995; Rayner & Duffy, 1986; Rello et al., 2013). The same is true for sentences. You can think of this as an efficiency problem. You can express any idea clearly or you can obfuscate the idea. In the first instance, you make your readers' job easier. Understanding the idea might require effort, but your style is not in the way. In the second instance, you make your readers' job harder. Regardless of the difficulty of the idea, readers now have to wade through burdensome prose. Why would you want to increase the costs of understanding your ideas? If you care for your readers, you will express your ideas in the simplest way possible.

Very few ideas are very complex. Most are made up of a set of simple ideas, each of which can be expressed simply. As a student, I hope you can appreciate this point. Many authors, whose works you had difficulty understanding, imposed a cost on you that they did not need to charge, but you had to pay. They could have expressed their ideas clearly but did not do so. Please try not to do this to others. Please respect your readers and strive for sweet clarity.

Unclear Writing Is Elitist

When you use uncommon, difficult to understand words in long, complex sentences, you are appealing to a tiny audience of elites. This means that others, with less education, cannot access your ideas. They must rely on other elites to interpret your ideas.

I write about crime and police. Because these affect all people, I try to make my ideas clear to as many people as possible. On occasion, I see the fruits of this effort. Last year, a police chief called me about a paper I published in an academic journal. He heard about it from his city manager. Usually, I have no idea who sees my work, but I try to write so that non-academics can understand my ideas.

Any social scientist in a public university, one whose salary is paid for by taxpayers, should write so members of the public can understand. This is also true of those who receive government grants and contracts. The public does not pay us to entertain each other in our journals and our conferences. They pay us to help accomplish something useful.

Very little that is useful can be implemented without public support. Therefore, you have an obligation to make your work accessible, within reason. There are honest technical topics that only people with special knowledge will understand: statistical modeling, for example. However, social science theory and research should be understandable to those in the public with at least a high school education. This is definitely the case with writing about any social science policies. You should make your ideas accessible to those with a high school education. If you can make your ideas clear to people with less than a high school education, that is even better.

In my field, criminology, there are many people who write passionately about the wrongs of society. They demand action. As self-proclaimed champions of the downtrodden they should be able to talk to the people they are trying to help. By writing in a manner that only a handful of other academics can appreciate, these privileged criminological critics perpetuate the elitist behavior they decry. Please do not do this. Please write so the public can understand.

Unclear Writing Discriminates

It took a long time for me to understand this point, although I should have understood it sooner. I suffer from dyslexia. This means that I have trouble decoding complex words and sentences. It is seldom the ideas that give me trouble: if expressed in short sentences or in diagrams, I am fine. However, my brain rearranges letters in long words. Sometimes words from the line below the one I am reading jump into the line my eyes are scanning. This confuses me. In a long sentence, with many clauses, I may skip over critical words. I sometimes miss the word "not" in a long sentence, reversing the meaning of the sentence. I find it hard to follow an author's thoughts in lengthy sentences, spanning several lines, and with numerous clauses separated by commas, dashes, and semi-colons. I have developed a number of coping skills. Applying these skills, however, requires time and energy. This means that to decode a passage, I have to expend more effort than others might. It is exhausting and it is extremely frustrating. I used to think it was just me. But my experiences are common (Ellis, 2016; Rello et al., 2013).

Many academic writers seem to care little for readers with dyslexia, or other cognitive impairments. This is discrimination, just like having a public building inaccessible to people in wheelchairs or pushing a baby stroller is discrimination. It is as much discrimination as not providing listening devices for people who have limited hearing. This is not just an ethical malfunction among academics. You can find unclear writing in numerous other documents: websites, instruction manuals, government reports. Unclear writing privileges some at the expense of others. Please do not do this. Please write so everyone can understand your work.

Unclear Writing Misleads

We all know that bad writing confuses people. We have seen this. We have been victims of this. Do you recall those classroom discussions where you and your fellow students could not agree on what an author was trying to express? This is fine in fiction, poetry, or music. It is not good in truthful writing.

Consider the ethics of research on human subjects. University human subjects review committees, usually called IRBs (Institutional Review Board), must approve all research involving people. If you are interviewing adults in your research, the IRB will require you to gain informed consent from these adults before conducting the interviews. Often, the researcher writes a letter describing the research and the subject's role. Often, the IRB requires that the subject sign this letter of informed consent before the interview. And IRBs often require that the researcher write these letters so that a subject with an eighth-grade education can understand them (Hadden et al., 2017). To be informed, the subjects must understand the possible consequences of their participation. Ethical research starts with being clear to research subjects.

Exercise 2.1

Find a piece of difficult, vague, or unclear nonfiction writing. Is the difficulty in the subject matter? Or is it difficult because of the author's choice of words, sentence construction, or organization?

Has the author ignored an ethical obligation to readers? Consider reasons for answering "yes" and reasons for answering "no."

When your writing is murky, you are misleading your reader. When it is murky because you have not taken the time and effort to make your ideas clear, you are deliberately misleading your readers. The confusion you can create has consequences. Here are some examples. A researcher seeking to test a theory must first decode someone's written theory. If the theoretician was not clear and precise, the researcher may be misled. Their study will be faulty and their tests inadequate. A scientist, attempting to replicate the research of another, depends on the first scientist's written reports of the original research. If these are unclear, the replication can be in error. A practitioner, planning an anti-crime effort based on a theory depends on a clear explanation of that theory. If the theoretician did not provide a clear description, the practitioner is likely to implement an inappropriate program. In the crime control field, inappropriate programs waste money and can waste lives.

Unclear writing not only misleads your readers, it misleads you. It is difficult to determine where poor thinking ends and poor writing begins. If you produce murk, your ideas can be bad and you will not know it. If you work hard at making your ideas clear, you are likely to detect gaps, inconsistencies, and errors in your ideas. Good writing cannot make an illogical idea understandable. But it can help you detect logic errors so you can correct them. Poor writing is like creating a poor map; the map user will get lost. Please do not lose your readers. Please write with sweet clarity so they know what you are saying.

When I read a difficult piece, I wonder why it is difficult. Sometimes the ideas the author is trying to get across are inherently complex. Usually, however, it is one of two other problems. One is that the kernel of the ideas is sound, but the author has not worked hard enough to make them clear. The other is that the ideas are not sound, and the author's unclear writing disguises this fact. When I find unsound ideas camouflaged by bad writing, I wonder if the author knows their ideas are faulty and they tried to disguise this with bad writing. Regardless, the author is guilty of unethical writing, for all of the reasons I just described.

Write a True Story, Credit Your Sources, and Do Both Clearly

Perhaps my proclamations about the ethics of writing frighten you. You may ask, "How can I avoid violating these rules of ethics?" My answer is simple. At the center of these ethics problems is a lack of conscious effort. If you do not work at helping your readers, then you are engaging in unethical writing. If you honestly try to make your ideas true, credited, and clear then you are writing ethically. Indifference to the reader is the issue. If you attempt to write ethically, then your mistakes are forgivable. If you do not attempt to write ethically, then we can judge your errors more harshly.

The simplest way I know of to demonstrate to your readers that you are an ethical writer is to follow the dictum I mentioned at the beginning of this chapter: *write a true story, credit your sources, and do both clearly.* You have to work at all three parts: none is more important than the others. An unclear truth is just as much a failing as a clearly articulated lie. A true story taken from others without attribution is just as much of a failure as a false story carefully referenced and told clearly.

Nevertheless, my emphasis remains on clarity. I assume you want to make a positive difference in this world, and you want to do this with the least possible harm to others. I assume you are trying to tell the truth as best you can. I assume that you will diligently credit your sources. I do not assume you will do any of these clearly. That is what the rest of this book is about. Before going on, however, print the ethical command and post it where you will see it.

3 A Writing Process

A Process

Writing creates anxiety. If you proceeded directly from high school to college, you mostly wrote term papers and other classroom assignments. If you hold a full-time job, you may have written reports for your work. Regardless of experience, you may find writing difficult or dreadful. Many smart students have told me they would not seek a PhD because they cannot imagine writing a dissertation. There are many reasons for not pursuing a doctoral degree, but that should not be one of them. Length is one reason we dread writing (but only one). Objectively, there is not much to dread; any long piece of writing is just a series of short pieces of writing.

Long or short, you need a process. So the first step on a serious writing project is to understand that process. That is the reason for this chapter.

I will describe a writing process. This is not the one true way of writing. Everyone has his or her own process. Not only do different writers have different writing processes, a single writer might follow different processes for different projects. I do not religiously follow a single process. Still, there are some basic things that I have found important for moving from the beginning to the end.

You might find this flexibility a relief: whew, I do not have to follow someone's rules; I can continue in my own weird ways. Alternatively, you might find this flexibility maddening: damn, I have to figure it out by myself; can't you give me a blueprint? If you are of the whew-set, then take any advice I provide as it strikes your fancy. If you are of the damn-set, then follow my process. Later you can revise it as you discover something better. In either case, it is your results that matter, not the process you use. A writing process is just a tool to achieve some end and there is no good reason to treat it as sacred.

I hope there is something here that you find useful. But if you have a process that works well, stick with it.

Figure 3.1 illustrates the process I will describe in this chapter. I wrapped this process around your potential readers. Readers are central and critical at each stage. The first three stages

DOI: 10.4324/9781003167532-4

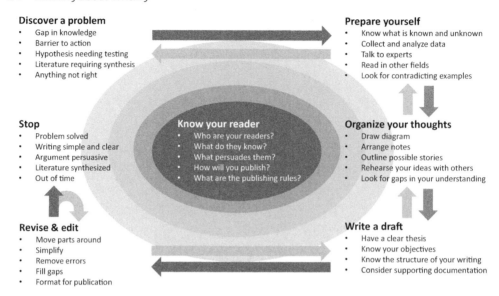

Figure 3.1 The Writing Process Begins before Writing and Includes Revisions

often come before you sit down to serious writing. Like the iceberg, most of your work is below the surface: it does not look like writing but it is essential to writing. I have connected the stages with arrows to illustrate how one stage leads to the next. And I have connected the stages with arrows to show how one stage leads back to the previous. I could have shown arrows connecting each stage to each of the others, in any direction. All connections are possible, but if I showed them all the figure would be confusing. If you want to jump directly from 1 to 3, and then to 2, do not let me stop you. Figure 3.1 is a suggestion, not a magic formula.

Stage 1: Discover a Problem

Whether you love or hate writing, you need a reason to write. You need a topic. You need to have something particular to say about that topic. You need a reason you should be the one writing about that topic. You need an audience who is interested in the topic and who will read your writing. And, you need to be sure no one else has addressed this topic, in the way you want to address it, for your readers.

"Why should I write this?" is one of the very first questions I ask myself. Did someone demand it, and if so do I need to pay attention to this demand? Will I be paid for it, and if so how much? Do I believe that when I finish the writing project, I will have something to say that contributes to something worthwhile? Am I sufficiently interested in this topic that I will find writing and researching it interesting? Am I capable of doing this job?

If I feel the writing is worth undertaking (or cannot refuse to take it), I ask another set of practical questions. How will my writing get to my readers? Who will publish it? In what format will they publish it? Will the readers I want to reach find my publication?

I always try to imagine my readers. When I began my career, my readers were police officials. I did not write for academics and had no interest in doing so. Police are a tough audience. Many people have told me over the last 40 years that "police don't read." I used to worry about this.

Now I realize this assertion is foolish. Police read just as much as anyone does: most read little, but a few are voracious readers. Even when my audiences were police, I never imagined all police being interested. I imagined a lieutenant who goes to work one morning and is assigned my report to read and summarize. I imagined a captain who tries to keep up with the latest ideas and discovers my writing. I imagine a sergeant who reads a news account (or blog) mentioning my piece and then tracking it down. I imagine a deputy chief who discovers my work when a colleague in a different agency recommends it. I imagine an officer studying for her master's degree reading my piece for class. They all turned out to be my readers.

For me, the idea for my topic is intimately connected to my readers. Your idea for a topic may pop into your imagination without warning. Or it might be something a professor or a supervisor inflicts upon you. Whether it was you who perceived a need or someone else who created the assignment, you have begun. The primary questions you are asking yourself at this stage are:

- What can I say about that topic that will help my potential readers?
- What has not been said?
- What has been said, but is probably wrong?
- What has been said, but is incomplete or deficient?
- What has been said, but has been said poorly?

Spend some time on these questions (see Chapter 5). Once you have a clear idea of your writing mission—because that is what these questions are about—then you are ready for the next stage.

Stage 2: Prepare Yourself

In Stage 2 you are doing your research. You will read what others have said on the topic. You should read what people have said about analogous topics, too. For example, years ago I was investigating police response time. I read the research. But I also looked at the literature on medical and fire response times. It turns out that many of the same issues that concerned the police, concerned medical and fire professionals. Heart attack victims, for example, delayed calling for medical help, even if they had prior experience with heart attacks.

It is at this stage that you will conduct your original research—collecting and analyzing data. You should talk to experts on the topic. Do not forget news media articles and other non-academic sources. Go out and observe things. I study high crime places, so I go to those places and watch. Often I take pictures.

As you are doing this, ideas about what to write will come to you. Some will be good, and some will not. As these ideas become clearer, start looking for ideas that contradict your original ideas. Look for evidence for your ideas. Then, look for evidence that challenges your ideas. Do not cling to any idea, but do not keep your mind free of ideas. Rather than pretend to start with a clear mind, free of theory (something that is impossible), for every idea you imagine, imagine its opposite. Compare the ideas. As your research continues you may settle on one or two ideas. Before you put any idea on a pedestal, try to break it with evidence and logic.

Sometimes you need to reverse Stages 2 and 1. You might work on a particular project investigating something. While doing so, you discover something new about which to write.

Therefore, I have an arrow going from Stage 2 to Stage 1. I included this arrow also because while you are preparing yourself to write, your idea of the problem changes. Perhaps, as you studied your ideas, you successfully broke them. Or, the gap that started you on this path may not be big enough, but you discover some other idea.

Take a lot of notes. Write down your ideas. Make sketches, diagrams, doodles. Come up with stupid ideas, silly ideas, wacky ideas, and outlandish ideas. They are part of a private conversation you are having with yourself. Treat them as disposable toy ideas. One or two might have something useful for later, but it may take you a long time to learn which. You are not promising any of these crazy ideas and ridiculous scribbles a place in your manuscript. Be prepared to throw every one of these ideas in the wastebasket.

Throughout, you should be asking yourself about your potential readers. What evidence will they need to be convinced? What expectations do they have that you need to overcome? What examples will they find useful? Imagine a fair, critical reader; someone who is knowledgeable, balanced, skeptical but will be convinced if you put forth a sound argument made of solid evidence. Then ask yourself, do I have the evidence and logic necessary to convince this reader?

How much time should you devote to this? How much time do you have? I like to spend a great deal of time on this stage. The less I know about a topic when I start, the longer I take. In many of my projects, Stage 2 is the longest stage. If you are writing under a deadline, you might not have the luxury I have. Carve out time to play with your ideas. This is why I like what cognitive psychologist Amos Tversky says at the start of this chapter, "The secret to doing good research is always to be a little underemployed. You waste years by not being able to waste hours."

Stage 3: Organize Your Thoughts

There are many ways of organizing your thoughts and the way you choose depends on you and the subject you are examining. I describe ways to order your ideas in detail in Chapter 6, so I will not spend much time on this stage.

Use outlines, note cards, scribbled diagrams, PowerPoint slides, Lego blocks, specialized software, or anything that helps you put things in order. When you are getting organized, you may discover that there are questions you have not investigated. Then you need to go back to Stage 2.

For me, the most common such discovery is the lack of a source for a critical point in my argument. I realize that I have no citation to back up what I thought was an obvious point, or I discover I did not do the statistical analysis necessary to draw a particular conclusion. Then I go back and find the reference or do the analysis. These are seldom big things, but they are important for a coherent argument. Sometimes, the source I thought would back my argument does not do so: it is mute on my point. I then have to reconsider how to proceed. Sometimes the necessary statistical results challenge my argument. I have to revise things.

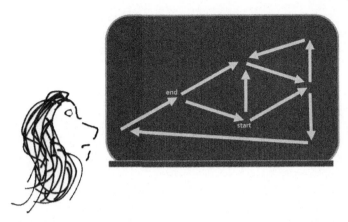

Here too, focusing on your reader is important. Will your readers be able to follow the organization you are considering? Will they imagine gaps in your argument that you have not filled, or even considered? Do your readers or publisher expect a particular organization to which you should comply? Is there an alternative organization for telling your story that will resonate with your readers?

You will find that you will have to go back and forth between Stages 2 and 3 if you are engaged in a complex writing task. So organize your ideas several times. Even when you get to the next stage, you may find that you need to revise your organization.

Stage 4: Write a Draft

At Stage 4 you are doing something that looks and feels like writing. Sometimes, if you have really absorbed all the background material, know your topic in and out, and have a convincing organization, you can just write the document. This seldom happens to me. I have heard tales about it happening to others.

The few things I have written flat out have been short: four pages at the most. A couple were summaries of longer studies I had already published. One was a satire of community policing I wrote as a joke and expected to show to only a few friends. My boss loved it and said we should publish it. The result was that I spent three times longer polishing the piece (see Stage 5) than I spent on the original draft. We mailed it to our membership of police chiefs and sheriffs. They loved it and ordered hundreds of copies for their departments. Several chiefs told me at our annual meeting that they loved it. I never have received so much praise for something I wrote, including papers that I spent years on.

There were several reasons this short piece was successful. I had a very particular axe to grind, and I knew the topic. The naïve and saccharine way advocates pushed community policing perturbed me. It was all hugs and did not reflect the reality of policing or communities. I had a clear aim: show how stupid this was. I had a tone: sarcasm. I saw my relationship to the reader: I pretended that they and I hated community policing. I had a simple structure: a list of ways to subvert community policing. And I knew my audience because I had spent several years studying policing and talking with police officials. I moved through Stages 1 through 3 before I came up with the idea.

In my experience, however, good writing takes a great deal of time. Only when you know a topic in great detail and have thought about it for a long time does writing seem easy. Whenever I take on a new topic, I know this will take time. Regardless of whether your first draft was fast or slow, your next stage will be the hardest.

Stage 5: Revise and Edit

Usually, I engage in a ping pong match between Stages 4 and 5. I typically go through at least five drafts: often more. It is difficult to count drafts, because I revise bits and pieces as I am writing. For example, when I start the day's writing I look at what I have already written to pick up the thread of my thoughts. I often find things to alter before getting down to adding new pages.

The writing, revising, editing loop goes on for so long that Stages 5 and 4 merge. The only reason I show them as separate stages here is that they require different thinking styles. Writing is creating and revision is killing. I can edit when I am tired but I can only write when I have energy. When I write, I dump words on the page and pay limited attention to all the advice I will give you later in this book. It's a creative process and I try not to interrupt the flow of ideas. Once I have difficulty coming up with new ideas, I switch to revising and editing.

At Stage 5, I am continuing my quest for sweet clarity. I replace fancy, long words with simple, punchy words. I convert passive voice to active voice. I look for sentences that my readers do not need and delete them. I do this even if I love my clever phrase. I fill in references in their correct format. I delete passages that readers may find confusing. I change the order of ideas. In the chapter on editing, I recommend a four-sweep process. If possible, I try to get someone else to read the draft to give me something closer to a reader's perspective.

As I oscillate between Stages 4 and 5 my work gets sharper and my changes get smaller. My massive changes and rewrites usually occur early. Several revisions later, I am often focusing on minor alterations. A friend used to call these "happy to glad" changes, but not because they are so pleasing. He called them this because they are trivial, like an editor telling you to use the word "glad" rather than "happy." This could go on forever, but at some point you need to go to the next stage.

Even when you think you are done, you may not be. Between Stages 5 and 6 lurks the purgatory of outside reviews. For your document to reach its intended readers, someone may have to review and approve it. I call these people "gatekeepers" and discuss them in Chapters 5 (Getting Started) and 17 (Reviews). If gatekeepers are part of your process, be prepared for several rounds of revisions. If they ask for revisions, then you go back to the Stage 5–4 loop. You might even have to revisit Stages 2 and 3.

Stage 6: Stop

All good things must come to an end. If I am under a deadline, then this forces me to stop editing. Sometimes I realize that my editing is not improving things, but just making happy-to-glad revisions. Once I become convinced that I have addressed the problem that started the process, created a reasonable argument for my case, and have done this with sweet clarity, I stop. Even after I have satisfied all review comments by gatekeepers, I am never 100 percent convinced that I have corrected all the difficulties. Nor do I believe there is nothing else I can do to improve the paper. But at some point I have to be done and now is that time.

Before you decide you are done, check again to make sure you have addressed your readers' concerns. If this is a grant proposal, did you answer all the questions, put things in the order asked for, and demonstrate why you are worthy of funding? If it is a paper for a journal, is it in the right format, is it appropriate for that journal, does it address reviewers' concerns? If it is for a professional magazine, is it the right length, does it have the right tone, is it interesting for the magazine's readers? If it is for your agency's leaders, does it answer the questions they asked, in the way they wanted?

As I said at the beginning, this process is far simpler than the reality of writing. Much depends on the circumstances. If you have a short deadline, for example, you might jump from Stage 1 to Stage 3 in a matter of minutes. Then go on to Stage 4 where you pound out your best effort. Then after a quick Stage 5, you submit your piece. The entire process may take a couple of hours or less. If you do not already know the materials (Stage 2), or you do not have practice at quick writing, this will be a nerve-wracking process. At the other extreme, you have an idea for an article that you take many months or several years to execute. You may bounce around these stages for quite some time as you sharpen your ideas and gather information. Most of the time may be going back and forth between Stages 2 and 3. Then, once you get to serious writing, that stage might go quickly.

I did not mention tables, graphs, diagrams, and other supporting materials (these I discuss in Chapters 13, 14, and 15). I produce these at all stages, except the last. I use them to illustrate my writing. Even more important, I use them to help me determine what I will write. I began writing this chapter, for example, with notes on points I wanted to cover. Then I produced the first draft of Figure 3.1. I made four more drafts of the figure until I settled on the one shown. Then I started writing. In this example, the written text was guidance for understanding a visual illustration.

Exercise 3.1

Consider how you write. Create a diagram of *your* writing process that begins with a vague idea and ends with a finished product. Is there a way of improving your writing by adjusting your writing process? If so, draw a revised diagram of the process you think will be better.

Conclusion

By now, you will have gotten the idea that this process is rather fuzzy, what with all that going back and forth. You are right. This process is a quick impression of something more complex, much like a cartoon is a caricature of a person; emphasizing a few prominent features but ignoring the details. Do not use this description as dogma. I don't. For example, I have no backward arrow from Stage 5 (Revise and Edit) to Stage 2 (Prepare Yourself). While editing, I often find a hidden knowledge gap, and this forces me to collect more information. Editing also reveals problems with my organization, so I also go back to Stage 3 (Organize Your Thoughts). Sometimes, reorganizing my thoughts makes me rethink the original problem (Stage 1).

Even with this admission there are definite products that mark when you are ready to move to the next stage. When you have a clear idea of what you want to write about–a mission statement—you are ready to move on. When you have a thick collection of notes and scribbles that cry out for organization, you are at the boundary of Stages 2 and 3. When you have a good enough outline, or something that serves that purpose, you can switch to Stage 4. When you have a sour first draft, you can move to Stage 5. When you have a draft that oozes sweet clarity, without grammar and spelling errors, and are down to trivial or imaginary problems, you are probably close to being done.

I am now done with the general discussion of writing. In the next part, I will describe topics that you need to consider when you have a specific writing task to accomplish.

Part II   Preparing to Write

4 Writing with Others

Comments on Working with Others

There can be no doubt that the tribe including many members who are always ready to give aid to each other, and to sacrifice themselves for the common good, would be victorious over other tribes.

Charles Darwin

One man alone can be pretty dumb sometimes, but for real bona fide stupidity, there ain't nothing can beat teamwork.

Edward Abbey

A False Assumption

I have lied to you. I will continue to lie. This chapter explains the lie; that is the truth.

Like every writing book I have read, this book assumes that you are writing alone. This assumption makes sense if you are writing fiction (see Anne Lamott or Stephen King, in *Further Reading*), or if you are engaged in nonfiction work for a popular audience (see John McPhee, in *Further Reading*). For most nonfiction writing in organizations and in academia, this assumption is false.

Most professional writing is done by teams of two or more people. Most of my work, for example, whether for academics, police, and or the public, has co-authors. Writing with others is a lot of fun, but it comes with a number of strains you and your co-writers need to address. Writing alone and writing with a team share much, but they do differ in one way: compromise. If you are the sole author, you get to make all the decisions. Even after you get responses from reviewers, you get to decide which of the reviewers' comments you will address and how you will address them. If you have one or more co-authors, you share these decisions. Unless you are an autocrat with all powers, you will have to compromise. With compromise comes complexity.

I write a great deal with current and former students. Even with my newest and most inexperienced students, I share decision-making. I do this for two reasons. First, I want them to learn how to make decisions. Even if I have a clear idea of what the piece should look like, I get their opinion so we can discuss the pros and cons of our options. Teaching aside, there are few settled answers to most writing questions. The fresh eyes of a new student often have given me

DOI: 10.4324/9781003167532-6

insights into the way a paper should be crafted. When I work with more advanced students and very experienced writers, it is even more critical that we discuss how to write a piece.

There are four closely connected questions you and your co-authors need to address.

Who Will Be the First Author?

One of the very first things I try to pin down is who will be first, second, and later authors. One criterion is status: the boss gets the top billing. This sucks, but it occurs even when the boss prefers to make a junior member of the team first author; organizational rules may force the boss to be first.

Another criterion is who came up with the idea, or initiated the writing effort. This is reasonable, if that person contributes substantially after his initial spurt of inspiration. It is not a good idea if the idea is simple, but the research and writing are difficult.

Clearly, effort matters too. However, often you do not know how much effort each member of the team will contribute until you finish.

Chances are some in your team have stronger personalities than others. Personalities do not predict who is doing the work or who should get the most credit. Before making a decision, ask if the quiet members of the group are getting fair treatment. Even if you can agree on authorship priority at the start, things can happen that may suggest revising this decision later.

Can you put off the authorship decision until the end? If yes, then come up with a fair process you can execute at the conclusion of the writing? That is, at the beginning you decide on how you will determine authorship later. This works if you can state the criteria for authorship order, you can measure these criteria with little dispute, and everyone agrees the results will be fair. You need to be able to deal with disagreements over who goes first: does everyone agree everyone contributed equally, for example? This brings us to coin flipping.

Can you leave it to chance? My favorite solution is a coin flip. If my co-authors and I cannot agree that one of us is the lead author, then we agree to flip a coin (two co-authors) or use some other gamble (drawing cards from a hat, for example). Why does this work? Before we flip the coin, each of us has an equal chance at first authorship. We both know if we lose the coin flip it has nothing to do with anyone's perceived deficiencies or status.

To add to the drama, I usually suggest we find a mutual fair friend who will flip the coin and report the results. We authors agree who has heads and tails but do not share this information with the flipper. Then we abide by the results. I prefer to do this at the beginning of a writing project. You can use it at the end, but you and your co-authors need to agree on the use of a coin flip early.

My Superpower

I have never lost an authorship coin flip in over 40 years. That is six flips. I calculated that the probability of this occurring is less than 16 chances in 1000 [< .016]. We used different coins. Each flip was made by a third party, using a coin of their choice. I warn co-authors that I have the superpower to suspend the laws of probability. No one believes me, because I only write with people who believe in the laws of probability. They always lose. You can make of this what you will.

Here is a simple process for selecting the first author. If you have more than two authors, just adapt it for your circumstance. After you agree on the topic, but before you have started your research and assembling of facts, you agree to follow the process in Figure 4.1. Start on the left side. You either agree on who should be first author, or you cannot decide, or you believe there is too little information to decide. If you can agree on an obvious choice of first author, then make that choice and go on to write.

If the choice is unclear, ask yourselves "Can we wait until later to make this choice?" If the answer is "No" then flip a coin and live with the consequences. If you can wait, agree on when you will make that decision. If at that point, the choice is obvious (e.g., one of you did far more work than the others), then make that choice. If not, flip a coin.

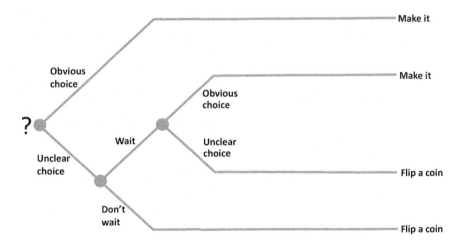

Figure 4.1 Deciding Who Will Be the First Author

Does it matter who is first author? Often not. Some status gets attached to this, particularly among academics who seem to need status markers. It seems fair that the person doing the most work gets the first position. My first professional rumpus was over this topic: I had developed and executed the project, and wrote the report, but my boss wanted credit, so I appealed to his boss and won. So although you can overestimate the importance of a first authorship, it is still meaningful and sometimes worth fighting for. But, is this fight worth it given everything else going on? Writing entails compromise.

Who Has Responsibility for What?

The next decision is how to divide writing tasks. The privileges of lead author come with greater responsibilities. The last author generally will have fewer responsibilities. That general rule is just a start. Who will do the research on each topic? Who will describe this research? Will the person running the statistical analysis write this section, or will she provide notes to a stronger writer? Who is responsible for the production of figures, charts, tables, and other graphics? Who will be the team editor/reviser? Will all share this responsibility or is it one person's job? Who is the contact person with the people who asked you to write the piece, or the journal to whom you are sending your article?

These are all decisions you will need to address. Some you can address at the start, but others might have to wait. Do not assume that once you have made a decision that is the end. Things can change. A task that you thought was relatively minor at the beginning turns out to be consequential, for example. Should other team members play a greater role in carrying out that task?

There are a number of ways to divide tasks. If your report has multiple sections, team members can have responsibility for preparing each section. Then one of you must have the responsibility of stitching them together. This assumes you have a clear idea of the report's organization: you have an outline, for example. So the team needs to organize the writing before this decision can be made.

You could divide tasks functionally. One person does the background research. Another conducts the statistical analysis. A third does the writing based upon what the first two produce. A fourth team member might edit the first complete draft. You may not need an outline to assign tasks this way, but you do need to have a clear idea of what the project looks like.

How Will You Assemble the Pieces?

If several of you are engaged in writing, you will have a first draft that reads like several people wrote it. Your readers will not appreciate this honesty. You need to decide how you are going to create a consistent voice throughout the document. Someone will have to edit the document from beginning to end and make it read as if a single person wrote it. The writing team needs to agree upon who will have this final and crucial crack at the document.

There is something you can do early that will help. Agree on a style. Select a writing book that can provide the guidance you need. Then, if there is disagreement among team members, you can look up some of the answers. Later in this book I show how to use a formula to judge reading difficulty. You could decide that your report will have a score of 12 (I explain this number later). Therefore, all team members will write to this standard. Making style and formatting choices early not only reduces conflict later, it saves time when someone has to edit the parts.

Who Has the Final Word?

One team member should have the final say in editing. Their eyes are the last of the team's eyes to go over the paper and make the final decisions. They have the responsibility of ending any disputes with a definitive call: this is how we are going to deal with this. There should be discussion to this point, but if the team members cannot resolve the debate, this team member gets the final word. You should decide on this person early, before the disputes arise. My rule of thumb is that this person is the lead author. They will take most of the heat for the mistakes, so they should have the final word.

How Do You Resolve Differences of Opinion?

It is difficult to keep your ego out of your writing. My only advice is to be honest and kind to each other. Do not worry about minor things that are difficult to resolve (e.g., if your co-author loves the word "utilize" and you know that this word sucks, do not go to the mat over it). Unless the document is extremely crucial, find a way for working things out even if you have to lose some arguments. Then, next time you have to write with someone, avoid writing with that person.

Consequently, before beginning you and your writing partners need to work out how you will resolve differences of opinion. Honest discussion about this in the beginning will help later. Do not assume that because you are all friends and have worked together before that you will be able to thrash things out. Friendship helps but even if you have worked together for some time, you will have differences. If you are new to each other, then each of you will have to put more effort into this.

I have discovered that the more discussion I have with my teammates prior to writing, the more easily things go during writing. I like having numerous meetings in the beginning. Each of us learns how the others think and what they expect. We can adapt ourselves to each other. These meetings can also increase trust and allow us to place our fate in the hands of the others without too much concern. Writing can be an intimate process, so trust is important. If you are editing my draft, I want to know that you are serious about writing and your edits are for the good of the team, the final product, and our readers. Then we can disagree as colleagues, and we can lose arguments without trouble.

Moving On

After this chapter, I will go back to using the lie that you are a lonely writer scribbling by your-self. That is just a convenient way to make my writing easier; I can use singular pronouns. If this assumption is wrong for you, adjust my advice accordingly. For most of my advice, that will work, if you and your co-authors are in agreement. Later I will push for simple words in short, active sentences with few adjectives. I will press you to include many examples, and to use figures and charts liberally. Your co-authors may have other ideas. They may love long sentences, immense words, numerous adjectives, and sentences so passive they appear comatose. They may dislike examples and hate figures and charts. You will have to work this out. Perhaps you can persuade them to write clearly, but maybe you cannot.

Life is a compromise in the best of circumstances. If your co-authors are people you like and want to keep as close friends and colleagues, then you will have to find a way of producing a product you can live with while maintaining your friendship. You might find that to preserve your friendship you need to sacrifice co-authorship. Only if you feel that your readers will be seriously harmed by unclear writing is it worth getting into a nasty argument. And a nasty argument is only worth it if you win.

Still, do not be a jerk. Make a strong but civil argument to your co-authors and live with the results. Rather than create a furor over the entire report, you should carefully select passages most critical to your readers. The abstract, introduction, and conclusions are my targets. If you cannot get the entire thing written clearly, seize control over the parts that matter most.

OK, now back to pretending you are writing alone.

5 Getting Started

Five Questions

I know you are eager to get to the writing, but before you put your fingers to a keyboard, answer these five pairs of questions:

1. Why do you need to write something? What is your *purpose*?
2. What new thing can you say about your topic? How will you be *useful*?
3. Who will read your document? Who is your *audience*?
4. Who will judge your document before your readers can see it? Who are the *gatekeepers*?
5. What do you need to write your work? What *resources* do you need?

Answering one pair helps you answer the other pairs. Therefore, be consistent. Consider how you will revise earlier answers based on your answers to later questions.

Each pair of questions is a section of this chapter. After I address each, I will conclude with a suggestion: write a very brief statement summarizing your answers. Write this "mission statement" in the simplest and clearest way possible. You are its primary audience.

Purpose: Why Do You Need to Write Something?

We write for a variety of reasons. Let us start with the reason most familiar to you. Someone told you to write it. It was not your idea. Someone gave you this task. Almost all course papers are of this type. Your instructor told you to write a paper on some topic. If they had not ordered you to do this, you would not have done so. Those of you who have jobs may have encountered this reason in your organization. You were happily minding your own business when your boss told you to write a memo, report, or other document. If this is your reason, your satisfaction depends on completing the assignment to the satisfaction of others. This might be the most common reason people write.

The second reason may be less familiar to you. You write something because you are interested in that topic and you think others might benefit from your knowledge. I mentioned that I once wrote a short essay lampooning community policing. No one asked me to do this.

DOI: 10.4324/9781003167532-7

I did it because it occurred to me that the many ways advocates described community policing were silly or self-defeating. I wrote my little essay as a joke I planned to share with my office colleagues. That was my purpose. You might recall that my boss, once he saw my joke, had another idea. Purposes can change. Still, always have a purpose when you begin.

I have a friend, Howard Rahtz, a retired police commander. Among his many tasks, he wrote reports for his department. These were assigned tasks. Before and after retirement he wrote five books on community policing, use of force, drug problems, riots, and mass shooting. These he wrote because he wanted to. I asked him what prompted him to write. He told me his books came out of various assigned projects, and his deep concern about how various problems were being discussed among police and the public.

You might not envision yourself deciding to write something. You might think, what do I know that is so deep or original that anyone else would want to read it? Unless you have a gift of prophecy, do not assume you will never have ideas worth writing. Of all the unforeseen things that will happen to you, self-initiated writing may be the least weird of all of them. As you gain experience, it is likely you will discover you have something worth sharing.

If, like my friend, you get the urge to write, then your satisfaction depends on pleasing yourself. In part, pleasing yourself depends on completing the writing and in part it will depend on how many people read your work and how they react to it.

The third reason is related to the second; you come to believe that there is a need for something written on the topic. Once I watched a friend present an idea to several police commanders. The idea was so good I felt she should share it with a larger audience. So she and I set out to create that paper. With the help of one of my doctoral students, we published it. Judging from the reactions I have heard, my friend's idea was something people needed to hear.

I wrote this book because I became tired of reading poorly written student papers, published articles, and other documents on crime. I talked to many students and colleagues. I discovered that they too did not like the current state of writing in our field and others. Over ten years of whining later, I wrote this book because no one else was likely to do it.

If this is your reason, then your satisfaction depends on how people put your work to use. For your work to be put to use, someone has to read your work. Further, these people need to communicate your ideas to others, who may not have read your work.

The last reason for writing is that you think you can earn some money from it. You can make money in two ways. The first is royalties. Royalties are what your publisher pays you for every book sold. Your publisher has to sell many books for you to make much. There are people who earn a great deal of money from writing. But very few are involved with social sciences. The exceptions are those few who write super-popular textbooks. Very little I have written has put money in my pocket, and the total amount I have earned from royalties is paltry. If money is your aim, prepare for a great deal of disappointment. You might become rich. However, you might earn enough to take a loved one to a nice restaurant (if you are not extravagant in your choice of wine). Even more likely, your publisher will send you a royalty check for $5.03. To make money this way, you will have to have many readers. To get those readers, you will need some help marketing your work.

The second way to make money writing is to have someone pay you up front to produce a document. Typically, an organization hires you as a consultant and your report is one of several things it expects you to produce. I have written several things like this. Usually, the payment is not great. On three occasions, my co-authors and I made a respectable amount. If this is your plan, you must have a good reputation as well as ideas to convince someone to pay you in advance.

You may have multiple purposes. Perhaps you have a deep interest in a topic that will help people do things better and someone is willing to pay you to write about that topic. Or, perhaps your organization tells you to investigate a topic and write up your results. After you begin, you discover that the topic is fascinating and your report could have a useful impact on people's lives. If you have multiple purposes, you should try to rank them. Give some careful thought to this. Would you write the report if you were not ordered? Not paid? Found the topic dull? Found the topic socially useless (or reprehensible)?

If you can answer the "purpose" question, you have some idea of how your writing can be useful, who will read it, and who you need to satisfy for your possible readers to get a chance to read it. Why you are writing is uninteresting to readers, but is important for you. Knowing your purposes helps answer the other questions. For example, if you are writing for your own needs, then you do not have to worry too much about what others have said, who will read it, or satisfying a gatekeeper. If you believe you have something useful that will help others, then you need to know the answers to the other four questions. If someone ordered you to write something, you need to know what they want and the format they want it in. If you expect a publisher to market your document, you need to know how they perceive the market for your ideas: the likely readers; what readers want; the alternatives readers can turn to; and the format readers expect.

Write a sentence (or two, but only two) describing your purpose. Save this, because you will need it again.

Usefulness: What New Thing Can You Say about Your Topic?

Why would a reader want to read what you wrote? They have plenty of other things to do, and they are probably not waiting impatiently for your document to arrive on their desks.

The answer is, you have something new to say. Your writing needs to give value to your readers. So put on your readers' assorted hats and consider how you will fulfill their needs. But also, look at your readers' situations. Do they have needs they do not realize? What can you say that will help them?

Here are some common ways a document can be useful:

- Lots has been said about a topic, but no one has summarized this.
- Lots has been said, but it is wrong in some important way.
- Lots has been said, but not to your readers.
- Few if any have investigated the topic, but the topic is important.
- Many have looked at this topic, but they missed the idea you are writing about.
- No one has provided guidance about how to do something your readers must do.
- Many have written on the topic, but they were poor writers and you can produce something better.

You need to create something original. It does not have to be earth shattering. It just needs to be better than what exists, for the people you want to read it.

Write a sentence (or two, but only two) describing why your planned piece will be useful to readers. Save this because you will need it later.

Audience: Who Is Supposed to Read Your Final Document?

If it were possible to take a picture of the people who will read your document, then I would urge you to put that picture above your desk (or wherever you write). Then, while you are writing, ask yourself, "What will they think of this? Will they understand it correctly?" Unfortunately, we seldom know who our readers will be. But you should attempt to imagine your readers.

I write for two kinds of readers, usually. For most of my professional life, my primary readers were police officials. I imagine this diverse group to include police chiefs, top-level commanders, middle managers, and line officers. For some of my writing I imagine crime analysts, both police officers and civilians. I learned that in any large police department there are a few voracious readers. They are often people below the rank of police chief.

A decade ago, two police friends called me to ask if I could meet them for coffee. They wanted advice on a project they were starting. At the meeting, one pulled out a copy of a book published the previous month. She had read it and made notes. She asked me what I thought of it. Embarrassed, I admitted that I had heard of the book, that I respected the author, and I planned to read it (all true), but I had not done more than look at its cover.

This officer and her lieutenant (now a police chief in another agency) are who I think about when I write. I also imagine police officials whose bosses give them my writing. They may not be avid readers, but they are important readers. There is an audience outside police agencies who have strong interest in improving policing. These community members, city administrators, and staffers to elected officials are a small but important subgroup of my readers. Even when I am writing for police, I am also aware that some academics may read my work. So I take them into account, as well.

Since the late 1990s, much of my writing has been for academics. They are not one group. Some are interested in policing. Others are interested in research design and measurement. And others are interested in crime patterns. Depending on what I am writing, I focus on one group more than the other groups. This is just a matter of degree, as the academics I write for are not respecters of watertight compartments. But I also try to write my academic papers in ways that police and other professionals outside of academia can understand. In the 1980s, on one of my visits to police agencies, I met a night commander of an investigations unit. I interrupted his reading of an article from the *American Journal of Sociology*. I think of him when I write academic articles.

Here are some audiences you should consider when you plan to write a document:

- Supervisors who will use it.
- Academic experts who will cite it.
- Students who might learn from it.
- Grant and contract reviewers who might give you money based upon it.
- Practitioners who will implement it.
- The press who might write about it.
- The public who might influence policy makers to act on it.

How diverse are your readers? If your imaginary readers look a great deal like you, you need to broaden your imagination. Your readers will have a range of expectations, knowledge, and beliefs that you need to consider. What do you know about them? What do they know that you need not explain? What are they unlikely to know that you need to explain? Whenever you make choices about writing, consider your reader.

Write a sentence (or two, but only two) describing your readers. Save this because you will need it later.

Gatekeepers: Who Will Judge Your Document First?

Are there people who must review your work before you send it to readers? These are gatekeepers. In an organization, your boss might be a gatekeeper. Others cannot see your report until she is satisfied that you did what you were supposed to do. Journal editors and their reviewers serve as gatekeepers for those of us who want to publish our research in academic journals. Publishers have individuals who decide whether your book proposal is worthy: they too are gatekeepers. If you apply for a grant or contract, your written proposal will have to be reviewed by someone in your organization. This person is a gatekeeper. Unless you are self-publishing a book, or writing a blog, there are always gatekeepers.

The upshot is that before you can get your work before the eyes of your readers, you must convince gatekeepers to allow your work to go forward. External reviewers sound dreadful. Sometimes they are. Nevertheless, good reviewers can help you improve your work and keep you from making a fool of yourself. I discuss reviewers in Chapter 17.

Gatekeepers can have objective and subjective requirements. Examples of objective requirements include type fonts, word limits, table layouts, and reference formats. These you can learn from websites and talking to gatekeepers. Subjective requirements are seldom explicit. These can include writing style, form of argument, research methods, and other things. You can learn these by reading documents from the organization (e.g., reports from your agency, articles from a journal). Study both types of requirements before starting to write.

Resources: What Do You Need to Write Your Work?

You might not think you need resources to write, but you do. You need time to complete your writing. You need access to reference works, you may need data, you may need analytical tools to process the data, and you might need quiet. Do you have these?

Time

Before you do anything else, you need to know when your writing project must be finished. The deadline is second only to the topic in importance. Time drives everything. If someone has asked you to write something, ask them for the last day you can put it in their hands. If they are wise, they will give you a date that is sooner than they really need it. You know that, and they know that you know. This can go on forever, so do not second, third, and fourth guess this person. Confirm the day, write it down, and plan to finish your project so they get it earlier. If their deadline is improbable or impossible, then negotiate a different due date. This is not a book on negotiations and I do not know the details, so that is all I can say on this.

Once you know when you need to be done—I mean done done: not sort of done because you need to edit it, or find some facts, or complete some other task—then create a schedule. Give yourself plenty of time to revise and edit. If possible, give yourself some time in which you do nothing on this writing project. This might be a week doing something else inserted between completing the first draft and revising. Even a day off is useful. You will need to see your writing with renewed eyes. Assume everything will take longer than you think. If your draft schedule has five days of writing your first draft, give yourself ten.

If you do not have a deadline, then set one. That is what I did for this book. I gave myself a year to complete the first draft. I set aside several months to reread writing books I last opened decades ago, and to examine newer books. I assigned myself the task to speak to publishers at a professional conference. So far, I have been reasonably good at keeping to my self-imposed deadlines. The COVID-19 outbreak disrupted my plans, so I adjusted them. This plan has helped me continue to make progress. When you are the one who commissioned your work, sticking with the project requires willpower.

Take into account interruptions. If you can remove yourself from distractions, do so. Turn off your phone. Put it in a box. Bury that box in your yard, or give it to a neighbor for safe-keeping. If you cannot remove yourself from these annoyances, then plan accordingly. If the cat loves sitting on your keyboard, and you love your cat, then make your plans with your cat in mind. The less experience you have with professional writing the more optimistic you will be in your plans. You cannot predict what will get in the way, but you can predict that something will get in your way.

Write a sentence (just one) describing the deadlines. Then write five or fewer sentences to outline your schedule. Save these because you will need them later.

Place to Write

It's hard to write in noisy conditions with many interruptions. So if your work space does not supply the right atmosphere, can you write somewhere else? I am lucky. My university office is pleasant for writing, and so is my office at home. Since I hate phones, I seldom have my cell phone turned on. Still, I find my mind wandering. When at the office, my mind wanders to who I should visit in the office (thus wasting my time and theirs). When at home, I consider snacks, or doing the dishes, or taking out the trash. So, sometimes I take my laptop to a coffee shop where I am unlikely to see anyone I know or have chores that need doing. I like the background bustling noise of such places.

Make a note of where you will write.

Access to Background Materials

If you are writing something off the top of your head, that is just your opinion, background materials will not be a problem. But for anything else, you will need access to books, articles, websites, and other materials. You may need access to special databases. You might need to speak to an expert or two. Make sure you can get this information in the time you have.

If you are a university student, you have access to the library. As a professional working at a proper job, your access to a university library may be limited. Seek your public librarians and ask for help. I have had several friends in police agencies who made good use of their public libraries. If you are in a large city, there may be several specialty libraries available (part of a museum or corporation, for example).

List where you are getting your background information.

Computer

You will need something that runs a good word processor, backs up your documents, and doesn't crash. Do not rely on your phone. If you want to write a long treatise on your phone, do it as a hobby. If you become great at this stunt, only then consider your phone a professional writing instrument.

Make a note about your equipment needs.

Helpers

These are proofreaders and others who will catch your mistakes and point out inconsistencies and awkward phrasing. They are people who will ask you if you have a source for some minor fact you describe on page 37, near the bottom. In my first 17 years of professional writing, I was blessed with several outstanding editors. They helped my writing look better than it deserved to look. Their efforts taught me a great deal. I have had a few graduate students who were fantastic editors: it takes courage to be a student editing your professor's work, along with intelligence, and an eye for detail. If you are fortunate, your organization will provide an editor. If not, find someone who can do this essential job. Be nice to them, regardless of what they say about your writing. If you find someone who ruthlessly turns your draft into something others want to read, lavish them with thanks and hope they stay in your life.

Make some notes about who can help you, or how you will find helpers.

Write a Mission Statement (or Proposal)

For any long piece of writing, create a mission statement (also known as a proposal). I hate organizational mission statements, so I had to take a deep breath before writing this advice. Organizational mission statements are vague and could apply to any organization. They are bullshit, most of the time.

Still, if they were clear, they could serve a purpose. Therefore, I suggest that before you begin your first draft, create a mission statement for your writing project. Remember all those sentences, notes, and lists I asked you to prepare? Use these to start your mission statement. Keep it to one page. Write how you will address each of the five things I described in this chapter: purpose, usefulness, audience, gatekeepers, and resources.

Exercise 5.1

Create a checklist you can use for beginning your writing. Include on it the things and conditions you need to start and continue writing.

The mission statement is for you, so do not bullshit yourself. Write it like you would say it to a friend over a beer (or coffee, or other beverage). Write it in first person: "My purpose is …"; "This will be useful for …"; and, "Delbert Smith needs to review the …" If you have a co-author or two write, "Our purpose is …" Make all sentences active voice. Keep all sentences in this statement under 15 words. Why one page and this style? Because it will force you to be specific, to cut out the qualifiers and padding. You need to be clear about what you are about to do, and it is easier to be clear with fewer words than many.

Your mission statement serves two purposes. The most immediate purpose is to force you to be clear to yourself about what you are planning to do. Even if you never look at it again, it has done its job (assuming you are not bullshitting yourself). The second purpose is to serve as a reminder. Later, deep into your writing, you might forget what it is you are trying to accomplish. Whip out your mission statement and get some clarity. Then either revise what you have been writing, or revise the statement.

If you have been assigned the writing task, you can ask the person who commissioned your writing to review your mission statement to make sure both of you agree on your task. If you are writing a book, your potential publisher will ask you for a proposal (which is a somewhat longer mission statement).

Once you have a mission statement, or proposal, then you are ready to pull out the keyboard, turn on your writing machine, flex your fingers, and put things in order.

Part III   Writing

6 Order

The Mystery of Order

Order is the most important feature of all writing. In the best writing, order is so natural that you cannot imagine an alternative. But there was one, perhaps more than one, and the author made choices to create that order.

When I began writing this chapter, I thought it would be easy to explain these choices. My next thought was: "Did any of my teachers teach me about order?" My earliest teachers tried to teach me about spelling: letter order. Being dyslexic, I had trouble absorbing those lessons. One year, in middle school, I failed all but one weekly spelling test. Another teacher tried to teach me to diagram a sentence: word order. I was as good at diagraming as I was with spelling. Another teacher showed us how to describe things: sentence order. I recall her telling us how to describe a room—beginning at the door describe the room in a clockwise circular sweep. That made sense, but when I described the room, my description bounced off random objects. I am not an orderly person.

DOI: 10.4324/9781003167532-9

Several teachers tried to teach me to outline my ideas before writing. I like outlines, but I do not recall a teacher giving me an assignment to outline something. I am not sure what my grade would have been. I also cannot recall any principles of why I should mention one thing before another.

When teachers and editors commented on my work, they would circle a sentence and move it elsewhere. These suggestions usually made sense. But I do not recall anyone giving me principles of orderly writing. I had to intuit order from their comments. I asked friends, who are superb writers, "Did anyone teach you principles of which sentence goes before the others, which paragraphs are first and which are second?" They could not recall any principle. They too learned by trial and error.

So when I thought about this chapter, I realized I had no rules of order.

Perhaps writers of writing books discussed order. Of the 40 books on writing I read, few gave more than artistic arm-waving advice. John McPhee showed how he used diagrams. I love diagrams and use them, so I was delighted to see an award-winning author use diagrams. To be fair, I did not understand his diagrams. But that is not important. He drew them, originally, for himself; as long as he understood them, they work. Jack Hart (see *Further Reading*) provides a good description of how to imagine the order of a long piece of narrative nonfiction. But most books I have seen on writing do not describe principles of keeping ideas in order.

By the time I read McPhee's and Hart's books I had written a first draft of this chapter. Their advice confirmed that order is far more complex than my teachers implied. So I begin with my four reasons why order is hard. Then I describe a zoological garden of orders, most are useful in particular circumstances but none are useful in all circumstances. It is one thing to see varieties of order, and something else to choose one. So after I discuss types of order, I have a section on the messy process of choosing order. Then I have a section about readers. Although the order may be plain to you, you need to make it plain to the reader. The last section does what all last sections do, concludes. I list some general points that might assist you in getting better at ordering your writing.

Why Is Order Difficult?

All clear writing is orderly. This is true even if the topic appears disorderly. If you are writing a piece of fiction, then you can appear disorderly. One of my favorite books is *Catch-22*, by Joseph Heller. Heller jumps back and forth in time, sometimes in mid-paragraph. I have read *Catch-22* close to ten times and I still do not have a sense of where it begins or ends. But I am not teaching you how to write fiction. Stifle your literary ambitions for a while and be orderly.

There are four difficulties in creating orderly writing. The first difficulty is that the written world and the actual world have different orders. The second difficulty is that you may not have a good idea of the order of your ideas. The third difficulty is that you may understand your order but your reader may not. The fourth difficulty is that order is necessary at multiple levels of your manuscript. I will deal with each.

Exercise 6.1

Reread the second paragraph of this section. It illustrates several principles of order. I started by saying there are four difficulties. Then I numbered them first, second, third, and fourth. I used the same sentence structure. Then I told you what I will do next. I designed this paragraph so you would know the order. I did not make you discover it on your own.

Difficulty 1: Conflicts between Writing and Ideas

Writing is linear. One letter follows another to make a word. If you mix up this order, either you produce a word different from the one you intended, or you produce nonsense. One word follows another to make a sentence. If you mix up this order, you either produce a sentence different from the one you intended, or you produce nonsense. One sentence follows another to create a paragraph's idea. If you mix up this order, either you create a fresh idea, or you produce incoherence.

Unfortunately, the subject about which you are writing may not be linear. Several things may occur at the same time, for example. Or, the past, present, and future get mixed up.

Here is an example. You are trying to describe how an offender decides. The decision is in the present. The decision has consequences. The consequences are in the future. However, the offender expects these consequences because he has had particular experiences. Those experiences were in the past. Do you describe the offender's decision-making in historical order: past, present, future? That seems natural. Do you start with the consequences and work back to the beginning? Criminal investigations seem to go this way: here is a dead body, here is a suspect, here is a motive, here are experiences that explain the motive. Do you start with now and then jump back to the past and then to the future? This too sounds reasonable. Many television plots, movies, and novels do this. So which order should you select to write about the offender's decision?

Writing involves imposing a linear order of words, sentences, and paragraphs on a world that is not linear. You must impose an order about the world in such a way that your reader can reconstruct the world's order from your writing order. This is a complex task.

Difficulty 2: What Is the Order?

The second difficulty is that you may not have a clear idea of the order of that piece of the world about which you want to write. What comes first? What comes last? What goes in the middle? Of the three things in the middle, which is first, second, and third? Sometimes, the answers are obvious. Unfortunately, almost all things interesting or even a bit complex have orders that may be unclear at first. You have to dig order out of the messiness of reality.

Your teachers, like mine, may never have taught you about order. They may have expected us to grasp order intuitively after a great deal of trial and error. But our math teachers did not do this. My math teachers did not tell me to divide 367 by 17 before giving me a set of procedures. Long division was difficult for me. It was difficult because I had to recall a series of steps in order. My math teachers had an order, I just could not recall the steps faithfully. If I made an arithmetic error, my teachers could point to the step I missed. It took me a while, but I did learn long division. This is not the case with writing.

To help you with this difficulty, I decided to list all the orders I could imagine. I came up with 16. I will describe them after we end discussing the four difficulties.

Exercise 6.2

Reread the paragraph above beginning with, "To help you with this difficulty." I had to resolve an order problem. In the above paragraph, I am describing the second difficulty. I introduce a set of orders. I could describe each now. However, there are many types and I suspect that introducing them now will confuse you. So, I mention that there are several types of order and tell you that I will deal with them later. This is how I deal with the third difficulty.

Difficulty 3: Does Your Reader Understand the Order?

The third difficulty is that your reader may not understand the order. It might be clear to you, but that does not mean anyone else understands your order. One of my peeves with much academic writing is the lack of clarity about order. An author might say they will discuss three things. The first thing takes three pages to describe. Then the author switches to the second thing but does not give a clear signal she is switching topic. I think we are still on the first thing and then get confused. Even worse, some authors do not tell me there are three things. After several pages, I have left the author's poorly marked road and I am stuck on a muddy trail going into the wily-wags. That is when I break out the post-it notes (if it is a library book) and reread that section. I label the topics on the post-it notes, along with rude remarks about the author's inconsiderate behavior. I would not have to spend this time if the author had road-marked her work.

It is easy to help readers navigate a complex argument, but it requires you to think about the reader. I will come back to this point toward the end of this chapter. I will list some techniques you can use to keep your reader on the road to your conclusions.

Difficulty 4: Order at All Levels

If you have had a research methods course, you know that you can study topics at multiple levels: micro, meso, and macro. For example, I am interested in high crime addresses: a micro-level topic. These addresses array themselves along streets. Some of my friends study crime on street segments: a meso-level topic. Other friends study crime in neighborhoods: a macro-level topic. This is a hierarchy: individual addresses cluster in street segments, which cluster in neighborhoods, and so forth.

Writing order is like this. We confront order within words, sentences, paragraphs, sections, chapters, and documents. It's order all the way up, and all the way down.

A word is an organization of letters. A misspelled word trips your readers. Sentences are organizations of words. A paragraph is an organized set of sentences that drive home an idea. When poorly organized, a paragraph gives the wrong idea or completely confuses the reader. A subsection organizes these ideas into a coherent and forceful argument. When it is badly organized, the argument is flaccid, hard to follow, or incomprehensible. Software can help you with spelling. Software can help with sentences. But I know of no software that will help you compose an orderly paragraph, or help you organize paragraphs into a coherent section.

Consider a section, made up of many paragraphs. The section organizes its paragraphs' ideas into a grand idea. But sections are components of something larger. The first section greets the reader on the reader's home territory; it connects to the reader's knowledge, beliefs, attitudes, and desires. The sections bring the reader along to the last section. It is a journey at many levels. For the reader, each paragraph is a step in that journey, each sentence is a knee flex, and each word is a heartbeat. You want the reader to have a pleasant walk with no stumbles, falls, or other accidents. You do not want the reader straying off the trail, or giving up. You need to signpost each fork in the path and provide guidance in places she could get lost. When your reader arrives at your last section you contrast what your reader knows now to what she knew at the beginning of her journey.

A difficulty arises when you lose track of the level and its order. You might have a perfectly orderly paragraph that drives home an important point. However, if that paragraph is out of order relative to its adjacent paragraphs, it creates trouble for your readers. Making things more difficult for you is the simple fact that the order you pick for one paragraph may not be the right order for other paragraphs in the section. You need to keep track of multiple orders, at multiple levels.

This chapter on order applies to all levels of writing. However, it may be most helpful to you for organizing paragraphs. Throughout this chapter, I refer to the order of ideas or topics. You should think of an idea or topic as a single paragraph or a cluster of closely related paragraphs. Which should go first? Which comes next? Which should be at the end?

Look at this example from a book on writing. The author starts his second chapter by talking about purpose, strategy, and style, in that order. Here is the paragraph that follows:

> Think of purpose, strategy, and style in terms of increasing abstractness. Style is imme-diate and obvious. It exists in the wiring itself; it is the sum of the actual words, sentences, paragraphs. Strategy is more abstract, felt beneath the words as the immediate ends they serve. Purpose is even deeper, supporting strategy and involving not only what you write about but how you affect readers.

(Kane, 2000: 9)

Do you sense the disorder? If purpose, strategy, and style are listed in order of increasing abstractness, then the sentences that follow are out of order. The author should have organized his lead sentence to say, "Think of style, strategy, and purpose in terms of increasing abstractness." That is the order of the sentences that follow, and that is the order of abstractness. No commercial software exists that can reliably flag disorder of this sort.

g

ve difficulty organizing your ideas, take heart. Everyone does. That is because order
xcept with the simplest ideas. In the next section, I show that there are at least 16
ose from. That is a lot. However, once you have a typology of orders and under-
...ere each has value, you may find the struggle to find order easier.

Types of Order

Several times, I promised you I would show you types of order. I will fill my promise now. Each order has its purpose. None is useful in all circumstances. In a long piece of writing, or in any writing describing a complex topic, you may use two or more of them. The Summary of Orders lists the orders that occurred to me.

Summary of Orders

Useful to the reader

> Given
> Convention
> Sequential
> Importance
> Familiarity
> Complexity
> Culminating
> Goldilocks
> Anti-Goldilocks
> Alternating
> Acronym
> Hierarchy
> Flow

Less useful to the reader

> Intuition
> Alphabetical
> Discovery

The reasons I came up with this list are simple and modest. I want you to be aware of many alternatives. I want you to be conscious of possible orders. I want you to think of order as something you help create. You will have to do the hard work of choosing and adapting the order that meets your and your readers' needs.

Use this as a guide that you can adjust to help you. Do not treat my list and descriptions as a deep, sacred text that you must defend against idolaters and heathens. There may be other orders I missed; this seems inevitable. So if you discover another order that helps your reader, use it.

I have divided orders into two groups. The largest group contains orders helpful to readers. I list these from the most obvious and simple to the least obvious and complex. None is more appropriate than another. The value of each depends on what you are discussing in your writing and what the reader expects. The second group contains orders that are less likely to help readers. Use these only when you are desperate. I list them from "possibly useful if nothing else is available" to "please do not use, ever."

Given

By "Given" I mean the reader expects the order. You are writing for a supervisor who has assigned you a topic and told you the order you are to use. Here is a simple example. A quiz question asks: "In light of the evidence we have examined, do hot spots patrols reduce crime? Explain." A perceptive student will realize the instructor has issued a *Given* order for their answer and they are better off answering in that order. The instructor's *Given* order is this: say yes or no, then explain the answer.

Given orders show up in many circumstances. When a government agency offers a grant solicitation for research or technical assistance, it will tell potential applicants the topics they want the applicant to address and the order applicants are to address them. Only fools ignore this and they seldom get funded. Research articles published in journals have a particular order for sections. A wise researcher learns that order and writes their articles to comply with what editors and reviewers expect. Some journals state you must write the abstract for your article in a particular order, or the editor will not examine your submission. Naïve writers sometimes ignore this rule. Guess what happens. Government agencies that issue routine reports often create a standardized order for these reports. If you are writing such a report, your supervisor will not be happy if you exercise creativity. Police agency policy and procedures have a standard order. If you have the task of drafting a policy or procedure, you should follow the *Given* order.

In these examples of *Given* orders, someone thought about the order. *Given* orders from an organization are not arbitrary. You can disagree with them, but they are seldom ridiculous. Even if you can imagine a far better order, use the one given. Your readers expect that order.

Convention

Often social *Convention* rather than explicit rules imply an order. In my department, we have no written rule saying how a doctoral student should organize her dissertation. I could let my students guess at our *Convention*, but I do not. I make sure my students organize their dissertations in a way that will not sadly surprise my colleagues. My students see this as a *Given* order, because I gave it to them. I see it as *Convention* because I am intuiting what my colleagues expect. *Convention* differs from *Given* in that there are no explicit instructions. You have to intuit what readers expect.

Experienced writers have an intuitive feeling about conventions readers expect, often based upon their mistakes. If you are not experienced, then you will need to investigate. Years ago, I had a six-month consultancy with the London Metropolitan Police. I had to write several technical reports for them. Before I did, I examined previously written reports. I also talked to my supervisor and gave her outlines to critique. I then organized my reports in ways that conformed to what I thought my readers would expect. If they were going to be surprised, then I wanted them to be surprised by my ideas not the packaging of my ideas.

If there is an order that others commonly use, or that your readers expect to see, then use it. Their familiarity with this order will make your writing clearer. Even if this order is stupid, consider using it.

There is one exception. If you feel that it is important to challenge this order, then create an original order. For example, by *Convention*, we mention males before females and then children, as in, "The refugee camp contained a mixture of men, women, and children." You might find this *Convention* off-putting: why do guys get the top billing? So you deliberately violate *Convention* by writing, "The refugee camp contained a mixture of women, children, and men." Violate *Convention* if it is important to make a point. However, avoid such violations if this distracts readers from more important points. Pick your battles wisely, but do not shy from important ones.

Sequential

I suspect that when most people refer to orderly writing, they are referring to *Sequential* order. Sequential order undergirds the old expression, "Life is one damn thing after another."

Example: SARA

SARA stands for Scanning, Analysis, Response, and Assessment. These describe the four stages of police problem solving (Eck & Spelman, 1987). Scanning means looking for, identifying, defining, and verifying problems that police should handle. Analysis means closely examining a problem to determine its causes and to lay the foundations for practical solutions. Response involves listing, selecting, and implementing solutions. Assessment is the evaluation of the solution to make sure it is doing what it is supposed to do. I show a diagram for this process in the chapter on diagrams. SARA is in *Sequential* order. It is also in *Acronym* order, which I discuss later. The acronym helps police recall the sequence. Police across the world use this process, in part because it is simple and easy to recall.

If you are describing something involving time, then a sequential order might fit. Imagine a relay team. The first runner holding the baton takes off. After running for a time, he hands the baton to the second runner. The second runner, after his interval, hands it to the third runner. This continues until the last runner crosses the finish line. You can think of each runner's interval as a paragraph or section. The handoffs are transitions.

With *Sequential* order, you describe the events in the order they occur. Simple processes such as recipes work this way: mix these two ingredients; then do something to another ingredient; put the first two ingredients into the third; next, cook this mixture; then serve warm.

Consider describing how a burglar breaks into a house. First, the burglar finds the neighborhood. Then the burglar selects a particular house. Then the burglar determines if breaking in can be accomplished safely. Then the burglar breaks in. Then the burglar finds what he is looking for. Then the burglar leaves. Then the burglar sells his loot to someone. If these are the major steps in a burglary process, you can describe each from the beginning of the burglary to the end.

Just because something evolves in time, does not mean *Sequential* order is your best alternative. Consider a literature review. This may seem *Sequential*. You could write about each document in the order they were published. This sometimes works. Often it does not. That is because the second study may not have followed from the first. The third, fourth, and fifth studies might overlook the second study and none build on the first study. Science seldom progresses in a neat sequence. A *Sequential* literature review will jerk the reader from one study to the next without giving the reader a coherent story. How do you deal with this? Try a different order.

Let us go back to the burglary process. Now, however, imagine you are describing more than a burglary process. You are describing the interactions among burglars, homeowners, and police. While the burglar is undertaking one of his steps, a homeowner is doing something else. The neighborhood's police officer is engaged in a third set of activities. In this example, you have parallel processes to describe. The process of writing conflicts with the reality about which you are writing. Writing allows you to describe one thing at a time, but in reality, several things are occurring at the same time.

You must impose a linear order on this parallel story. You could describe the burglary process, then the homeowner's activities, and then the police. Or you could describe the homeowner first, then the burglar, then the cop. Or, you could start with the police officer, and move to the other two. Alternatively, you could identify a general temporal framework, such as before, during, and after a burglary. Then for each you first describe the homeowner, then the burglar, and then the police officer.

Here is another example. Imagine you are describing three theories of burglary that have some elements in common, but conflict on key points. Like the second example, the writing process conflicts with the subject you are writing about. You have to wrestle that subject into a linear order without mangling it. What order do you use?

Many textbooks describe theories in the order they appeared in the literature. This is helpful if the second theory builds on the first and the third builds on the first two. If the theories do not share a history (for example, one theory comes from a marketing theory of shopping and the other theory comes from a sociological theory of neighborhood deviance) then there is not an obvious order. You could describe them in the order of their popularity. Your readers might be familiar with one theory but not the other two. Therefore, you could start with the theory they know and then move to theories of increasing obscurity. Regardless of the order you pick, you will have to make the non-linear reality conform to the linear requirements of writing. For these circumstances, look at the orders that follow.

Importance

Try ranking your topics or ideas by importance from most to least, or least to most. Here are some examples: biggest to smallest, most to least harmful, most people affected to least. If your readers expect this order, or you can justify this order to your readers, *Importance* is a nice choice. Whether you should move from least to most important, or the reverse, depends on your argument.

Familiarity

Are some things you want to discuss more familiar to your readers than others? If so, then consider ordering them from most to least familiar. This works well when descriptions of the most familiar items teach principles that apply to less familiar items. You begin with something your readers understand well and then proceed by adding concepts of decreasing *Familiarity*. The last concept you add is a topic your readers do not understand when they began reading your work. At the end, they do.

Complexity

Like *Familiarity*, can you rank your topics from simple to complex? This works well when you are describing a few topics that vary in *Complexity*. Because *Complexity* is difficult to measure, if you have many topics, you will have difficulty determining which topic is the most complex; several will compete for that title. However, much depends on your readers. If your readers understand the simplest idea, you can start with that and build to the most complex. But maybe your readers understand a complex topic, and you want to show them how this familiar topic is just one manifestation of a simpler process. Then, you start with the complex and move to the less complex.

Culminating

Are you are building to a specific point? Then order your ideas accordingly. For example, there are four ideas, A, B, C, and D. You want to explain D, but you have to mention the other ideas. Some of your readers might already understand A and B, but are weak on C. So that all readers have the same foundations, you cover all three, A, B, and C. Having dispensed with these, you can focus your readers' attentions on D. *Culminating* is much like a set of stairs: the stairs help bring you up to the landing where you want to spend some time. Often you will combine *Culminating* with one of the above orders.

Except for the first order, *Given*, so far I have described orders involving ranking. Your job is to find the ranking that is most useful and then order your ideas accordingly. The next two orders have rankings, but you do not start at the top or bottom.

Goldilocks

Remember Goldilocks and the three bears? When she was sleepy, she had to choose among three beds. One was too hard. One was too soft. And one was just right. Because the "just right" bed is difficult to understand before understanding the other two beds, it is mentioned last. The hard and soft bed form a context for the just-right bed. Levels of analysis are like this. There are macro-, micro-, and meso-levels. Meso-levels are in between the first two so they are difficult to understand until you understand the extremes. Use a *Goldilocks* order if the reader easily understands the extremes, but might have greater difficulty understanding the middle.

Anti-Goldilocks

This is the opposite of *Goldilocks*. Here, the reader understands the middle position but may not understand the extremes. Therefore, you explain the middle first, then use it to explain the extremes. We often use the *Anti-Goldilocks* order in statistics. Imagine you are describing the ages of offenders that you are studying. With an *Anti-Goldilocks* ordering you write, "The mean age of the offenders was 24, but this varied from the youngest offender, age 18, to the oldest, age 47." The *Anti-Goldilocks* order is related to *Familiarity*; readers are more familiar with the middle category so you start there.

The next two orders are not based on the relationships among the topics. Instead, they focus on the readers' expectations and ability to recall your topics.

Alternating

Imagine you are writing about a crime program. You have written a description of it. Next, you want to give a set of arguments, pros and cons. You could write about all the pro-arguments and then switch to writing about the con-arguments. However, imagine that the pros and cons are pairs; for each pro-argument there is a matching con-argument. Here, if you wrote about all the pros and then all the cons, your poor reader might become confused. Instead, an *Alternating* order might be useful. You describe the first pro-argument and then describe its twin con-argument. Next, you describe another pro and its partner con, and so forth. When you are done you summarize all the pros and all the cons. You might even provide a verdict.

Acronym

Another approach is to create a memorable *Acronym*. An acronym is a series of initial abbreviations that create a word. CRAVED is one of my favorite *Acronyms*. Ronald V. Clarke (1999) created it do describe the attributes of items thieves like. It stands for Concealable, Removable, Available, Valuable, Enjoyable, and Disposable. The more of these attributes an item has, the more likely thieves will want to steal it. Clarke could have listed these attributes in another order: Disposable, Available, Concealable, Valuable, Enjoyable, and Removable, for example. He could have used different words: common instead of available, or expensive instead of valuable, for example. But the CRAVED order makes his list memorable.

It is memorable because you can pronounce it. CRAVED also has the feature of being a real word that suggests the mental state of a thief viewing an object. If you remember that CRAVED describes things that tempt thieves, the six letters prompt you to recall the words they represent.

The letters in the *Acronym* dictate the order you must explain the topics. In a document about thievery, you would introduce CRAVED and then explain the six attributes in C-R-A-V-E-D order. If someone invented a better acronym, perhaps because they discovered a seventh attribute, they would have to explain it in a new order.

You can become too pleased with your cleverness and forget about whether the acronym helps your reader. Be careful. If your items have some natural order that your reader can easily grasp and recall, do not scramble their minds with a new acronym.

The next two orders are more complex than the ones I have discussed so far. For these reasons, draw a diagram of your ideas if it helps you determine which topics come first and which come later. Your diagram is your diagram; you do not have to share it with anyone else. So do not worry about its beauty. Draw it on anything that is handy using any tool that is useful. If you decide the diagram will help your readers, then you can take the time to make it beautiful and put it in your report (see Chapter 15 on Diagrams).

Hierarchical

Sometimes your ideas nest within each other. Classification schemes work this way. You first describe the top category. You then point out that this class has several subcategories. You describe each. As you describe a subcategory, you describe its sub-subcategories. Biologists use this system for the classification of all living organisms. This works best if there is no overlap among categories at any level. There are cats and there are dogs, but there are neither cogs nor dats.

Sometimes there are small overlaps that are not consequential, so you can still use a *Hierarchical* order. Here is a specific example: dog breeds. There are eight groups: sporting, hound, working, terrier, toy, non-sporting, herding, and miscellaneous. Within each group, there are numerous specific breeds. Within herding dogs, there are many breeds including Collies and the Welsh Corgi. There several Collie types and two types of Welsh Corgi: Cardigan and Pembroke.

This example illustrates the groups-within-group structure of *Hierarchical* organizations. It also illustrates the problem of overlaps. In college, I owned a Huskie–Labrador–German Shepherd. This classification system only works for dog fanciers by focusing on so-called "pure" breeds and ignoring my lovely pet.

Outlines are a *Hierarchical* order. Your paper has four sections. Section one has three parts. Part one of Section one has two parts. Part two of Section one has one part. Part three of Section one has four parts, and so on.

Writing about hierarchies presents a problem. Do you describe first all the items at the top level, then all those at the second level, then the third level, and so forth until the bottom? Or do you pick one top-level category, describe that, then go down a level and pick one subcategory and describe that and go down, and so forth? Figure 6.1 is an illustration of a *Hierarchical* classification of crime places that Tamara Herold and I created. It describes a classification system for crime places. Our primary interest was in proprietary places. We drew a version of the diagram before we wrote about the elements in the diagram.

With this illustration, the order is reasonably clear. There are only three top categories, and two have no subcategories. We explained these using size as the order (small to large): proprietary, proximal, and pooled. If we used *Culminating* order we would have done the reverse.

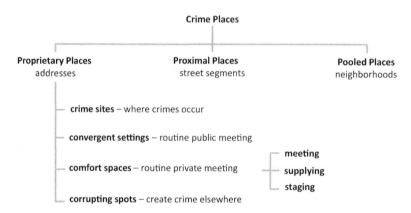

Figure 6.1 A Hierarchical Organization of Crime Places
Source: Revised from Madensen & Eck (2013).

Having described the top level, we then described each of the proprietary places. We described the proprietary types in rough order of *Familiarity*: most obvious at the top and least at the bottom. We explain the three comfort space types when we describe comfort spaces.

Hierarchies are common and varied. My advice is to draw the hierarchy first. You may have to revise this diagram as you go. In my experience, it is easier to revise it if you sketch it first. Then, consider a strategy for leading the reader from the top to the bottom. You may have to experiment, as the pitfall of a choice may not appear until you fall into it. As you discover problems in describing the hierarchy, consider revising your diagram in addition to revising your writing (that is why I sketch on scrap paper). When you have written the description, ask yourself, "Does the diagram help the reader, or can they easily understand what I am saying without it?" If the diagram is not very helpful, then discard it. It is scaffolding: once builders complete their structure they remove the scaffolding. If the diagram is still useful to your readers, keep it. In this case, its purpose is the same as a staircase within the building: it helps the building function. Now take the time to do a final drawing.

Flow

Flow charts combine features of the above types of order. They show branching, as in *Hierarchical* orders, but reveal a sequence of the choices. For an illustration, I selected one that has been circulating since before the internet. I have seen a number of versions of Figure 6.2, most of which use stronger language than is appropriate here (search on "problem-solving flowchart"). Unlike the *Hierarchical* order, a *Flow* chart can have loops. When you trace a path from the beginning of a hierarchy, you come to a unique end, depending on which branches you select. With a *Flow* organization, several paths can lead to the same conclusion.

How do you describe a set of ideas that has this form? What do you describe first, second, third, and eventually, last? It depends. I suspect that if I gave this chart as an assignment to my students, they could come up with several plausible alternatives. That said, for every good way of describing ideas that have this structure, there are several that are not good.

Here is my suggestion. First, recognize that you are dealing with a *Flow* order. Second, draw it. You may need several versions before you have one you like. Keep it as simple as possible.

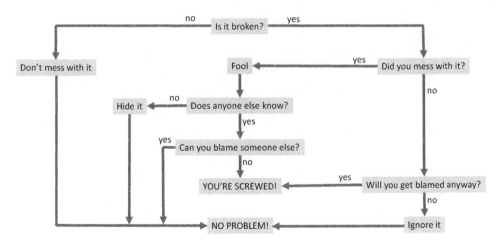

Figure 6.2 A Problem-Solving Flow Chart

Sometimes you can eliminate parts you do not need. Try to draw the diagram so that lines do not cross. This is not a requirement: crossed lines may be necessary. However, the fewer the crossed lines, the sooner you will find a simple way of writing about it. Third, circle a set of boxes and lines that you will describe first. Circle the group you will write about second. Do this until you have explained the entire chart. Before you write, ask yourself, is there is a simpler way? If not, start writing. If there is, reorganize things and then write. Then revise the chart and your draft. At the end, you can discard or keep the diagram, depending on whether you think your readers will benefit from seeing it.

Exercise 6.3

Write a description of this flow chart for a reader who will not see this diagram. Once you have a draft you think might work, give it to the friend and have them draw the diagram you have described. Their diagram and my figure should look similar. Your friend should have all the same boxes and all the same arrows connecting them. They should not have extra boxes or arrows. However, the position of the boxes on their page may be different from my figure. "Did you mess with it?" for example, could be on the right or left. Their diagram could start at the bottom of the page and go up, for example. If they cannot reproduce this chart, examine your description to detect where you should make changes.

Intuitive

Finally, I turn to desperation orders. These are not very helpful to your readers. Please avoid these when there is something better. Still, there are better and worse ways of writing poorly, so if you are desperate, pick the best of the worst.

Sometimes, even after careful thought and experimentation, you cannot imagine a useful order. If you cannot come up with an order that is useful, then order your ideas by intuition. A pair of ideas may have an order but you could place the third and fourth ideas anywhere, for example. There is some order involved, but there is no overarching order for everything. This is what I did for the first group of helpful orders. Their usefulness depends on circumstances so I listed them intuitively. I am not particularly happy with this, but I suspect that intuition is better than the next two alternatives. If you know your topic and understand your readers, intuition might work well. If you just take wild guesses, then it probably is not a great way to write.

Alphabetical

This is almost the worst order. This is only helpful if your readers know the names of each topic and the topics are few. Usually, there is a better choice than this. If you are writing about crime in several cities, you could write about them in *Alphabetical* order. Then if a reader is curious about Albuquerque, Kalamazoo, or Yazoo they can easily find the city about which they are most curious.

Discovery

Here you list things in the order they came to your mind. This is the worst order. It is only good when you are starting out and need to keep track of things. This order—really disorder—is only meaningful to you. Your reader was not privy to your thinking. Throwing things down in your text in the order you discover them is a sad way to engage your reader. Think about order from your readers' perspectives, rather than in the order they occur to you.

Creating Order while Writing

It is one thing to know that there are many ways to order your writing, and quite another to choose one that works. Like any creative process, there is much fumbling in the fog. Here are some ideas I have used for making that fumbling productive:

*   Select the most obvious order and revise it later.
*   Pin down the beginning and end then plan a story to connect them.
*   Talk it over with others, particularly if you are part of a team. Plan for a great deal of talking and false starts. Treat this as play and you will discover things you would not discover otherwise.
*   Create a presentation and deliver it. Thinking about talking may be easier for you than thinking about writing. Then use the presentation as your guide. Explaining your topic to your cat, dog, or ferret is often as helpful as explaining it to a room full of people.
*   Pick an order. If stuck between several alternatives, just choose one (flip a coin). The failings of that order may reveal better orders.

The trick is to never treat your first order as sacred. Always be willing to sacrifice it. Your aim is to produce order at the end of your writing. Do not expect it at the very beginning. I use the dump and sort method often. Before writing, I arbitrarily list all the topics I can imagine. If I know the subject well, they will be reasonably orderly. If I do not, then they are a mess. I do this on note cards. I do this on legal pads. I do this using my tablet with a drawing app. I do this using writing software. I use whatever is handy. Once, while on a beach, I used a stick to organize some ideas in the sand. I do not recommend the stick and sand technique, especially below the high tide line.

After you throw down topics, look for ways to sort, lump, and split. Lumping is combining and splitting is separating. I try to sort the topics so that those that are similar are next to each other. Often, two or more topics are so similar they are really the same thing. Then I lump them. Sometimes a topic seems bulky and hard to describe. Then I look to see how I can split it. After lumping or splitting, I usually have to reorganize again.

I draw diagrams, particularly if I think a *Hierarchical* or *Flow* image will help. I then work back and forth from the diagrams to the text until I think I have a sensible, useful order.

Once I have a useful order, I organize my writing from the big to the small. From my thesis down to the word. I then revise in the other direction: from word to thesis. Then I reverse and revise again from thesis down to word. As I continue to revise, I move up and down these levels. I added this paragraph, for example, on the sixth set of revisions because I felt I had left out some critical ideas about organizing writing. I then went back over it to make sure it fit into the overall section. Throughout, I tried to be conscious of order at multiple levels. Long ago,

I learned that I must revise things multiple times to discover all the errors in the order. How many revisions? As many as your readers need and time permits.

I have been discussing the order you are trying to create in your final document. It is only the last draft that matters. That is what your readers see. If you have a complex document, create a reasonably solid draft order. Then start writing anywhere. You do not have to write from beginning to end. You can write the middle first, then the second section, followed by the last section. So if you get bogged down on a particular piece of your writing, set it aside and work on another piece. Stitch these pieces together in your first draft and edit out the seams. Let the order provide a structure while you write, but always be prepared to change the order.

Keeping Your Readers in Order

I mentioned at the beginning of this chapter that one of the difficulties with order is communicating that order to your readers. There are a number of simple ways to solve this problem.

Tell Them

Yes, it can be as simple as that. Tell your readers the order of things. Once you introduce your writing and get your reader interested, tell them how you organized your document. Something as simple as this will do.

> I have organized this paper into six sections. You are at the end of the first, introductory section. The next section describes two competing theories and the research supporting or contradicting each. The short third section describes my research hypotheses, in light of the earlier research. Following that, the fourth section describes the data I use to test these hypotheses and the principal analytical procedures I apply to these data. The fifth section describes my statistical findings. In the final section, I describe the implications of my findings, for both research and policy.

Now your readers know how your work is organized. You should be sure that what you write complies with this description!

Use Section and Subsection Headings

These serve as navigational aids. They should correspond to the outline of your writing that you described to the reader in the introduction.

Use Bullet Points or Numbered Lists

The bullets or numbers clearly distinguish each separate item. This is much clearer than a set of sentences in a paragraph.

Signposts

If there are 12 things, tell readers, "There are 12 things. They are … [list of 12 things]. I will discuss them in this order." Then give each thing its own paragraph, or even a heading. This is particularly important if each of those things takes one or more paragraphs to describe. It is easy for your readers to get lost. You do not want your readers asking themselves, "Is this still part of the ninth thing, or has this author moved on to something else?"

Diagrams

I have mentioned this earlier regarding how you can keep yourself organized. Here I am emphasizing communicating the order to your readers. Diagrams are useful when you are describing something with many points that are not sequential. This is one reason I have a chapter on diagrams: illustrations help readers see the order. Nobel Prize-winning author Gabriel Garcia Márquez shows a family tree before he begins his book, *One Hundred Years of Solitude*, for this reason. Without it, I would have been lost.

Use Alerts and Reminders

Alerts tell your reader something is coming. You might introduce a topic early in your work, but discuss it in depth later. You can say something like: "I will have more to say about this topic in the third section. For now, it's only important for you to consider _____." A reminder is a reference to an earlier passage where you discussed the topic. You can say something like, "In the second section I mentioned _____. I described one important characteristic. Here I am returning to this topic to describe several other characteristics."

Use the Same Terms

If you give things names early on, use those names throughout. Do not refer to those things by other names. If you were studying countries and referred to "Great Britain" in the beginning do not call the country England or the United Kingdom just to create variety. Besides creating confusion, you would make errors: these names refer to different, but overlapping, areas. If you are discussing a theory that has several names, acknowledge the names in the beginning, pick one to use, and then stick with it.

Be Consistent

Use the same order in lists, diagrams, and in text blocks. If you say, "I am going to talk about four things: B, X, W, and Q," do not then describe these four things in a different order, like Q, X, B, and W. I gave you an example of this sort of mistake earlier. Change either your introductory sentence or the order of the paragraphs that follow. If you have a diagram that conveys a particular order, then use that order in your writing. If you use an acronym, then explain it in the order of the letters. This advice might sound obvious, and it is. However, I have read too many papers by students and colleagues that violate this obvious advice. Remember, when you revise your order you risk errors, so make sure you revise everything connected to it. For example, if you revise a diagram, revise the order of paragraphs that describe the diagram.

As you near completion, keep asking yourself how a reader might be confused. Look for points where your reader could go astray, then fix them. If you have someone read your work, ask her or him to describe confusing areas.

The End of Order

Order is more obvious than easy. We overlook organized writing when the author has done such a magnificent job we cannot imagine an alternative. Disorderly writing stands out because we suffer its consequences. Probably the most important pieces of advice I can give you are these:

Be very aware of order. Look at all your writing, at all levels from words up, and ask yourself, "Does this order make sense? Can I improve it?" My list of 16 orders may help you find something that fits. Or if you have an order, review the list to check if there is a better order.

Pay attention to how other authors order their ideas. If the author has produced a work you like, look carefully at her order and try to understand it. If the author has produced a piece you struggle with, look carefully at this work and search for ways the author might have improved their order or communicated it better. Try your hand at reordering his work to gain practice.

Prepare yourself to reorder and then do it. Think of the order as a plan and consider that "No battle plan survives first contact with the enemy" (attributed to Prussian General Helmuth von Moltke). The order I start with usually differs from the order I end with. My first attempt, and the order that drives my first draft, never survives the completion of that draft. My second draft changes it even more. You will find that the value of the first order is to reveal the better order that you could not see when you started.

Complex writing can hide disorder in a fog of long sentences and big words. In the next chapters, I discuss simple and clear writing. If you follow my advice in these next chapters, you will be better able to detect disorder in your writing and fix it. It will also help you prevent disorder so you will have less to fix.

7 Words

Bloviated Narratives of Discourse

Conceivably, you presuppose elongated utterances demarcate the intellectual from the multitudes; that the use of obesely stretched and wretchedly obscure declarations monumentally obligate others to venerate your discourses, narratives, and chronicles. Conceivably, you imagine bloviated words demonstrate the cerebral; that ginormous textualized ramblings intensify your picturesque philosophies, and catapult disdain upon the pronouncements of inferiors utilizing the speechification of the hoi polloi. If so, you are wrong.

It is difficult to get through college without feeling obscure words are the best. That happened to me, too many of my students, and possibly to you. Enough. Let's write with sweet clarity. Use words that are short, precise, common, and clear. That is this chapter's lesson.

A pompous word addiction is hard to overcome. You must practice writing with short, precise, common, and clear words. Let's start now.

I begin by tackling why simpler words are best. Then I discuss seven commands:

1. Use short words.
2. Use common words, words you understand.
3. Use precise words, not jargon or fad words.
4. Do not make up silly words.
5. Limit adjectives and adverbs.
6. Shun euphemisms.
7. Attend to gender.

DOI: 10.4324/9781003167532-10

Following the chapter's conclusion, I present an appendix that summarizes several tests for bad words. Enough with the preliminary chit chat, let's start.

Why Word Choice Matters

Do long words help you or your readers? In "Consequences of Erudite Vernacular Utilized Irrespective of Necessity: Problems with Using Long Words Needlessly," Daniel Oppenheimer (2006) answers with "no." His title is a joke, but his findings, published in the journal *Applied Cognitive Psychology*, are serious. Oppenheimer experimentally varied word length in five studies to determine how long and short words affect readers' understanding of the text and their perceptions of the writer. He found that unnecessarily long words reduce the reader's ability to understand. Unnecessary complexity makes the readers think the author is less reliable or maybe foolish. Many other studies he reviews come to similar conclusions.

Exercise 7.1

Read Oppenheimer's paper, "Consequences of Erudite Vernacular Utilized Irrespective of Necessity." Write a two-page summary of his research a person with only a high school education can understand.

So here are two reasons to choose short words: they help your readers, and show that you are not a fool or a jerk. Now, let's illustrate these points.

Here is the opening paragraph of a book recommended by a friend:

> This book is about the relationship between people and place. It's about how race and gender, sex, and place interact. It's about the geographic lessons Black Chicagoans learned during the twentieth century and the role housing and architecture, politicians and police played in those lessons. This book argues that policing, surveillance, and architectures of confinement were used to "spatialize blackness" in Chicago, which produced racialized and gendered consequences for Black people on the city's South Side. Through examining interracial sex districts, cramped apartments, project housing, street gangs, and Chicago's AIDS epidemic, this book delineates the workings of spatialized blackness in Chicago. The term "spatialized blackness" underscores how mechanisms of constraint built into architecture, urban planning, and systems of control that functioned through policing and the establishment of borders literally and figuratively created a prison-like environment. These mechanisms were put in place by a police force determined to put a lid on interracial vice, greedy landowners who exploited poor Blacks, race theorists who advocated segregation, city planners who sought to control Blacks, the public-housing authority that wanted to contain crime, and federal policy that waged war on drugs. As a result, parts of Chicago's South Side were confronted with daily forms of prison or carceral power that effectively *prisonized the landscape*. By "prisonize" I mean that techniques and technologies of prison punishment–policing, containment, surveillance and the establishment of territory, the creation of frontiers–functioned in the quotidian space of Black Chicago.
>
> (Shabazz, 2015: 1, emphasis in original)

The first three sentences are clear. Then the trouble begins. Consider these terms:

- Architectures of confinement. Why not just confinement, or buildings?
- Spatialize. This obscure word hides more than it reveals. What's wrong with "Segregate"?
- Racialized consequences. This is too vague and mushy for the serious results the author is describing.
- Gendered consequences. Another euphemism that sucks the air out of the argument.
- Mechanisms of constraint. Are these mechanisms of control?
- Carceral power. More mush. Imagine protestors chanting "Fight carceral power," instead of screaming "Break down prison walls."
- Prisonized. I think the author means that the government made entire neighborhoods prisons. Imagine chanting "Free the prisonized!"
- Quotidian. This word means "every day." Why not say "every day"?

Each word is another wall frustrating understanding. Combined, they create a maze obstructing knowledge. This is unnecessary. I have read many books on race that use everyday words. They are clear and powerful. They make me want to know more. They yank on my emotions. They command me to act.

If you want your readers to read, to feel, and to act, you must entice them. Make it easy. Here is how.

Use Short Words

Once my mother gave me a sweatshirt emblazoned with two words, "Eschew Obfuscation." She gave it to me because, during the 1972 Nixon v McGovern campaign, we had joked about the front-page *New York Times* headline, "McGovern Impugns Nixon, Defends His Owns Veracity" (Lydon, 1972). The words "impugns" and "veracity" are weak. They lack punch. Imagine if the headline had said, "McGovern Calls Nixon a Liar." When Nixon defended himself in 1973, he did not say, "My veracity should not be impugned." He said, "I am not a crook" (The Learning Network, 2011). Senator McGovern, in 1972, also used direct short words. Near the end of his campaign, he responded to a heckler with "Kiss my ass" (Heineman, 2012). He did not say, "Osculate my posterior." To raise funds, the McGovern campaign in my town sold buttons abbreviating "kiss my ass" to "KYA." I proudly wore my KYA button until Election Day.

I am guessing that you had to look up "osculate." The English language has over a million words. Even if you knew most of them, the rest of us would not. If you want to appeal to a small group of elitists, pick long, obscure words. It is harder to find short, obscure words, although scrabble and crossword puzzle enthusiasts have plenty. If you want people to read and understand your prose, pick short words when you can.

"Utilize" is a symbol of word bloat. It contains three syllables and seven letters. Two syllables and four letters are not needed. Use "use" anywhere you could use "utilize." I ban my students from using this ugly utterance. This is a lost cause. Writing experts have been losing the fight against utilize for over 120 years.

One warning sign of bloated words is the three-letter ending "ize." The term "accessorize" was popular for a while, but never with me. A number of my colleagues are in love with "contextualize." It means to put something in context, as in: "He was convicted of mass murder, but once his attorney contextualized his rude behavior, the judge gave him a light sentence accessorized with a small fine."

The word "weaponize" means to change something into a weapon. For some things, this makes sense: weaponizing anthrax spores or uranium, for example. Unfortunately, people are weaponizing all sorts of stuff. I ran across an article about weaponizing psychology (Gray, 2014). Apparently memes have been weaponized, too (Donovan, 2019). Perhaps, inmates weaponize their mashed potatoes. Please try to resist the temptation to accessorize perfectly good words with "ize." There is no need, usually.

Other abuses of language come from "ism" and "ist." There are sensible isms: absenteeism, abolitionism, socialism, and baptism, for example. Their siblings are abolitionists, socialists, and Baptists.

My rule of thumb is to use "ism" or "ist" only if it is a word that has been around for some time and there is no shorter word that will serve my purposes. I choose not to use the newer "isms," like "ableism" (discrimination against people who have a disability). In the ethics chapter, I stated that bad writing discriminates against people with learning disabilities. Did I use "ableism"? No.

Why? Creating longer words by appending "ism" or "ist" makes readers' lives more difficult. They are show-off words, elitist words. And isms and ists are often just elitist ways of calling people names. People on political extremes seem to love flinging "isms" and "ists" at their enemies. I refrain from using them for the same reason I mostly refrain from calling people assholes.

Appending "ization" to the ends of words is common too. I will deal with this later in the chapter. Until then, you can guess my feelings.

Use Common Words

I do not know why so many social scientists choose unclear words (e.g., quotidian) to say everyday things. Some may just like their sounds. Others may be bored with plain words. Or perhaps they think it makes their ideas sound important. They cannot be choosing these words to aid their readers.

To help your readers, embrace plain; avoid obscure terms. Obscure words block readers' understanding and undermine your credibility. They also increase the risk you will choose the wrong word.

Consider "extant." It means, existing, present, or surviving. Now consider these three examples:

> In this paper, we draw a connection between population heterogeneity and state depend-ence processes and extant criminological theory.
>
> (Nagin & Paternoster, 2000: 117)

> The extant research on this topic, however, suggests that community members have posi-tive reactions to these focused policing actions.
>
> (Braga et al., 2014: 634)

> Wilson and I wrote together for the last time in *The American Interest* in 2006. After assessing the extant literature on broken windows, we concluded the following ...
>
> (Kelling, 2015: 628)

What is wrong with these uses of "extant"? Obviously, the authors could only examine existing theory or research; they could not review forgotten or as-yet-to-be-discovered theories. So, telling readers you reviewed *existing* studies tells them nothing. To see why, ponder this: "Not yet conducted research on this topic suggests that community members have positive reactions to these focused police actions."

"We reviewed the extant documents on noodle theft in 14th-century Venice. Unfortunately, earlier records on this heinous crime were destroyed by an earthquake in the 13th century." In this invented example "extant" makes sense because there were documents that had disappeared. Here is another correct use:

> And, perhaps more important, the CAPS program and the problem-solving initiatives therein are extant in all city neighborhoods.
>
> (Carr, 2003: 1283)

But why use an uncommon word when the plain "existing" fits? Consider this fix: "And, per-haps more important, the CAPS program and problem-solving initiatives exist in all city neighborhoods."

Extant is not the only abused word. A colleague sent me an example from a paper on video games and violence:

> However, a strong version of the competition hypothesis states that violent content has no impact beyond its effects on competition and its sequela.
>
> (Anderson & Carnagey, 2009: 732)

Sequela has little to do with sequels, as in "The first Star Wars movie was much better than its eight sequela." Nor does it have much to do with sequences, as in "Things went from bad to worse in a sequela of stupid sentences." It is a medical term. It is the consequences of a disease or injury, as in "The short-term sequela of contracting COVID-19 was that he could not submit his term paper on time."

The authors of the quote should have used "consequences," "results," "outcomes," or "effects." Not only do the authors confuse readers, but they also confuse themselves. Replace "sequela" with "consequences," to produce "However, a strong version of the competition hypothesis states that violent content has no impact beyond its effects on competition and its consequences."

Do you see the muddle? The effects on competition *are* "consequences." Were the writers talking about the consequences of consequences? If the authors had used a plain word in their first draft, they would have detected this confusion. They could have put a period after "competition" and deleted the last three words.

These are examples of *The Princess Bride Disorder* (PBD). In the movie, *The Princess Bride*, one character uses "inconceivable" whenever he is surprised. Another character states, "You keep using that word. I don't think it means what you think it means." If I owned a rubber stamp with that retort I could grade papers faster.

Look around and you will see PBD everywhere. In the 1940s, the painter and poet Marsden Hartley rented the room I now use as my home office. He slept where I am writing this. He almost died here too, but the homeowner put her foot down. She had a friend drive him to a hospital, where he died the next day. Cleaning out Hartley's room afterward, the homeowner found a manuscript for a poetic elegy to three men drowned in a storm, *Cleophas and His Own*. One line states, "Life must literally burn to mean anything at all." Decades later, a friend of mine made a movie of the poem and used this line on the poster announcing the film's debut. As a reminder of the history of my office, I pinned the poster to the wall.

But that line is infected with PBD. The word "literally" is wrong. If Hartley had written "Life must burn to mean anything at all" the line would have been true and have punch. If he had lived longer, he might have deleted "literally" before publication.

Many people use "literally" when they mean "virtually." If you say, "The man was literally shot before my eyes" then you saw him as someone shot him. If you came around the corner a second after he was shot and watched him slump to the ground, you did not literally see someone shoot him. Literally does not mean "almost" or "sort of." It does not help describe your feelings, trauma, or excitement.

Exercise 7.2

Write a description of something simple using the longest and most obscure words you can find. You can use a dictionary or thesaurus. You can turn this into a party game, too. Someone selects a topic, say, "Slicing cheese." Then each person (or team) writes the most bombastic description possible. The group then compares descriptions and votes for the most bombastic. Why do I suggest this game? Ridicule and parody are great teaching aids. Once you learn to laugh at the use of long uncommon words, you will see them when you write them. Then you can delete them before anyone notices.

In conclusion, know what your words mean and know how you are supposed to use them. This is easiest if you choose common words.

Use Precise Words

Long words are seldom precise. The exception is in highly specialized fields like medicine, law, biology, and statistics. Here is an example of a technical word that is not jargon: heteroscedasticity. Statisticians use it to mean unequal variances. The term "variance" has a particular meaning defined by a mathematical formula. It too is a word I would not use on an unsuspecting reader. However, if I need to talk about unequal variances, I do not have a compact alternative word to heteroscedasticity. If my readers do not know this word, I must explain it.

In economics, the term "marginal" has a distinct meaning difficult to translate into a few common words. It means the effects of producing or consuming one more thing. Imagine drinking beer. The effect of the last beer you drank is the marginal effect of beer. Marginal effects change. The marginal effect of your first beer differs from the marginal effect of the fourth one.

Jargon can be a technical word ripped from the loving context of its discipline and plonked into a strange field where it makes little sense. Writers use jargon to pad out sentences to make them appear sophisticated.

Fancy words popular at the moment are fad words. Jargon and fad words have these characteristics: they are not needed; they are vague and undefined; and there are simpler words that have meaning.

Exercise 7.3

Rewrite this sentence in plain English that an eighth grader could understand.
   "If you have some pharmacologically induced compulsion to utilize an expansive lexicographic device, look it up in a dictionary!"

A friend sent me this example from a state government website. I have put the jargon in bold:

> **Growing proactive** traffic safety is a **novel** approach that **strategically shifts** our focus to the **engagement** of the larger majority of safe road users to influence the behaviors of the smaller group engaging in risky behaviors. Previous research sponsored by the Traffic Safety Culture Pooled Fund to understand **traffic safety citizenship** revealed a variety of opportunities to bolster **proactive** traffic safety to reduce traffic crashes and fatalities. However, in order for state highway safety agencies and **stakeholders** to embrace this **strategic** approach, information learned from research must be translated to practice. This final report provides the final drafts of four **proactive** traffic safety communication tools that can be used to communicate and **integrate proactive** traffic safety into existing traffic safety efforts. The communication tools include: a **proactive** traffic safety primer, PowerPoint presentation, conversation guide, and poster.
>
> (Montana Department of Transportation, n.d.)

Let's start with "proactive." A "proactive strategy" is always better than a "reactive strategy." Toss a few "proactives" into your common speech to see how useless it is. For example, "Let's go out for a proactive beer." Or, "Should I get a proactive flu shot?" Or, "The bad egg salad gave her a proactive bowel movement."

The test of the uselessness of a word is removing it. If the sentence's meaning is unchanged or improved, the word is useless.

"Growing" is an example of a useful word forced to serve as jargon. You can grow a plant, but how do you grow a "proactive traffic safety." Take "novel." Maybe the author wanted to say that the strategy was special. However, there are many special ideas that are bad. If this strategy is special, it should be especially good at something. Being "novel" is only useful if you are in the fashion or Halloween costume business.

Sometimes a string of words loses meaning, although each word is meaningful on its own. "Traffic safety citizenship" is such an example. In an introductory paragraph, this phrase has no meaning. It might have been useful later if the author had defined it.

I rewrote this paragraph without jargon and fad words. I also shortened the sentences and eliminated passive voice (I discuss passive voice in the next chapter). The term "stakeholder" gave me some trouble. I looked at some documents on the website and found that the author meant government agencies. I did not eliminate the name of the fund sponsoring the research. It is the name of a real entity. Here is my rewrite:

> The majority of safe road users can influence the behavior of the smaller group who create most of the road safety problems. Research sponsored by the Traffic Safety Culture Pooled Fund reveals a variety of ways government agencies can reduce traffic crashes and fatalities. We designed this set of tools to help agencies put these research findings into practice. The tools include a traffic safety primer, PowerPoint presentation, conversation guide, and poster.

Because I work at a university, I see jargon and fad words a lot. Here are two examples from emails I received.

The first example announces a talk a faculty member will give on an important topic. I have redacted the faculty member's name and topic to avoid my having uncomfortable hallway conversations. I have put the jargon in bold.

> Dr. ____'s research focuses on designing **impactful support interventions** for [particular people]. She has conducted multiple needs assessment studies to understand the support needs and the **support ecology** of [particular people] of various socioeconomic statuses. Findings from these studies identified a gap in the expected and received support for [particular people]. This gap can lead to adverse outcomes for both the [particular people] and the [particular people], including [particular people]. Prior research shows that compassion motivates people to act upon their empathy for another person's suffering through helpful behaviors to alleviate that suffering. In this presentation, she will discuss her research **utilizing design thinking methodology**, which informed the design of a **potential compassion-cultivating intervention**.

Maybe this talk was for those who know exactly what these words mean. "Design thinking," for example, is a way to look for solutions to difficult problems. However, the college sent this announcement to all the faculty, most of whom know nothing about the topic (I had to look up this term).

In contrast, look at this example from my university's Office of Public Safety. It too describes an important topic. It too was sent to everyone. Notice the lack of jargon.

> Earlier today, an employee received an anonymous bomb threat for [building name]. The employee called the UC Communications Center, where dispatchers immediately sent

police to the building. Upon their arrival, officers interviewed the employee who received the call. Based on the information available, officers were unable to discredit the threat.

The building was evacuated, and officers and K9 teams checked the building for potential explosives. An emergency message was sent to the entire University community, using the Rave Alert system, asking the community to evacuate the building and avoid the area. Several K9 teams were on campus training at the time, allowing us to quickly check the building. It was determined there was no threat to campus. A follow-up message was sent notifying the UC community that the building was safe to re-enter. UCPD is investigating the source of the false threat.

The difference between technical words that are necessary and jargon words is difficult to pin down. Consider "rubric." Among other things, it means how a religious service is to be conducted. People in the field of education appropriated this technical word. In education, a rubric is a set of grading criteria. Although my colleagues in education administration treat this as a technical term, I treat it as jargon. Why? If an educator, spoke about grading criteria to parents, the audience would understand. If this educator used the term "rubric" most of the audience would not understand. The only reason for a technical word is when there is no short clear alternative. Rubric fails this criterion.

People who are serious do not use jargon. So the more jargon I see, the less attention I give. If you want readers to take you seriously, eschew jargon and fad words.

Every year brings new fad words. Most die out after a few years. The term "influencer" is hot at the moment. "Groovy" was popular when I was a teen. Only someone costumed for Halloween as a hippy would use the term now. For serious writing, do not use fad terms.

Here is another example, "move the needle." It seems to mean to make a small change, presumably in a positive direction. It is fine in a casual conversation when you are wearing a ripped T-shirt and dirty sneakers. Do not use in serious writing. Do not write, "Diddlysquat and Humphknagle's (2018) examination of rutabaga theft moved the needle in the study of root vegetable crime." Instead, write, "Diddlysquat and Humphknagle's (2018) study of rutabaga theft added a tiny amount to our understanding of root vegetable crime."

I asked friends to nominate jargon or fad words. Here is a list of their submissions with which I strongly agree:

- *Bandwidth*: My dial-up modem has limited bandwidth. Unless you are talking about the transmission of signals over wires or radio waves, use a precise word. The word, "capacity" springs to mind.
- ___*centric*: I just received an email from my university's Ethics Center seeking nominations for speakers on "relevant ethics-centric" topics. Why isn't "relevant ethics" topics sufficient?
- *Dialogue*: Use only as a noun and never as a verb. "After the dragon and St. George dialoged they went their separate ways." No. "After the dragon and St. George had a heart-to-heart talk, they hunted down a wild boar and had a pig roast."
- *Empower*: The word is too vague to be used without specific examples of what you mean. I am disempowering you to use this word.
- *Etiology*: It means "cause." To study the etiology of crime is to study the causes of crime. If you want to appear to be a stuffed-shirt academic, use this word. Otherwise, find a word normal people will understand.

- *Explicate*: A pretentious word meaning to explain, "He explicated the etiology of empowered dialogue within carceralcentric bandwidths." I will not explicate further my reasons for disliking this word.
- *Functionality*: Something has a function. It does not have functionality.
- *Impactful*: Presumably this word means something did what it was supposed to do. Why not effective?
- *Incentivize*: Sadly, I have used this word too often. It means to provide incentives to do something. Its partner in crime is "disincentivize." I am practicing using "encourages" and "discourages."
- *Initiative*: If you want a great bullshit phrase, put this word after other words on this list. For example, an impactful incentivizing initiative.
- *Input*: Programmers are wonderful people with computer languages. I just wish others would stop hijacking their terms. As in, "Please provide your input." No, I will not. I will give advice. I will offer comments. I might complain. I might even rejoice. But I will never provide you with input.
- *Irregardless*: As Yoda should have said, "There is no irregardless. Regardless only there is."
- *Narrative*: Use story. Does the library have a section called "Children's Narratives"? No.
- *Neutralized*: As a member of the ize mob, this word is automatically on the "Don't Use" list. It is a euphemism (see below). If the SWAT team kills a barricaded shooter, say "killed." Save "neutralize" for chemicals to hide body odors.
- *Not unlike*: this is a double negative. Just say "like." Consider this publisher's book advertisement: "'Nihilism, not unlike time (according to Augustine) or porn (according to the US Supreme Court), is one of those concepts that we are all pretty sure we know the meaning of,' ..." Instead, how about, "Nihilism, like crime and porn, is one of those ..."
- *Paradigm*: Thomas Kuhn made the word famous and it has meaning in the philosophy and history of science. Outside of that, no. A friend of mine demanded, "Whenever anyone uses the word paradigm, they should have to cite Thomas Kuhn. For example, 'There has been a massive paradigm-shifting event in the world of breakfast pastries (Kuhn, 1970).'" But if you cite Kuhn, you must read him. It's easier to skip this word.
- *Parameter*: Unless you are discussing statistics or mathematics, do not use this word. Do you really mean "boundary" or "limit" or "range" or something else? And do not use "parameterize" either.
- *Problematize*: Just say "made into a problem" or "created a problem" or anything in plain English. Of course, you could claim that I "problematized parameterization." But few people would get the joke.
- *Scenario*: This word means a set of scenes in a play or movie: a screenplay. Herbert Kahn, a Cold War strategist, created "scenario planning" to help the military and others make long-range plans. Do not use this word to mean "situation," "circumstance," or "example." Don't use it unless you are planning a war.
- *Sophisticated*: If you mean complex, advanced, or knowledgeable, then say complex, advanced, or knowledgeable. Its earlier meaning suggested corruption or adulteration. You could say, "Nixon was a sophisticated president." Please avoid saying things like, "The authors used a sophisticated research design." Explain the research design and let the reader decide if it was complex or advanced.

- *Synergy*: It should mean that the parts are greater than the whole. If that is what you mean, say it that way. Most things that people claim have synergy do not.
- *Ubiquitous*: If something is ubiquitous, it is everywhere. Perhaps you mean "common" or "widespread." Air is ubiquitous. Bad writing is common, but not yet ubiquitous.

Many of these words can be useful in specific contexts (e.g., bandwidth and scenario), but some are just useless in any context (e.g., problematize). How do you know if a term you hear or see often is wrong? A dictionary is helpful but time consuming. And new fad and jargon words pop up weekly. What we need is a rule of thumb to flag words at high risk of foolishness. Here it is.

I call it the RULE test because you determine if the word is Recent, Uncommon, Long, and Extraneous. Words that fit all four criteria are at greater risk of being fad words than words that fit one or none. Let us look at each criterion separately.

Is the word's origin *recent*? Has the word been in common use for a decade or longer? I picked a decade because most jargon words do not stick around that long. Pick words that have been in use for many years. If you must use a new word, make sure it refers to something that someone discovered recently.

How often do you see or hear this word in general writing or speech? By general, I mean by a broad range of people: not just 14-year-olds, business commentators, sports broadcasters, politicians, military bureaucrats, or university administrators. If you have an *uncommon* word, treat it with suspicion.

Is it *long*? Of the 22 words in my list, all but two (bandwidth and input) have three or more syllables. This suggests a simple way to detect jargon and fad words. Count the syllables: one or two might do. Three or more, bar the door.

Do you need the word? If you don't, it's *extraneous*. Being extraneous is so damning you should cut the word even if it is short, common, and venerable. I wish, however, I could find a short common word that means the same thing as extraneous because it is neither short nor common. But my desire to create a cool acronym overcame my good sense.

In short, Recent, Uncommon, Long, or Extraneous words may be bad choices. Write with RULE words only when you have no alternative. The RULE test will pass some jargon, and will mark as risky some sensible words. Even if a few stray bits of jargon sneak past the RULE test, you will still have less jargon than you would otherwise. Strive for Venerable, Ordinary, Tiny, Effective words. Just remember, VOTE words RULE.

Do Not Make Up Silly Words

Not happy with jargon or fad words, some writers invent their own silly words. One of my students submitted a paper that contained "responsibilization." I asked her if this was a real word. She sent me the article she referenced. The offending word is from a 1996 paper by David Garland writing in the *British Journal of Criminology*. More people should read Garland's paper; it makes some fine points. One reason his paper may not have gained more readers is his use of language. Here is the passage where he introduces "responsibilization":

> These new criminologies are far from being fully translated into government policy, but already one can trace the emergence of new strategies and techniques which form this framework. In particular, there has developed a new mode of governing crime which I would

characterize as responsibilization strategy. This involved the central government seeking to act upon crime not in a direct fashion through state agencies (police, courts, prisons, social work, etc.) but instead by acting indirectly, seeking to activate action on the part of non-state agencies and organizations ... Its primary concern is to devolve responsibility for crime prevention on to agencies, organizations and individuals which are quite outside the state and to persuade them to act appropriately.

(Garland, 1996: 452)

Let's ignore Garland's long convoluted sentences. I deal with long sentences in the next chapter. Let's focus on "responsibilization."

What is wrong with it? If fails the RULE test on all criteria: it's recent, uncommon, long, and extraneous. In addition, it is hard to pronounce. That means it is hard to remember and hard to spell. That it is unnecessary is its most damning feature. Garland invented this word although there are common shorter words that his readers would understand.

"Responsible" means several things—to be accountable, answerable, in charge, in control, in authority, liable, guilty, blamable, answerable, dependable, conscientious, trustworthy, reliable, sensible, mature, or in other ways not irresponsible. None of these meanings suggests shifting a burden to some other person or organization. In fact, they mean the opposite. Garland is suggesting that governments are holding others responsible for the crimes their actions facilitate (e.g., holding a bar accountable for drunken fights promoted by the bar's serving policy). Responsibilization does not immediately convey that sense—it is ambiguous as to who is being held responsible: the government or third parties. Even if it was a memorable word, readers are likely to misuse it in later discussions.

What might be a better term or set of terms? If Garland wanted his word to catch on, what should he have chosen? Here are some criteria for selecting his term. The ideal term would be short, easy to pronounce, not pretentious, and fitting. If that word met these criteria, it would be memorable. Herman Goldstein, who has been at the forefront of pushing the types of policies that Garland is discussing, uses the words "shifting and sharing" (Scott, 2005). This is three words, but each word is short. The phrase is fitting. It is anything but pretentious. And it is easy to pronounce; in fact, it is lyrical. If you read Garland's paper (and I recommend it for its content, not its style) simply substitute "shifting and sharing" for "responsibilization."

Another way to think about Garland's idea is to ask, precisely what is it that the government is doing? Do we have a name for this activity? Yes. The name is "regulation." Therefore, Garland could have simply called it a "regulatory strategy." Regulation is well-known and it fits.

Limit Adjectives and Adverbs

Adjectives and adverbs are modifiers. In the sentence, "The black dog rolled in stinky poop," the words "black" and "stinky" describe the nouns "dog" and "poop," respectively. They are adjectives. In the sentence, "The dog ran rapidly toward the poop" the word "rapidly" is an adverb because it describes the verb "ran." Adverbs can modify almost anything except nouns, but they have a special affinity for verbs, like dogs have for poop.

Sometimes you need an adjective or adverb. Often you do not. If there were two dogs, of different colors, then the adjective "black" helps distinguish one dog from the other. But, if there was only one dog, then "black" might be a useless word. If you are trying to create a vivid picture in your readers' minds, then the color of the dog may be important. Otherwise, drop it.

The adjective "stinky" is unnecessary in any circumstance regarding poop. Unless the author is comparing "sweet-smelling" or "odorless" poop to "stinky" poop, the author can eliminate the word because almost all poop stinks. If you must mention the odor, then do so when the odor is surprising—"The dog rolled in the lavender-scented poop"—or when the odor helps explain what is going on—"The dog rolled in the cheesy-scented poop."

Here is an example of a redundant adverb. I copied it from an email sent to my university's faculty:

> Geographic Information Sciences (GIS) is broadly applicable to many fields of study as almost all data can have a spatial component.

"Broadly" is redundant. The words "many fields" mean the same thing but are precise. So "broadly" adds nothing. Reread the sentence without it and you will see what I mean.

> Geographic Information Sciences (GIS) is applicable to many fields of study as almost all data can have a spatial component.

Whenever you think you need an adjective or adverb, examine the sentence with it and without it. If leaving it out does not change the meaning, or if the sentence becomes clearer, drop the adjective or adverb. I call this the drop test (see appendix).

Adverbs and adjectives can make your ideas mushy. When you pile them up, they can be misleading or ridiculous. An email sent to the faculty advertised a website for a new "Faculty Virtual Scholarly Writing Community." There are four adjectives ganging up on "community." How does one make sense of this? Let's apply the drop test to this five-word email title.

First, faculty and scholarly are redundant in the context of this community. Further investigation of the website revealed that this community considers a wide range of writing, not just academic papers and books. So let's drop "scholarly"; the group is for faculty members, but not just for those writing academic papers. This gives us "Faculty Virtual Writing Community."

The Order of Adjectives

My first recommendation is you do away with the adjective. But this does not always work. My second suggestion is to have only one adjective. Once you get past one adjective your sentence becomes prone to silly interpretations. Pick the one that is most essential then provide additional qualifications in separate sentences. On special occasions you may need two. My third recommendation, should you be forced to use two or more adjectives, is to pay very close attention to their order. If you conduct a web search on "adjective order" you will find numerous sites listing the order in which you should use adjectives. The British websites differ somewhat from the US sites, but there is also variation within each country. Still, they agree with each other about 80 percent of the time. These guides may help you avoid errors. The most important thing you can do, if you are cornered by an adjectival herd, is to reread the sentence multiple times and look for ways it could be misinterpreted. Or, have someone else read the sentence and offer suggestions. All of this is a great deal of work, so I urge you to heed my first two recommendations.

Next, look at "virtual." One gets the impression it modifies scholarly writing. If so, the title implies the group writes things that are not quite scholarly: almost scholarly. Dropping scholarly, unfortunately, produces the impression the community is interested in imitation writing rather than real writing (like calling margarine virtual butter). I suspect the author meant that the community meets online, rather than in person. Moving "virtual" up against community addresses this, but gives us "Faculty Writing Virtual Community." This is ugly. Dropping "virtual" solves this problem.

So we have "Faculty Writing Community." It gets across the most important points: it's a community for faculty members who write. That it meets online, or that it emphasizes scholarly writing, can be said in a descriptive paragraph that follows. I virtually responded to this sad email, but I literally ignore the community.

When you use unnecessary adverbs and adjectives you can disrespect your readers. You are telling them how to think rather than trusting them to come to their own conclusion. This is why it is better if you demonstrate rather than tell. Rather than "I collected information from a large sample of women" say, "I collected information from 1263 women." The second sentence is precise. A reader can judge for herself whether this is a large sample or not.

Here is a test to kill off adjectives and adverbs. Look at a sentence and then switch the adjective (or adverb) to its opposite. If the sentence is still meaningful, then the adjective (or adverb) may be useful. If the new sentence is absurd, then the adjective (or adverb) is useless. I call this the opposite test (see appendix).

Earlier, I used this test on "extant." Compare "I reviewed the extant literature" to "I reviewed the non-extant literature." Because the second sentence is absurd, "extant" is extraneous. Imagine teaching extant students, or walking extant dogs, or slurping extant soup. When I walk in cemeteries, however, I only talk to extant people. There are people who talk to non-extant people in cemeteries.

Shun Euphemisms

I write about crime and justice. Therefore, I have to write about nasty, ugly, brutal, and disgusting things. Consequently, I am tempted to sugarcoat, to sidestep, and obfuscate. Recently, a friend directed my attention to a piece entitled "Research Points to Gender Inequalities for Justice-Involved Youth" (Espinosa, 2020). It is a well-written blog on an important topic. But who are "justice-involved youth"? Are these young people removing injustices and increasing fairness in the world? Could they be prelaw students? Do they intern with judges? No. In the article, they are girls whose behaviors have alerted the police and probation officials. The article below the title discussed the difficulties police and probation officials have in helping these misbehaving girls, and why so many girls are locked up for minor infractions. Justice-involved youth is a euphemism because it hides the real subject. The blog post has power, but the title saps it. A better title might be "Why Do We Arrest and Lock Up so Many Girls?"

James J. Kilpatrick, in *The Writer's Art* (1984), suggests that there are three forms of euphemisms: those that inflate, those that are mannered, and those that deceive.

Inflationary euphemisms puff. When I was a child, the head of a corporation was its president. Now it is the Chief Executive Officer. In the late 1980s, you could order a small coffee. Now the same size cup is called regular or large. These days a slight improvement in knowledge is a paradigm shift.

Exercise 7.4

Look for euphemisms in the statements of public officials and the writings of academics. Rephrase their declarations with honest, direct, and clear words. Find words a public official could use in public.

What euphemisms do you commonly use? Why? Under what circumstances? Are there more honest ways of expressing yourself?

Mannered euphemisms make the less palatable writeable. You have seen them most often regarding sex, elimination, and death. In conversation, we use euphemisms to avoid causing offense. I had a male colleague who, when he had to break off a conversation to go to the toilet, would say, "I need to visit the little professor's room." He never said whether the room was little, or whether it was reserved for small professors. His euphemism was a joke. Two of my female colleagues just say, "Excuse me, I need to go pee." They are more direct. My mother refused to say someone "passed away." She would always say, "They died," until she did at age 93. In casual conversations, euphemisms can be useful to avoid creating unnecessary grief or vulgarity. In nonfiction writing about crime, they are likely to soft-peddle the consequences of actions and help us become comfortable with the horrid.

Deceptive euphemisms hide things. Discussions of the public agencies killing people are often filled with euphemisms. While editing this chapter I saw a CNN article stating Navy security personnel had "neutralized" an active shooter. CNN put the euphemism "neutralized" in quotes, suggesting that the Navy used this term (Hassan et al., 2020). Another article, in the *Atlanta Journal Constitution* stated that Navy security officers "killed" the shooter (Barak, 2020). It did not put quotes around killed.

Consider "collateral damage." This can be a euphemism for a government action that tramples upon the rights of people, injures them, or kills them. It is a terrible side effect. "Collateral damage" is not vivid. That is why someone created this term. If you are writing about the costs of incarceration on the children of inmates, do not use the words "collateral damage." Describe to your readers the precise harms these children suffer. If these harms are suicide and murder, then say it.

You will have to struggle with this problem if you are writing about something relatively complex and nasty and you need a summary word or phrase. No single word or phrase can impart the awfulness of your subject, but the practical requirements of writing require short labels. What words should you choose? If you select a jarring word, it might capture the essence of your topic but offend your readers. After seeing that jarring label multiple times, its impact may wear off. On the other hand, selecting a bland, emotionally neutral phrase (e.g., collateral damage) undermines the importance of your topic. Picking a label that misdirects the reader (e.g., justice-involved) borders upon speech we expect from venal political leaders.

Exercise 7.5

Create your own euphemisms for common things. The more you do this, the more aware you will become of the euphemisms that surround us.

Although there is no specific solution to the euphemism problem, being aware of the problem and puzzling through it will help you stay honest. If you suspect something is a euphemism, look it up in Holder's (2007) guide (see *Further Reading*).

Attend to Gender

How do you deal with gender? I have struggled with this as long as I can recall. Writing books published in the 1970s and 1980s show that I have not been alone. The problem has become more complex. Here are some thoughts.

Consider this example:

A student should not use stupid words in his narratives.

In 1950, no one would notice the gender glitch. We could say,

A student should not use stupid words in her narratives.

This might be useful if we wanted to remind readers that women write, too. Or we could write:

A student should not use stupid words in their narratives.

Dreyer (2020: 93) notes that the singular "they," "them," or "their" has been in use for a long time. Some now see it as a solution to the gender pronoun problem.

Be careful. Consider this sentence:

When they write, a student will frequently avoid revising their first draft.

To my ear, this sentence seems awkward. By mixing singular and plural it sounds like the author does not know what they are doing.

With some thought, you can minimize the gender problem. First, rewrite the sentence so you need not use a pronoun. If you describe a single person doing something, you are likely to have to use a singular pronoun. Recast the sentence so it involves many people. Then use "they" or "them." For example:

Students should not use stupid words in their narratives.

Alternatively, make the example specific. Give the person a name and gender and use the appropriate pronouns. This is useful in hypothetical examples. Suppose I invented a writer, Rowena, and used her writing as examples. Then I might say,

Rowena should not use stupid words in her stories.

If you are discussing an actual person, use the gender terms they prefer.

Another method, recommended by Steven Pinker, is to vary the pronouns. In his book, *The Sense of Style*, Pinker (2014) uses "he" in one chapter and "she" in another. I try to vary the gender of subjects in my hypothetical examples, though I am not as systematic as Pinker.

Occasionally I will use "him or her" or "he or she." I try to use these phrases when the extra syllables fit the rhythm of the sentence and do not draw attention away from the idea I am expressing. Also, I mix it up. Why should the male pronoun always go first? I sometimes use "she or he," even though this draws attention away from my subject.

Avoid words that contain an unnecessary gender. When I started work, in 1977, "policeman" was the common way authors wrote about sworn employees of police departments. This must have annoyed the relatively few policewomen of the day because a female police inspector once complimented me for not using this word. I thought "policeman" had been tossed on the compost heap of history until a female student used it in her answer to a test question. When I asked her about this, she said she comes from a family of police officers, some of whom are women, and among them the word is fine. Although I respect their choice, I do not aspire to make everyone happy. I am sticking with "police officer."

Sometimes there is no good word substitute. In my Maine village, we call all people who trap lobsters, fishermen, or lobstermen. If you asked one of the few women who captain a lobster boat what she does for a living, she would say, "I fish." Most locals use neither fisherperson nor lobsterperson. The few people who do are people from away (few things annoy Maine locals more than people from away telling locals what to do). We could use "captain" although this sounds stuffy for a one or two-person boat. Still, it is more nautical than "owner." Another solution is to respect the preferences of those who take their boats to sea.

The other person on a lobster boat is the "sternman." A number of women have this job. Some stern for their husbands or fathers. Others stern for female captains. A friend told me that occasionally someone will call the deckhand the "sternperson." This raises the question, "Why are there angry people at the back of the boat?" Would "mate" work? That too might raise an eyebrow. No one calls this person a "deckhand." What to do? Ask the people involved.

My last inadequate advice on this topic is to think about your readers. Your readers will probably be a diverse crowd. So you will not please all of them. You can make choices that offend the fewest. Until someone solves this problem, you would be better off not chiseling a line in rock and guarding it with all your vigor.

A Few Last Words

All writing experts I have consulted recommend using short, clear words instead of long obscure words. This includes experts on fiction, nonfiction, business, and academic writing. Long, imprecise, and obscure words will cause your readers problems. They do not show that you are smart and insightful. Such words signal that behind the elongated vocabulary lurks a pretender. And brontosaurian words—be they jargon, fad, or invented—are signs you have contracted Princess Bride Disorder.

The cure for PBD, and a hallmark of sweet clarity, is to practice *using few words that are short, precise, common, and clear.* In the following chapters, I will extend this lesson to sentences, paragraphs, and eventually to tables, charts, and graphs.

Appendix: Tests for Word Selection and Deletion

With so many words on the banned list, you may fear having to spend all your time in a dictionary. You should use a dictionary because looking things up is useful, but it disrupts writing. So, here are several tests you can apply quickly and without a dictionary. They are just helpful rules of thumb. If a test marks a word as risky, and you do not have a sensible alternative, open the dictionary.

Drop Test: Delete the word you are testing. If the sentence continues to make sense, throw out the test word. If something vital disappears from the meaning of the sentence, then the test word might be useful.

RULE Test: This is a test for jargon and fad words. Words that have these characteristics, individually or collectively, are at risk: Recent, Uncommon, Long, and Extraneous. If the application of this test suggests a risky word, apply the substitution or drop tests. A positive alternative to RULE is the VOTE test: words that are Venerable, Ordinary, Tiny, and Effective are good words to use.

Substitution Test: I did not mention this test by name, but I did apply it. Use it when you have a word that could be jargon or a fad. To apply this test, consider what that word means and then substitute short, common words for the possible jargon or fad word. If the sentence conveys your meaning as well as or better than the original word, use the substitutes. If you cannot find short, common words to substitute, you may be stuck with the original word. You can use this test to determine if a word is a technical word or just jargon. With a technical word, you will have to substitute a great many words. If it's jargon, you need only substitute a few words.

Opposite Test: You substitute a word with the opposite meaning of an adjective or adverb. If the sentence with the opposite adjective or adverb makes sense, then the original adjective or adverb may be useful. "The carceral policy" v "The non-carceral policy," for example. If the new sentence is absurd, impossible, or meaningless, then delete the original adjective or adverb. "The carceral state" v "The non-carceral state," is an example. As a non-carceral state is virtually impossible, carceral is meaningless in this context. "A carceral policy" v "a non-carceral policy" results in the opposite conclusion. Because it's possible to have a non-carceral policy, this adjective may be useful.

Picture Test: Can you picture in your mind what the word or phrase describes? Can you give vivid, plausible examples of this? If not, the word might be too vague and you should find a word or phrase that creates a picture. A more powerful variant of this test is to ask someone else to read the phrase and describe the picture they see. If they cannot give a picture, are confused, or describe a picture you did not intend, change the words.

8 Sentences

Short and Active Beats Long and Passive

The same principles governing word selection govern sentences. *Write short, common, and clear sentences.* I did not learn this in school; college taught me the opposite. Reading academic papers gave me a template for academic writing and my professors never told me to write differently. Outside the university, my boss would not put up with such gobbledygook. So I had to retrain myself, to write with sweet clarity.

Like me, you might believe that long sentences make you sound sophisticated. Like me, you might believe that long sentences give your writing weight. Like me, you might believe that long sentences make readers take your writing seriously. If so, you are wrong, like I was. Long sentences confuse readers, who start resenting the writer. Long sentences mislead readers, just as they mislead the writer.

Half of this chapter is an attack on long sentences. The weapon I use, and the weapon you should learn to operate, is the Flesch-Kincaid Grade Level formula. We will start with that and then apply it. Once you can detect long sentences, you can substitute short ones. But this is not a take-no-prisoners attack; occasionally, a long sentence works well.

The second half of this chapter is an attack on passive voice. I show you how to wield passive voice detectors against this brain-eating scourge. Once you have the s
voice, you will see how to write in active voice. This too is not a take-n
passive voice in the right place is fine.

Flesch's Readability Formulas

A single long sentence is far more confusing than several short sente
idea. Try using mostly short sentences. Intersperse them with mod

DOI:

create a lively style. Once you have become experienced at this—once you write short sentences instinctively—include a few long sentences. Even then, short sentences should be your basic building block.

Creating short sentences without conscious thought is easy in theory but hard in practice. It takes two things: repetition and ruthlessness. You need to repeatedly attack long sentences. You cannot just do this when you are in the mood. And when you do, you must be harsh. Mercilessly throw words away. Cleave sentences at their joints. Kill entire sentences. Think of your favorite movie assassin (e.g., The Bride in *Kill Bill*, Nameless in *Hero*, Cal in *Assassin's Creed*, or John Wick in *John Wick*). Take on that persona. But before you go killing words, you need a magnificent weapon with a deep back story.

I recommend the Flesch-Kincaid Grade Level. I discovered this weapon decades ago. I am passing it on to you. But to wield it well you must know its history.

For over 80 years, researchers have measured the ability of readers to comprehend written passages. Rudolf Flesch was one of these researchers. He first created a formula using the average sentence length, word difficulty, and personal words (such as names). He measured sentence length by dividing the number of words in a passage (e.g., a paragraph or group of paragraphs) by the number of sentences. That makes sense, because longer sentences impose greater burdens on readers.

For word difficulty, he counted affixes. What are affixes and why do they matter? An affix is a suffix at the end of a word (e.g., able, ability, less, or ism) or a prefix at the front of a word (e.g., dis, ex, and un). The word "unreadable" has two affixes, un and able. "Read" is easy to understand. With a suffix, the reader requires a smidge more effort. The same is true of a prefix. If only one word with affixes appears, the reader is OK. But as the number of affixes increases, the difficulty for the reader increases.

Flesch included personal words in his original weapon, such as the names of people. He thought these words would aid comprehension. A writer who referred frequently to specific people would produce easier to understand text than a writer who did not.

Others tested his formula. It proved to be so useful that it became popular. Not satisfied, however, Flesch conducted more research to create a weapon that was easier to use (counting affixes is tedious and prone to error).

Flesch's revised formula used the number of syllables per word as an indicator of word difficulty (more syllables = greater difficulty). He continued to use the number of words per sentence as an indicator of sentence difficulty (more words = greater difficulty). He dropped personal words.

The result was a lighter, sharper weapon, that he called the Flesch Reading Ease Scale. Using the average word length and average sentence length of a passage, the formula produces a number between 0 and 100. Higher scores are better. To be comprehensible to a wide range of people, a passage needs to have a score of 60 or more. This corresponds to a 12th-grade education. Higher scores are understandable to readers with less education. To understand passages with lower scores, readers need more education. A writer seeking a higher score should use more short words and reduce the length of his sentences.

In the 1970s, consumer advocates complained that the federal government's rules and guidance to the public were hard to understand. Flesch assisted government agencies, particu- ly the Federal Trade Commission, to make their regulations understandable to those who had ply with them. His book, *How to Write Plain English* (1979), comes from this effort. It had ence on my writing than any other book.

While Flesch was trying to make civil government understandable to the masses, the US Navy was trying to make their manuals understandable to sailors. It undertook a comparison of three readability formulas, including Flesch's. J. Peter Kincaid, a consultant to the Navy, led the study. Kincaid stated the reason for the Navy's interest in his report:

> The ability of military personnel to understand narrative technical material has for many years been a problem. Studies conducted by all three military services have verified that the material that must be comprehended to do the job is written at a level of difficulty well above the reading ability of the man reading the material. ... The effects of faulty communication are well known and disastrous. One recent Air Force study ... has traced many costly errors to the reading difficulty level of the instruction in manuals to be followed. The more difficult the material, the more mistakes were made.
>
> (Kincaid et al., 1975: 1)

Pause here. Consider the implications of that statement. Imagine the Navy producing manuals written like the articles your professors have assigned to you. Imagine such a manual explaining how to affix a bomb under the wing of a jet on an aircraft carrier. Imagine the consequences. Clear writing saves lives and money. We are done pausing now.

Kincaid's team revised Flesch's formula. It too uses average sentence and average word length but adjusts the formula to calculate the lowest educational level of a reader who can comprehend the passage. A score of 12 on this scale means that someone with 12 years or more of education can understand the passage. This is someone who graduated from high school but has received no college education. A score of 16 shows that the reader needs a college education, or more, to understand the text. A score in the 20s means that the reader needs a PhD. This scale is called the Flesch-Kincaid Grade Level. This is the weapon I use now, and it is the weapon I bestow upon you. Add it to your sweet clarity arsenal, and use it wisely.

Table 8.1 compares these two scales. Both scales reward short words and sentences and punish long words and sentences. Because it is easier to interpret the Flesch-Kincaid (F-K) Grade Scale, I prefer it. If you search the web, you can find a number of software packages to do the counting of syllables, words, and sentences, and then generate these scores. Word processing software often has these scales among their grammar checking options.

I choose 12, on the F-K Grade Scale. This is the highest number I will tolerate. But if I can achieve 8, I am even happier. To do this, I must eliminate every extraneous long word. If

Table 8.1 Comparison of the Two Flesch Scales

	Flesch Reading Ease	*Flesch-Kincaid Grade Level*
Formula*	= 206.835 - 1.015 X ASL + 84.600 X AWL	= .039 X ASL + 11.80 X AWL - 15.59
Most readable score	100	Lowest score
Least readable score	0	Highest score
Score's meaning	It has no direct interpretation. You look up the number in a table to learn readers' grade level.	Readers' grade level necessary to understand the passage
What do you need to count to calculate a score?	# syllables # words # sentences	# syllables # words # sentences

* ASL = average sentence length = # words / # sentences; AWL = average word length = # syllables / # words.

necessary, I substitute a short equivalent word. I also must keep my sentences short. I must have a very good reason for any sentence over 20 words. I attack my writing paragraph by paragraph.

Despite the availability of automated tools, I recommend you start out by using your eyes (and a calculator). Select a paragraph. Count the syllables, words, and sentences. Calculate the score. Revise the passage and repeat until you obtain an F-K score of 12 or lower. This forces you to pay very close attention to words and sentences. You will notice the long words you did not realize you were using, and that many of your sentences are too long. Examine many paragraphs and revise them. Once you have an intuitive feel for your weapon, switch to an automated version. If you use Microsoft Word, look in the grammar options.

Exercise 8.1

Look at your writing software and locate the settings for checking spelling and grammar. Nose around and find the setting for enabling readability scoring. If it's there, turn it on and start using it.

Poke around on the internet and find websites that will give you readability scores. Test them with the same passage. Bookmark the ones you like.

Whether you do it by hand or use a computer, it is the effort you put into revising your writing—paragraph by paragraph—that is important. Scoring and revising one paragraph at a time helps you pinpoint very specific problems you might miss if you scored your entire document. Remember, you're imagining yourself as a precise assassin, not a mass murderer. And there is a bonus. Because applying the F-K formula one paragraph at a time forces you to look at each word and sentence, you will find other ways to improve your writing.

I should note that there are many other scoring systems. I will leave it to you to investigate them, should you desire to collect interesting weaponry of that sort.

OK. We are done with the background information. Let's put our weapon to use.

Applications

Here is an example of a long sentence. It is from a book by a former English professor. Her book describes how medical doctors at the University of Cincinnati intentionally irradiated 86 unsuspecting African American cancer patients, during the 1960s, for military research. Over 20 died. Read this and ask yourself if you felt an emotional tug.

> In my own mind, the public information campaign about the tragedies of radiation within our school was a valuable part of the crusade to redress the balance of the past; such a campaign could play a small part in helping people understand the continuing need in our own decade, the ever more pressing need in fact, for a measure of public authority over medicine—and all the other systems that control our lives.
>
> (Stephens, 2002: 141)

It does not tug me. Why? It's ponderous. Editing this paragraph helps explain.

This single sentence contains 73 words! The author divided these 73 words among six distinct parts (separated by commas, a semi-colon, and a dash). I applied the F-K Grade Level to this sentence. A reader with 16.5 years of schooling is the least educated person we can expect to comprehend it. Yet the author is not explaining anything that is complex.

Here is my first rewrite:

> The public information campaign about the tragedies of radiation within our school was a valuable part of the crusade to redress the injustices of the past. This campaign could make a small, but vital, contribution to helping people understand the continuing need for a measure of public authority over medicine.

I eliminated 23 words and divided the original sentence into two sentences of modest length. I chopped out "In my own mind." A reader already knows that the statement comes from the mind of the author. Who else's mind would it be? We do not need that phrase. The phrase, "the ever more pressing need in fact" is an aside. It distracts our attention from the critical point. We do not need that either. So I killed it. Then, I whacked "and all the other systems that control our lives" for the same reason. Finally, I terminated "balance" and inserted "injustices." It is not clear what the author means by "balance." Perhaps, the author is referring to the scales of justice being out of balance. If the author wanted readers to be outraged and storm some barricades, demanding balance is unlikely to motivate them.

The revised paragraph has an F-K Grade Level of 14.6: a college senior might be able to understand it. The sentences in this passage are still too long. I rewrote it again.

> The university's public information campaign was a part of the crusade to redress the injustices of the past. It could make a small, but vital, contribution to helping people understand the need for a measure of public authority over medicine.

I eliminated "about the tragedies of radiation within our school." Readers who have made it this far in the book know the author is writing of these tragedies at this school. I put "university's" upfront to show who was campaigning. I removed "valuable" because the author never provides evidence that it was valuable. Further, the following sentence casts doubt on the value; the author describes it as "small." I deferred to the author about "but vital." But I sliced "continuing" because the word "need" implies continuing.

The paragraph now contains 40 words and has an F-K of 12.5. You can probably find more to cut. I will leave that to you. Notice I revised the paragraph twice. I find it easier to go after an awkward section several times, rather than trying to succeed in a single effort.

Let me summarize. Write brief sentences, mostly. Use the Flesch-Kincaid Grade Level to assess a paragraph. If it has a score greater than 12, revise it. Start by shortening sentences. Separate very long sentences into several short ones. Eliminate unnecessary clauses and unhelpful words. Once you have a new set of sentences, attack needlessly long words. Be ruthless. Make difficult decisions. If all your choices are easy and obvious, then you may not be trying hard enough.

If the paragraph's score is 12 or less, you are doing well. Set a lower limit, like 10, and try again. Do not mindlessly aim for the lowest score possible. Always make sure that you are communicating your ideas. Sometimes a word is needed, or that long sentence fits. You are striving for balance.

I use a rough guide to assess my sentences' lengths. I aim to have most of my sentences range from 10 to 20 words. I call these "short sentences." I use long sentences (over 20 words) but not too frequently. I intersperse some very short sentences (four to nine words) among short and long sentences. On occasion, I pop in a tiny sentence (one to three words). A tiny sentence can be dramatic following a long sentence, acting like an exclamation point. What is the fewest number of words you can have in a very short sentence? One. But do not do this often. And do not write entire paragraphs of sentences of only one, two, or three words.

If I have spilled out a 20+ word sentence, I look at it to make sure it is clear, despite its length. Even if it is, I compare it to shorter alternatives. Usually, breaking it up makes it clearer.

Exercise 8.2

Find long sentences in your writing and break them into two or more short sentences. Do this with long sentences you find written by others.

But even if I suspect a long sentence is useful, I break it into a series of short sentences, make sure each part is clear, and then reassemble the parts into a long sentence. Then I reread it. I reread it by itself. I reread it along with the sentences before and after it. I read it aloud. Frequently, I rethink its usefulness and chop it into short sentences.

This editing helps me think. It will help you think too. The more difficult the idea, the more important it is for you to use short clear sentences. So practice short sentences until it becomes a habit. You can use long sentences, but use them rarely and with care. Never pile one long sentence on another.

Repetition and the Uses of (Occasional) Long Sentences

The bishop of Rome had a large household staff, as befitted his princely rank; he had a huge entourage of courtiers, advisers, clerks and servants, as befitted his political office and his ceremonial significance; he had an enormous chancery, as befitted his juridical power; and he had a massive religious bureaucracy, as befitted his spiritual authority.

(Greenblatt, 2011: 137)

This single sentence contains 56 words, yet, it is understandable. Its F-K Grade Level is 11.7. How can that be? The author was very careful and used repetition. Notice the repeated phrase, "as befitted." Notice that these two words come at exactly the same place in each sentence. Notice that each clause, except the first, begins with "he had." Notice that each clause ends with a word describing dominance: rank, significance, power, and authority. Although the author could have written this sentence as four sentences, he harnessed repetition to create a powerful description.

This long sentence is the last of eight sentences in a paragraph describing the 15th-century Vatican. The previous seven sentences are short, ranging from five to 20 words. The sentence following this long sentence has only 13 words. In other words, the very long sentence is not typical.

The point is simple. You should mostly write short sentences and very short sentences. On occasion, you can insert a long sentence. When you do introduce the occasional long sentence, pay careful attention to its construction.

Use Active Voice Rather Than Passive Voice, Mostly

Now that you understand why short sentences are your most basic tool, let's turn to the active voice. Much writing in social science is in the passive voice. Let's look at why overdoing passive voice is a mistake.

A business or government agency screws up: innocent people are dead; numerous people are injured or sick; someone ran off with lots of money; a highly touted project becomes a fiasco; people's rights are trampled. At first, the business or agency is silent or denies the screwup. Media wolves circle. Snarky memes race across social media. Pressure builds. Finally, the organization's public relations person stands before the assembled press and mutters, "Mistakes were made." That is passive voice. If the leader of the business or agency said, "I made a mistake," she would be speaking in active voice.

Keep your passive voice down. Learn to write in active voice, mostly. Before explaining why you should write mostly in active voice, let's discuss what active and passive voice do.

Table 8.2 provides several simple examples of active and passive voices. In active voice, we have a subject (the dog in the first example) who acts (eats a cheeseburger). The emphasis is on the thing doing the acting. In passive voice, the subject (the cheeseburger) is acted upon (by the dog). The emphasis is on the action. Often, a passive writer omits who or what is doing the acting. That is why I put them in parentheses.

There are automated tools for flagging passive voice. For longer passages, these tools tell you the percent of the sentences with passive voice. Microsoft Word has a passive voice detector you can enable in the software settings. It does a reasonable job. There are a number of web-based programs to flag and correct passive voice. I enjoy The Passive Voice Detector: https://datayze.com/passive-voice-detector.php. One of its delightful attributes is it uses zombies. If you ask it to apply the zombie test, it will put "by zombies" after the appropriate verb. If the sentence makes sense with "by zombies," it's in passive voice.

Although these tools can help you, you should learn to spot passive voice without them. So if zombies are not your thing, you can use almost any noun you want (e.g., vampires, fruit flies, orthopedic appliances). I love Corgis, so I will use these dogs when I go hunting passive voice.

Table 8.2 Examples of Active and Passive Voices

Active	Passive
The dog ate the cheeseburger.	The cheeseburger was eaten (by the dog).
We interviewed 35 people.	Thirty-five people were interviewed (by us).
Residents failed to exert informal social control.	Informal social control was not exerted (by residents).
"I shot the sheriff, but I did not shoot the deputy." From Eric Clapton's, *I Shot the Sherriff*.	The sheriff was shot (by me), but the deputy wasn't shot (by me).
"I fought the law and the law won." From The Clash's, *I Fought the Law*.	The law was fought (by me) and the law won.

Applying the Corgi test to the table's first passive voice example gives us "The cheeseburger was eaten by Corgis." Applying it to the standard organizational apology produces "Mistakes were made by Corgis." These are reasonable sentences. And self-evident, if you've any experience with this breed. The last passive example in the table is also reasonable, once it has been put to the test (by Corgis): "The law was fought by Corgis and the law won."

Let's see what Corgis do when set loose on a sentence from a classic criminology book, Shaw and McKay's, *Juvenile Delinquency and Urban Areas*. Here is the original:

> This segregation of population groups on an economic basis does not always proceed in the manner described, because it may be complicated by conditions which serve as barriers to the free movement of population within the city.

> (1967: 22)

Here is the passage after bedeviled by Corgis:

> This segregation of population groups on an economic basis does not always proceed in the manner described, because it may be complicated *by Corgis* which serve as barriers to the free movement of population within the city.

This makes sense to me; Corgis always complicate things. I will come back to Shaw and McKay later. For now, here is my rewrite of this sentence in active voice:

> This segregation of population groups on an economic basis does not always proceed in the manner described, because non-economic conditions may complicate barriers to free movement of population within the city.

There is no room for Corgis in this revision.

Why should you avoid using passive voice? First, it is boring. This is why songwriters seldom use passive voice. Would "The law was fought and the law won" become popular? Passive voice is why so much of what you read for your classes is boring.

Here is famous quote from the movie, *Dirty Harry*. This is Active Voice Dirty Harry Callahan talking to an offender. The offender is thinking about grabbing a shotgun. Harry has his gun trained on the offender when he says:

> I know what you're thinking. "Did he fire six shots or only five?" Well to tell you the truth, in all this excitement, I kind of lost track myself. But being that this is a .44 Magnum, the most powerful handgun in the world, and would blow your head clean off, you've got to ask yourself one question: "Do I feel lucky?" Well, do ya, punk?

Now imagine another world, in an alternative universe, where a gun is pointed by Passive Voice Dirty Harry. In this other world, here is what is being said (I asked my Corgi to sniff at the first sentence; you can have your beastie examine the other sentences).

> Your thoughts are known [by Corgis]. "Were six shots or only five fired?" Well truth be told, in all this excitement, the number of shots fired is unknown. But being that this is a .44 Magnum, the most powerful handgun in the world, and your head would get blown off by it, one question must be asked: "Do I feel lucky?" Well, do ya, punk?

I know what you're thinking. "In the other world, would this be one of the most quoted movie lines of all time?" Well to tell you the truth, in all this excitement, I am kind of in the dark. But being that active voice is the most powerful way to describe action, you've got to ask yourself one question: "Do I want to use passive voice?" Well, do ya?

In addition to boring readers, passive voice can confuse them. This is why misbehaving organizations use "mistakes were made." It draws attention away from the people who made the mistake. It allows the organization to acknowledge a problem without taking responsibility for creating it.

Active

Passive

The third reason to avoid passive voice is that it can confuse you, the writer. It blinds you to who is doing the acting. It hides from you important questions you should be asking. If you wrote, "The deputy was shot," you might forget to ask "Who shot the deputy?"

The rare use of passive voice is not a sin. Used sparingly, in the right place, it is helpful. The three problems I just mentioned become serious when you use passive voice repeatedly. Let's return to Clifford Shaw and Henry McKay to illustrate this.

Shaw and McKay, earlier in their book, asserted that some natural process gives rise to the residential patterning of cities. Governments, businesses, and other institutions do not trigger this process, it just happens, much like the weather. When Shaw and McKay discuss the segregation of European immigrant groups, they point to economic processes. Supply and demand segregates ethnic groups. Newer immigrants are poorer than earlier immigrants, so they can find lodging only in neighborhoods with cheaper rents. The newest immigrants migrate to these areas. As these immigrants, their offspring, and their offspring's offspring prosper, they leave these poor neighborhoods and move to areas with better housing. As they leave, their former landlords rent the newly vacated dwellings to newer immigrants. This is, according to Shaw and McKay, a natural process; it's not directed by anyone.

But there is an exception Shaw and McKay feel a need to address. They do not want to abandon their notion of a natural process. That is the purpose of the paragraph I quote here (underlines are mine and I will explain them later).

This segregation of population groups on an economic basis does not always proceed in the manner described, because it may <u>be complicated</u> by conditions which serve as barriers to the free movement of population within the city. In northern cities, barriers of racial prejudice and established custom have prevented the Negroes, the group now in the least advantageous position economically, from occupying certain low-rent areas, into which they otherwise <u>would have been segregated</u> by the economic process, and from moving outward into communities of their choice when economically able to do so. As a result, <u>many have been restricted</u> to neighborhoods which have most of the characteristics of inner-city areas but where often the rentals are disproportionately high, partly because of increased congestion and the resulting demand for homes. In southern cities the segregation of the Negro and white population corresponds in general to differences in economic status but <u>is sustained by</u> more elaborate caste mores and taboos.

(1967: 22)

This paragraph has 158 words in four sentences: almost 40 words per sentence. Its Flesch-Kincaid Grade Level is 21.4: mostly unreadable even if you had over two years of doctoral studies. Further, each of these four sentences contains a passive voice clause. Those are the bits I underlined.

If the authors had written these sentences in active voice, they would have had to identify who or what is complicating conditions (sentence 1), who or what is segregating Negroes (sentence 2), who or what is restricting Negro access to neighborhoods (sentence 3), and who or what is sustaining elaborate mores and taboos (sentence 4).

I rewrote this paragraph by breaking up the long sentences and rearranging out-of-order ideas. I also put the sentences into active voice. Still, I tried to keep as much of the original phrasing and words as possible.

The separation of population groups does not always proceed in the way we have just described. This is because XXX have created barriers to the free movement of populations within the city. In northern cities, YYY have created racial barriers that prevent Negroes—the group in the least advantageous position economically—from occupying certain low-rent areas. These barriers of prejudice restrict many Negroes to particular inner-city neighborhoods. These restrictions create congestion within these neighborhoods and drive up the prices Negroes must pay for homes. In other words, Negroes suffer from two forms of segregation: economic and racial prejudice. Without this second form, they would be able to move outward into communities of their choice when they become economically able. In southern cities, economic status differences also contribute to racial segregation. However, ZZZ apply more elaborate caste mores and taboos to sustain these differences.

My rewrite has fewer words (143) and more sentences (nine), so it has much shorter sentences (averaging 15.8 words). The Flesch-Kincaid Grade Level is 12.3; a smart high school graduate could understand it, just.

My rewrite has no passive voice. To write it in active voice, I had to identify the subjects who were acting. Shaw and McKay do not tell us who was acting. So I substituted strings of Xs, Ys, and Zs for the subjects Shaw and McKay forgot.

By writing in passive voice, Shaw and McKay avoided telling the reader who was discriminating against African Americans. By using the active voice, I had to tell. Readers of Shaw and McKay's passive paragraph may not have noticed the missing information. Readers of my active version confront this missing information. It is possible that Shaw and McKay deceived themselves with passive voice, believing they had a satisfactory explanation. If they had written in active voice, that would have been impossible.

Recall, Shaw and McKay believed that group population changes occur naturally within Chicago, without government action or the interference of others in power. But African American communities presented Shaw and McKay with an anomaly that natural processes could not explain. By using passive voice, they could preserve their "natural process" idea.

Passive voice allowed Shaw and McKay to shirk the ugly task of pointing fingers at institutions that promoted and enforced racial segregation: city government, courts, the association of real estate agents, white neighborhood organizations, and others. Passive voice allowed Shaw and McKay to delude the reader into assuming that "established custom" and "elaborate cast mores and taboos" is another natural process. Passive voice gave the impression that the racial segregation of Blacks is just as natural as free-market economics. Passive voice allowed Shaw and McKay to recognize an anomaly in housing patterns that threatened their assumptions and then write over this inconsistency without explaining it. Their use of passive voice may have allowed them to delude themselves.

In active voice, it is clear that the natural process thesis is false. If these authors had written in an active voice would they, and generations of researchers following in their wake, have clung to the natural process thesis? Who knows?

We do know that passive voice is more powerful than a Jedi mind trick. The Jedi are not confused by their own mind tricks, but writers can confuse themselves with passive voice. Writing in passive voice means thinking in passive voice. So you hide things from yourself. Jedi mind tricks wear off quickly. Passive voice can leave a lasting impression.

When you train yourself to write in active voice, you force yourself to ask, who or what is acting? This question and its answer are vital to you and to your readers.

Is there a reason to use passive voice? Yes. Here are five circumstances where passive voice makes sense. I list them in declining order of validity:

1. You do not know who is doing the acting. I have no idea who shot the deputy, for example. If this is the case, then use passive voice. The deputy was shot. Be sure to admit your ignorance to the readers in other sentences.

2. You are sworn to secrecy about who is doing the acting. If so, warn your readers that you cannot divulge names. For example, the Institutional Review Board of my university forbids me to tell you who shot the deputy. Give this warning early. Also, consider giving a fictitious name to the actors and use active voice. A person I will call Fred shot the deputy.

3. The person or institution or process doing the acting is inconsequential. The song is about the sheriff, not the deputy. Use this test. Write the sentence in the active voice and then rewrite it in the passive voice. Compare them. Only select passive if you are confident the actor is irrelevant and there are no other passive voices sentences nearby.

4. You have already established who is acting (we discussed the deputy thing several pages earlier), and you discover that a passive voice sentence aids the rhythm of the passages. Keep these passive sentences widely spaced.

5. You must cover up the shenanigans of people or institutions. The sheriff shot the deputy, but he would fire me if I told anyone. Do this only if your job is in jeopardy. Then seek another job (and consider leaking the information to the press).

You should be able to say, I seldom use passive voice, but when I do, I do it for sweet clarity.

The Last of the Sentences

I gave two lessons in this chapter. Keep your sentences short, mostly. Use active voice, mostly. Using long sentences and passive voice resembles an addiction. Once you have succumbed to the habit of writing this way, it is difficult to shake it off. Learning to write with sweet clarity often requires unlearning old habits. My first drafts contain an embarrassing number of long sentences in passive voice. And I have been fighting long sentences and passive voice in my writing for decades. Still, I relapse into long passive sentences far less frequently than I did when I started out. One reason is that routinely I use software tools to analyze my writing. They force me to scrutinize my sentences and improve them. They are imperfect tools, so I have to take their advice with caution. Still, these imperfect tools are far better than no tools.

Exercise 8.3

Find a paragraph in a reading one of your instructors assigned to you. Identify every passive voice sentence. Now, find and apply an online passive voice detector. Does it agree with your results? If not, consider why. Then, rewrite the passage in active voice and reapply the on-line passive voice detector.

Pick an important passage, particularly one with which you are struggling to understand. Then, when you complete this exercise, you will have a better understanding of that reading. In class, you can ask your instructor if your interpretation is reasonable. It may not be a good idea to do this if you have selected something your instructor wrote. Keep that to yourself (or share with your close friends).

How do you unlearn bad habits? Practice. Lots of practice. Practice seeing long or passive voice sentences. Then practice correcting them. Practice with and without software tools. Do not despair if your first drafts have many crappy sentences. Remember, these are your first drafts and only you see them. Work at rewriting these sentences before showing them to others. If you do, in some mysterious way, you will train your brain to create fewer terrible sentences in your first draft. This is much easier to state than to do. It will take more time and more effort than you think. So get started.

9 Paragraphs and Longer Passages

On Beyond Sentences

I gave you a chapter on words. Then I gave you a chapter on sentences. Now I give you a chapter on all those things that comprise more than a single sentence: paragraphs and clusters of paragraphs. A paragraph tells a tiny story. A section tells a small story. A group of sections, like this chapter, tells a modest story.

This paragraph is about paragraphs. It defines a paragraph and introduces this chapter. This paragraph, like all paragraphs, is more than a grouping of sentences. It is an organized set of sentences on a single thought. The first sentence introduces the thought. It is followed by a series of sentences, in a logical order that brings the reader to the last sentence. The last sentence closes the thought. It hints at the next paragraph.

A section is a group of paragraphs that have stronger connections among each other than they have to paragraphs in other sections. It has the same structure as the paragraph: lead, middle, and end. So the first paragraph in a section introduces the set of ideas the section will examine. Then there is a logical progression of paragraphs that tell the section's story. The last paragraph in a section draws some conclusion or sets up a transition to the next section.

This section comprises six paragraphs. Its purpose is to tell you about the content of this chapter. The purpose of each paragraph is to give you one piece of that description. The common feature uniting these paragraphs is that each helps lay the foundation for what is coming later in the chapter.

DOI: 10.4324/9781003167532-12

In a large document, like this book, sections coalesce as chapters. Guess what? They have the same structure. Chapters usually have an introductory section (you are reading one). They have a wrap-up section that often has a connection to the following chapter. And in between, the chapter has a logical progression of sections. After this, I will not mention chapters separately: there is nothing special about them that you cannot understand if you understand paragraphs and sections.

With that overview, here is what I will cover in this chapter. After this introductory section, I have four sections. The first deals with the importance of a central idea. I illustrate this with a paragraph that contains several ideas. The second section deals with the necessity to keep the elements of a paragraph or section in a logical order. I illustrate this with a paragraph that does not. The third section deals with the need to stick to the point: exclude irrelevant comments. I illustrate this with a paragraph that contains ideas that do not belong. I use the analytic tools I discussed in the previous chapters to help improve each of these paragraphs. I conclude this chapter with a reminder that the principles of a central idea, orderly presentation, and absence of irrelevancies, also apply to larger blocks of text. So, although my examples are of paragraphs, they suggest larger lessons. I choose paragraphs for illustrations because quoting larger blocks of text is cumbersome. I believe you can generalize from the examples I use.

Stick to One Idea

A paragraph's lead sentence states the topic of the paragraph. Sometimes that introduction is blunt: see the first sentence of this paragraph. Usually, the first sentence is more subtle. Blunt or subtle, when you form that first sentence, ask yourself, "What is this paragraph about? What is its purpose? Who or what does it describe?" These sorts of questions help you craft a useful start. Answering these sorts of questions will help you stay on task for the rest of the paragraph. They help to keep you from drifting from the chief topic to side or irrelevant topics.

In your shitty first draft do this intuitively. When you revise, then you should be explicit with these questions.

Budget your ideas. Each paragraph gets one, and only one. Just like you need to connect ideas in sentences to make a paragraph, you need to connect the ideas in paragraphs to make a section. That each paragraph has one idea, different from the ideas in the preceding and following paragraphs, does not mean you can create a section out of a heap of paragraphs.

Most sentences sit between other sentences. Together, a sequence of sentences drives the idea that makes the paragraph important. Imagine a 19th-century train. The first sentence is the engine. Following it are a series of cars. Each car carries a specific load. The last car is a caboose. Like the train cars, the sentences need to have some connection. If they do not hook together, the paragraph, like the train, comes apart. Connections between sentences may be subtle.

Connections between paragraphs may be subtle or obvious. The lead sentence in a paragraph should connect to the previous paragraph. As an entrance, its job is to link the previous paragraph to the interior of its paragraph. The last sentence provides a connection to the next paragraph. It's the exit. Like all entrances and exits, you do not want people stumbling over thresholds or falling down stairs. Connections are key to sweet clarity, making the transitions easy and pain-free.

Exercise 9.1

In readings, look at the beginning and end of paragraphs. Note how they hook to each other (or fail). Check a paper you wrote. Examine the hooks you use. Can you improve them? How? Try it.

Connections may be a single word or phrase. If you look at the paragraphs above, you see that I often use a word in the last line of a paragraph, and then repeat it in the next sentence. Sometimes I use different words that have similar meanings (link and connect, for example). Even when my paragraphs are short, I try to provide a link.

Try to keep your paragraphs to modest lengths. There are no hard rules about paragraph length. A single well-crafted sentence can be a sensible paragraph. I have seen very long paragraphs, although I am not fond of them either, as a writer or a reader. In most cases, follow Goldilocks's advice: have a paragraph that is neither too short nor too long. I know this is not very helpful. What matters most is that you deal with the paragraph's topic. Usually, if the topic is worth bringing to a reader's attention then it requires multiple sentences to make it clear.

Here is an example of a paragraph that does not give readers a place to pause. It is from page 2 of Amos Hawley's book, *Human Ecology*, published in 1986. Read it and ask these questions. Is this one paragraph, or are there more than one in this passage? Are the sentences in a logical order? What is the story this passage tells? Can you understand it with ease? Are you confident in your interpretation?

> Many of the features of the plant community seem to have analogies in the urban community. The notions of an association of species join in a division of labor and thereby forming a distinguishable adaptive unit, of dominance diminishing on a gradient with distance from a center of influence, and of a naturalistic development moving through a sequence of stages appeared to be transferable with slight modifications to the urban community. Although these ideas were subsequently elaborated with analogies from animal ecology and from physiology, the model constructed by the early human ecologists from these borrowings retained the imprint of the plant community. The persistence of that influence was doubtlessly due to the fact that both plant and human communities exhibited highly visible spatial patterns. Sociologists seized upon the spatial dimension of human interrelations as the sine qua non of human ecology and proceeded to produce a great volume of field research on the spatial pattern of the city and the correlates of that pattern. So confined to that preoccupation were the early researchers that human ecology came ineluctably to be regarded as a study of spatial distributions. Indeed, Robert Park (1929) went so far as to suggest that sociology would become scientific to the extent that social relations could be reduced to measures of distance.

Did you answer the questions I put to you? If not, do it now before I give my opinion. ... OK, here are my answers.

Is this one paragraph, or are there more than one in this passage? There may be two or more paragraphs here. Slicing the passage just before the S in "Sociologists seized ..." seems reasonable. The first part deals mostly with plant ecology as an analogy. The second part looks primarily at sociologists' use of this analogy.

Are the sentences in a logical order? I cannot tell. They may be. But the complexity of the passage gives me doubts.

What is the story this passage tells? I am unsure. I suspect Hawley claims sociologists made an analogy between plant ecologies and urban neighborhoods, then they produced a pile of studies. And this led sociologists to believe urban processes could be analyzed geographically.

Can you understand it with ease? No. If I had understood it with ease, I would not have selected it as an example.

Are you confident of your interpretation? No. I have the feeling I am reading some ancient religious text that sect leaders argue over. Your answers may be different. But if you and I differ then Hawley is not being clear. I will come back to this point later. Now, let's analyze the passage using the tools I described in the previous chapter.

Hawley favors sentences that snake over several lines. He also is keen on words that trip readers (e.g., dominance, gradient, and ineluctably). This is reflected in the Flesch-Kincaid Grade Level for this paragraph: 18.1. Sociologists of his generation often fill their pages with such prose. So this ponderous paragraph is no surprise.

Mercifully, Hawley has only one passive voice sentence: "So confined to that preoccupation were the early researchers that human ecology came ineluctably to be regarded as a study of spatial distributions." Using the Corgi test, it reads "So confined to that preoccupation were the early researchers that human ecology came ineluctably to be regarded *by Corgis* as a study of spatial distributions."

We can apply the Flesch-Kincaid Grade Level tool to each sentence. This can help us find ways to improve the paragraph. Table 9.1 lists the sentences with the number of words and Flesch-Kincaid Grade Level. The first two columns show the number of words and Grade Level for each sentence, and the paragraph.

Although the first sentence is reasonable, the second is a gargantuan swamp. With 55 words, a reader needs 28 years of schooling to understand it easily (someone with a PhD has about 22 years of schooling). The remaining sentences are better but still murky.

I rewrote each sentence. My goal was to keep Hawley's meaning but improve the ability of readers to understand it. Here is my translation:

> We can draw an analogy between an urban community and a plant community. Consider several features of plant communities. Species of plants cluster. They work together, with each species carrying out a particular function. Together, this group of species creates a

Table 9.1 Readability Changes

Original			Revised		
Sentence	Words	F-K Grade	Sentence Number in Original	Words	F-K Grade
1	16	11.3	1	13	11.2
2	55	28.1	7	56	8.6
3	32	21.5	3	26	11.3
4	22	13.9	2	16	8.9
5	40	19.7	2	29	12.0
6	23	16.9	1	17	11.1
7	28	15.1	2	17	12.7
total	216	18.1	18	174	10.2

unit. The unit's influence declines from its center. The unit's characteristics change, going through a series of stages. These features, with slight modification, appear to describe urban communities.

Early human ecologists expanded this analogy. They added ideas from animal ecology and from physiology. Still, the model they constructed kept the mark of plant communities. Plant communities kept their influence for good reason. They and human communities display distinct spatial patterns.

Sociologists made spatial patterns the core of human ecology. They produced a great volume of field research showing the spatial patterns of city characteristics and correlations among these patterns. Spatial patterns so ruled sociologists' thoughts that they saw human ecology as a study of spatial patterns. Robert Park (1929) even said that sociology measures social relations by distance. Then sociology could become scientific.

I divided sentences when necessary, particularly the gargantuan swamp. The last three columns of the table show how I split sentences, the number of words, and the grade level. As I showed in the last chapter, writing clearly may increase the number of your sentences, but you use fewer words.

In addition to splitting sentences, I changed the single passive voice sentence to active. I used common short words when possible. And I split the paragraph into three.

Why three paragraphs? Because there are three ideas. Paragraph one describes the plant ecology and how urban communities might be like plant communities. The second paragraph shows how adopting this analogy directed human ecologists' attention to spatial patterns. The third paragraph describes how spatial patterns ended up dominating sociologists' imaginations.

Now, let's return to those questions I could not answer with confidence. Are the sentences in a logical order? Yes. They start with the analogy and proceed to the dominance of spatial patterning in sociological thought. Do you agree?

What is the story this passage tells? Sociologists started by using plant ecology as an analogy to urban processes. This analogy so dominated their thinking that they published lots of research on spatial patterns and came to believe everything urban could be shoehorned into this framework. Was that your interpretation?

Can you understand it with ease? I did the translation, so of course I am going to say yes. How about you?

Are you confident of your interpretation? I am. Are you?

Exercise 9.2

In a book or article, find a very long paragraph. Read it carefully to see if it contains more than one idea. List those ideas. How would you break the original into several paragraphs? Do the same for something you wrote.

Could someone claim my translation does not convey all of Hawley's ideas? Yes. However, if they are correct, then his paragraph is so unclear that two educated people could come to different conclusions. That is not something that any author of truthful writing should desire. And it should discomfort a reader of science. We can disagree over how to interpret a painting or poem; many artists leave interpretation to observers. We should all agree what authors of truth are trying to say, even if we disagree with their conclusions. That is the point of writing with sweet clarity.

What did we learn from this example? Two things. First, you need clear sentences to make clear paragraphs. Second, lumping several ideas into a single paragraph hides your story. We did not learn much about order because Hawley is orderly. To really understand order, we need to look at a passage that is disorderly.

Keep Things in Order

Hawley did keep his sentences in order. Now I provide an example where order is a problem. It is from the book *Dorm Room Dealers: Drugs and the Privileges of Race and Class* (Mohamed & Fritsvold, 2010: 145). The authors interviewed a number of drug dealers who are part of a network. The drug dealers the authors talked to describe being robbed. The authors recount their story to illustrate how these college student dealers interact with the police. The paragraph below describes events leading up to calling the police, and the paragraph that follows it (not reprinted here) describes the dealers' interactions with the police once the cops arrived. Ignore the numbers in brackets for the moment; I will explain them later.

> [0] In fact, what proved to be among the more audacious undertakings by any of our network's dealers revolved around a summoning of police in response to one of the very few acts of drug-related violence experienced within the network over the entire time we studied the drug market. [2] One evening relatively early on in the research process, three armed men forcibly entered the home and operations center shared by three of our network's dealers. [1] At the time, two of the three dealers were home and the third was on campus attending a class. [3] In classic home-invasion robbery form, while holding them at gunpoint, the robbers proceeded to restrain the two dealers with duct tape and robbed them of substantial amounts of cash and drugs recklessly strewn about and high-end electronics. [4] Shortly after the robbers fled, the third dealer-roommate arrived home to find his partners still bound up. [8] Rather than retaliate in the style more true to form in the world of drug-dealing gangsters, without a moment's hesitation, these dealers of privilege dialed 911. [5] In quickly putting together the pieces of the robbery, the dealers deduced that the robbers were from another Southern California town approximately two hours' drive away. [6] They went on to conclude that the robbers were associates of someone who accompanied a trusted buyer during a drug transaction at their place a week or so earlier. [7] Apparently, this buyer's associates described to his friends and soon to be robbers our dealers' operation as an unfortified drug outlet and easy robbery target.

Table 9.2 provides statistics about this paragraph.

To their credit, the authors use no passive voice. Given that they are telling a story with plenty of action, this is as it should be. Still, the writers make a simple story complex. To understand

Table 9.2 Original Paragraph's Summary Statistics

Words	253	Sentence Length	
Sentences	9	Longest	Shortest
% passive voice	0	48 words	17 words
F-K Grade	14.5	Average 28.1 words	

this paragraph a reader needs 14 years of education (roughly the equivalent of an Associate's degree). This is absurd; the story is not that complex. The fault is in the long sentences. The first sentence is especially elongated. But even the shortest sentence is not very short.

There are greater problems not reflected in the statistics. The authors use the word "associates" for two different sets of people. This makes the final sentence ambiguous. The authors embed moral statements in the story; they tell rather than show. Readers should be able to conclude without aid that these dealers are "privileged." Readers should be able to see without aid that these dealers are not behaving in a stereotypical way. Readers cannot tell without aid if the dealers are being "audacious." But the authors do not provide evidence that readers need to draw that conclusion. If the robbers were behaving in "classic home-invasion form" then the authors should have described the classic form. Judgments of stereotypicality, privilege, and audaciousness are best left to readers. If the authors felt their judgments were needed, they should have put their judgments at the end of the story. Weaving judgments into the story interrupts the story's flow, creating turbulence in readers' minds.

Most of the turbulence, however, comes from telling the story out of order. They jump back and forth through time, as shown by the bracketed numbers. The numbers tell the order of the sentences in the sequence of activity. I put a zero in front of the first sentence as it is not part of the story. It is an editorial statement.

Here is the paragraph with the sentences arranged to account for how events unfolded. I removed the authors' first sentence.

> [1] At the time, two of the three dealers were home and the third was on campus attending a class. [2] One evening relatively early on in the research process, three armed men forcibly entered the home and operations center shared by three of our network's dealers. [3] In classic home-invasion robbery form, while holding them at gunpoint, the robbers proceeded to restrain the two dealers with duct tape and robbed them of substantial amounts of cash and drugs recklessly strewn about and high-end electronics. [4] Shortly after the robbers fled, the third dealer-roommate arrived home to find his partners still bound up. [5] In quickly putting together the pieces of the robbery, the dealers deduced that the robbers were from another Southern California town approximately two hours' drive away. [6] They went on to conclude that the robbers were associates of someone who accompanied a trusted buyer during a drug transaction at their place a week or so earlier. [7] Apparently, this buyer's associates described to his friends and soon to be robbers our dealers' operation as an unfortified drug outlet and easy robbery target. [8] Rather than retaliate in the style more true to form in the world of drug-dealing gangsters, without a moment's hesitation, these dealers of privilege dialed 911.

Next, I edited the rearranged paragraph to eliminate useless words, break up sentences, and improve the flow.

> Early in our research, our dealers told us this story. One evening, while one dealer was attending class on campus, the other two dealers were home. They had left drugs and cash strewn about their house. Three armed men forcibly entered their home. The robbers pointed guns at the two dealers and then bound them with duct tape. The robbers stole a substantial amount of cash, drugs, as well as some high-end electronics. Then they fled. The third dealer arrived home to find his partners bound up. The dealers quickly deduced that the robbers were from another Southern California town, approximately two hours'

drive away. They also concluded that the robbers were connected to friends of a trusted buyer. This friend had accompanied the buyer during a drug transaction at their home a week or so earlier. Apparently, the buyer's friend described to his friends the dealers' operation, noting that it was unfortified and an easy robbery target. Rather than retaliate, without a moment's hesitation, the dealers dialed 911.

My chronologically correct version has 169 words, compared to 253 in the original. It has 13 sentences, compared to nine in the original. It has an average sentence length of 13 words, compared to 28 in the original. The revised paragraph has a Flesh-Kincaid Grade Level of 7.8, compared to 14.5 in the original. An eighth-grader could follow this story.

In addition to putting the sentences in order, I did several other things to make this story clear. I struck the first sentence; it did not help tell the story. It only reflected the authors' surprise, which is not part of the story. I straightened out the problem with who was an associate of whom. I removed editorial comments such as "in the style more true to form in the world of drug-dealing gangsters." Now, the paragraph has a natural beginning, middle, and end. The paragraph ends with a surprise and connects to the paragraph that follows: about the arrival of the police.

There are two lessons we can draw from this example. First, keep things in order. If the story has a distinct chronology, then follow it. If it has a different order, use that. Second, show rather than tell. You, the author, might be surprised by some finding, but your surprise does not matter to your readers. If there is a surprise, you should arrange things so the reader is surprised. If there is a moral, then tell the story so the reader can find the moral. The same lesson applies to your delight or repugnance. Tell the story so that the reader experiences the delight or repugnance. Leave editorials out or put them in the final summary paragraphs.

Exclude the Irrelevant

Editorials are not the only thing you should leave out of most of your work. You also need to leave out some facts. Just because it happened does not mean you need to mention it. And if you need to mention it, put it in the right paragraph or section. To see this, let's look at another example. This comes from the journal *Criminology* (Kochel et al., 2011: 475). Here too the length of sentences bury the story. They also bury the fact that some parts of this paragraph belong elsewhere (or nowhere). I have put numbers in the paragraph so that I can refer to them later. Ignore them for the moment.

> Although police detectives [1] define success almost solely in terms of making arrests, most arrests in America are made [2] by the ordinary patrol officer in the course of his or her everyday work on the streets, and the bulk of these arrests are made without the use of a warrant, essentially a legal mandate that at least in theory eliminates the discretion of the officer.[3] Therefore, it is impossible to observe on a case-by-case basis the true scope of influence the suspect's race may exert on the arrest decision. To the extent that race is a conscious factor, nowadays [4] we have many social and legal disincentives for American police to manifest obvious indications (e.g., uttering a racial epithet) that race influences their decisions: civil lawsuits and penalties, internal discipline, and bad publicity. Similarly, they are unlikely to reveal any such motivation in the official documents they complete or even in confidential interviews. [5] That is not to say that such events seldom occur but only that their absence is no reliable indicator of a lack of an effect of race on arrest. Race may not even be a conscious factor in decision making, but it could still be a powerful one.

This six-sentence paragraph has 199 words, making the average sentence length 33.3 words per sentence. This is too long. Its Flesch-Kincaid (F-K) score shows that a reader needs 17.4 years of schooling to understand it.

The paragraph has several other problems, which I have numbered. [1] The authors mention detectives in their lead sentence. They do not mention them again. These irrelevant detectives mislead the reader into suspecting they are the subject of the paragraph. I will drop them in my revision. [2] The second clause uses the passive voice. I will change this to active. [3] "Legal mandate" is confusing. The authors seem to want to distinguish arrests with and without judicial supervision. Unfortunately, they seem to imply that everyday arrests may not be legal. I will eliminate the mandate from my revision. [4] "Nowadays" is a word that calls attention to itself but does not appear to help the authors' story. I will drop this word. [5] The sentence begins with "official documents" but "confidential interviews" are not documents. They go in a different sentence or go out.

> In the course of their everyday work, ordinary patrol officers make most arrests in America. They make the bulk of these arrests without the use of a warrant. Therefore, it is impossible to observe the influence of a suspect's race on an officer's arrest decision. Police agencies, local governments, courts, and society impose on police many disincentives to make overt racial decisions: internal discipline; civil lawsuits and penalties; and bad publicity. Therefore, officers are unlikely to reveal any such motivation in their official reports. Nor is it likely they will admit to racial bias in confidential interviews. In short, the absence of obvious racial bias is an unreliable indicator that race does not affect arrest. Race may not even be a conscious factor in decision making, but it could still be a powerful one.

My rewrite has eight sentences with 134 words and almost half the average sentence length of the original. The F-K score for my rewrite is 11.8; a high school graduate can understand it. I dropped several ideas: detectives, nowadays, and the legal mandate. Nevertheless, the revised paragraph makes the same essential points as the original.

The main lesson from this example is that just because something is true, or even important, does not mean it belongs in a paragraph (or anywhere else). Unless it helps tell the paragraph's story, you should eliminate it. Clear away anything that is not the story to emphasize the important facts of the story. Extra words, clauses, and sentences hide from the reader the central idea you are trying to make.

Exercise 9.3

Apply the Flesch-Kincaid formula to books and papers your instructors have assigned to you. Pick a few paragraphs. Compare the scores. Try rewriting the high scoring paragraphs.

If you cannot scan the paragraph to obtain a word document (it might take several steps) then retype it. Remove any errors you created.

You might find that you understand the passage better. Or, you might find that you cannot rewrite it with the assurance you accurately translated it. Figure out the reason. There is a lesson here.

So you might be saying to yourself, "Is he saying I should eliminate facts that do not fit the story I want to tell? Wouldn't this be lying, distorting the truth, and unethical?"

If I were advocating that, it would be unethical. Instead, I am saying, find the true story first. Then tell that story. While keeping to the truth, eliminate everything that is not essential to the story. Truth is first, story second. If you were telling the story of a police shooting of a citizen, you do not need to tell us that the citizen's boxer shorts had red polka-dots, what he had for breakfast two weeks ago, or that his great grandmother was named Maud. These all may be true and worth including in your next crime novel. But they are not relevant here where we are responsible for truth and striving for sweet clarity.

Conclusion

I have used three examples to illustrate common problems with paragraphs. One is putting several ideas in a single paragraph. A paragraph should have one idea. If you have several ideas, then make several paragraphs and call this group a section. Another problem is failing to attend to the order of sentences. While banging out your first draft you might fling down sentences in the order they pop into your mind, after that, you need to put them in order: an order readers can follow. The third problem is adding irrelevant material. After your first draft, discard this stuff or put it somewhere else.

These same lessons apply to subsections, sections, chapters, and larger bodies of text. Each should have its own idea. Anything not strongly connected to that idea should go elsewhere. The paragraphs that make up a subsection, the subsections that make up a section, the sections that make up a chapter, and the chapters that make up a book should have a clear order.

This is much easier to say than to do, as the examples in this chapter show. Your starting point is to ask, what is the central idea for this block of text? If you know this, you can judge the component parts. You can eliminate the parts that go elsewhere, or nowhere. You can put the parts in order. If you do not know the point of the paragraph or larger passage, then you will be unable to sort things out. This also applies to your use of examples, the subject of the next chapter.

10 Examples, Analogies, and Related Matters

The Uses of a Platypus

What are more powerful than clear, fact-filled logical arguments? The subjects of this chapter: examples and analogies. If you can explain your ideas with potent examples or analogies, your readers are more likely to understand, agree with, and recall what you say. When your readers repeat these ideas to others, they will talk most about your examples or analogies.

Consider this book. I state that I want you to write with "sweet clarity." What do I mean by that term? I use the noun "gobbledygook." What do I mean by that word?

I could have defined these concepts using other abstract words. Instead, I give examples: unclear passages or gobbledygook. Then I translate them into passages that are clearer and not gobbledygook. Definitions are helpful but examples, lots of them, are even better.

Often our words are too abstract to create vivid and accurate images. Readers have a ghost-like understanding of abstractions. You have had the experience of reading a complex idea and

DOI: 10.4324/9781003167532-13

finding that it flickered in and out of your mind. Even if you could form an image, a day later you may not have been able to find that picture. If asked to describe that idea, you produced a fuzzy account. You needed examples or their cousins, analogies. These are the topics of this chapter.

Examples and analogies help assure that the ideas in your readers' heads are like the ideas in your own head as you wrote. You are giving your readers something unfamiliar, so you must connect these ideas to familiar ideas your readers already possess. Examples and analogies connect abstract ideas to concrete images. And they help your readers remember your concepts, even if they cannot recall definitions.

Without resorting to the internet, consider this statement. "Monotremes are a fascinating group of mammals." Six of the seven words in this sentence gave you no trouble, but the seventh probably stumped you. Here is the sentence with a snippet of a definition, "Monotremes, egg-laying mammals, are a fascinating group." This helps, but you still may not have a clear picture. Now here is the sentence with an example. "Monotremes, such as Australia's platypus, are a fascinating group of mammals because they lay eggs." I choose the platypus because I suspect you have seen its picture. Because you recall the image of a platypus, you have some insight into what a monotreme is.

What if I had given you the steropodion as an example? Would steropodion spark an image in your head? A monotreme fancier knows this critter hung out with Tyrannosaurus Rex. As you are probably not an expert on who was cavorting with whom back then, steropodion is a terrible example.

That was an example of the use of good and bad examples. Let's examine an example of an analogy. Many people refer to the platypus as the duck-billed platypus because its snout looks like a duck's bill. It does not have a real duck's bill, but we can describe its snout by analogy to a duck. An analogy explains one thing in terms of another. Here, the platypus's snout gets explained in terms of a duck's bill. Most people know a duck or two. So for those who are platypus ignorant, but duck smart, the duck helps form an image.

Examples and analogies perform similar functions. In both cases, the writer wants to explain something that she believes the reader will have trouble understanding. In both cases, the writer explains her unfamiliar ideas using something the reader already knows.

Though they serve similar purposes, examples differ from metaphors. With an example, the writer explains her idea by selecting a concrete case: one of many cases that she could select. She selects that case because she suspects her readers will be familiar with it. The platypus is a specific case of the concept monotreme, for example. Since you know about the platypus, you know something about monotremes. The upper diagram in Figure 10.1 depicts this.

Examples are short true statements or stories about members of a group. A Welsh Corgi is an example of a dog. Dog is a concept describing a class of things with the same characteristics (e.g., four-footed, furry, mammals that usually come when you call and lick your face). A Welsh Corgi is one member of that class. The concept "dog" is abstract. An example of a breed of dog is more concrete. In this sense, examples are like pictures. Was "Welsh Corgi" a good example for you? Would a "Golden Retriever" have been a better example? Why?

An analogy compares an entire unfamiliar idea to an entire familiar idea. The lower part of Figure 10.1 shows this. The writer selects the analog because it has some characteristics of his idea. He suspects his readers understand the analogy better than his idea. The platypus shares some important characteristics with a duck: both lay eggs and have a long flat snout. Since you know about ducks and their bills, you can visualize a platypus.

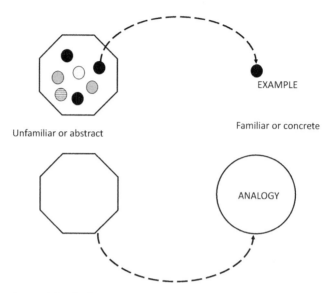

Figure 10.1 Examples and Analogies

Writers on crime often compare it to disease, a medical analogy. You have read or used sports, military, and business analogies.

A simile is a very short analogy, where you use the words "like" or "as." Raymond Chandler, the detective fiction writer, produced some doozies. Here is one from *Farwell My Lovely*: "He looked about as inconspicuous as a tarantula on a slice of angel food cake." This simile gives a deep impression of how much the guy stood out. If Chandler had written, "He was very conspicuous," no one would have noticed or remembered.

A metaphor is an analogy without the words "like" or "as." Here is metaphor describing how we should write, also from Chandler, "Throw up into your typewriter every morning. Clean up every noon." Chandler compares writing to barfing and editing to removing vomit. It is vivid because everyone has experienced throwing up, but many people have no experience with writing. If Chandler had written, "writing is like throwing up and editing is like cleaning it up," he would have been using a simile but no one would remember it.

"Punish the Monkey," a Mark Knopfler song, uses metaphor. It describes an employee anxious he will be punished for the crimes of his boss. Here is a line from the song: "Punish the monkey and let the organ grinder go."

The employee is the monkey and his boss is the organ grinder. The unfairness of his predicament is obvious with this metaphor. This metaphor has infected my mind. Whenever I hear of someone getting the shaft while their boss skates, I refer to it as a "punish the monkey" moment. For me, punish the monkey is now a category of situations, not just a phrase from a song.

United States President Harry Truman had a sign on his desk saying, "The buck stops here." "The buck," a dollar bill, is a metaphor for responsibility, a rather vague concept. Truman's metaphor expresses the opposite of punish the monkey.

Your metaphors and similes may not be as vivid as Chandler's or Knopfler's, but then they write crime fiction and songs. Your job is to communicate the truth, so your image creation needs to be in keeping with your mission.

This chapter has three parts. We are at the end of the first. Examples are the subject of the second. The third part looks at analogies, including similes, metaphors, and clichés. Except for clichés, these are useful ways to illustrate what you mean. They also have their limitations and dangers.

Examples

It is hard to have too many examples. Jane Jacobs in her celebrated book, *The Death and Life of Great American Cities* (1961), used 346 examples in 434 pages. That is eight examples every ten pages. In two chapters she averages one example per page. How do I know this? I counted them. Jacobs uses examples from the works of others, she uses examples from her observations as a reporter, she uses examples from her personal life, and she uses hypothetical examples. Many examples are a single sentence. Other examples cover several pages. Each example illustrates a specific idea.

If you want to understand the value of examples, try to make sense of the chapters in this book on words, sentences, or sections without them. Some of my examples come from actual writing. But I also use hypothetical examples.

Examples of real things have two benefits. First, truth is more compelling to readers than something made up. Second, a real example demonstrates that something could be true because there is at least one example of it being true.

The principal value of examples is to make vivid your general points. A good example helps your readers and it helps you. If you find yourself unable to give a convincing example, then this is a warning that your ideas may be off in the willywags, far from a paved road, with no cell services, and without help from a GPS signal. If you can provide a good example (better yet, two or three), then your ideas are on a marked road with strong cell service and accurate GPS.

Exercise 10.1

Did "willywags" throw you off? I have only heard this expression from natives of Maine. It refers to somewhere far from a major paved road, deep in the brush-tangled countryside. If it did throw you off, I chose the wrong expression. But perhaps you could rapidly intuit its meaning based on its context and sound.

Over a decade ago, Ronald Clarke and I wrote a guide for police crime analysts on how to solve problems. The British government's Home Office (analogous to the Department of Justice in the USA) commissioned the manual for police crime analysts. Ron and I realized that if this manual were to be successful, we needed to define "problem." We settled on a set of six criteria that had the acronym, CHEERS. For a troublesome circumstance to be a problem, it had to meet all six criteria.

Table 10.1 describes each criterion. The first three columns provide abstract principles. Realizing that our readers might still scratch their heads, we provided examples in the last two columns. In the text that accompanied this table, we explained these examples in greater detail and gave more examples. What are anti-examples? Stay tuned. I will come back to these in a moment.

Table 10.1 Using Multiple Examples to Clarify Ideas

Criteria	Explanation	Reasons	Examples	Anti-Examples
Community	The trouble must be in the community	Rules out managerial concerns	Break-ins	Police car collisions in a police parking lot
Harm	There must be a tangible harm involved	Rules out concerns about status	Injury	Disheveled people hanging out
Expectation	Some part of the public must expect the police to handle it	Limits police involvement	Traffic accidents	A flu outbreak
Events	There are discrete events	Rules out intangible concerns	A prostitution transaction	Concerns about teens wearing baggy pants hanging below their butt cracks
Repeating	The events repeat	Rules out singular events	A series of shootings	A one-off sensational crime
Similarity	The events have something in common	Points to characteristics to be analyzed	Copper theft from abandoned single family homes in one neighborhood	An assortment of unconnected crimes in an area

Source: Clarke and Eck (2003).

Consider the second criterion, Harm. As an example of Harm I used "injury." That is obvious. The anti-example I used is "disheveled people hanging out." Because style of dress does not indicate anyone is harmed, the Harm criterion is not met.

Several years later, I worked with a friend and colleague, Rana Sampson, on a paper to describe an idea she had developed. As a police problem-solving trainer, Rana found many examples of problem-solving failures. And she learned how some police avoided these failures. From these examples, she created the idea of super controllers. Super controllers are people and institutions who provide incentives for others to prevent crime. They are important because police can work with super controllers to encourage prevention practices. As we invented the idea of super controllers, we could not expect readers to understand it, even with a definition. Can you form an image of what we mean by super controllers?

Exercise 10.2

Find a concept. Define it. Give as many examples of the concept as you can imagine. Then, give as many examples of things that do not fit the concept, but that people could mistake for the concept.

Apply this exercise every time you read about a new concept. Did the author do this for you? Why? Can you do better when you write?

Our published paper (Sampson et al., 2009) described ten types of super controllers and gives examples of each. One type of super controller, for example, is regulators. But "regulator" is an abstract term. State bureaus of alcohol control that regulate bars and county health departments that regulate restaurants are two examples. Another abstract category was "financial." Examples of this type include banks and insurance companies. Without examples, the abstract terms are almost meaningless. In the absence of examples, readers' minds can run amok.

Here is some advice about using examples.

Two Forms of Examples

It's useful to consider two sorts of examples. Some are very brief, as short as a single word. These are the types in the CHEERS table. The ever popular platypus is another. Very brief examples have no explanation. They should be self-evident to your readers.

The other sort are long examples. These are stories. The "punish the monkey" example of a metaphor is of this type. Since I could not be sure you have heard this song, I needed to wrap it in a short explanation. There is no limit to the size of an example. When they are not self-evident to the reader, you must construct them carefully.

Make Sure Your Examples Connect with Your Readers

Imagine a fetid swamp labeled on Google Maps with "The Quagmire of Confusion." Your reader, with her understanding, stands on one side of the swamp. You and your idea are on the other side. You want her to cross this mire without getting her feet wet, or worse. Using examples, you fabricate a bridge allowing her to cross with the least effort. To do this, you must pick examples your readers understand immediately or can grasp quickly. The more effort a reader has to spend understanding your example, the more rickety the bridge, the less likely it will withstand the weight of your reader's ignorance, and the more likely she will flounder in the bog. Always strive to keep your readers out of The Quagmire of Confusion.

You may believe that most readers understand your example without explanation. But remember, you have many readers, some of whom can cross your bridge with ease and others who struggle. So consider what information to provide in your example. Too little and some readers do not make it across; they turn back, scared of the rickety bridge, or fall into The Quagmire of Confusion. Too much information and the bridge becomes too long, boring readers and wasting their time. By the way, the bridge I have been describing is a metaphor.

Keep the Example Simple

When selecting examples, I discard many candidates. Usually, I discard an example because I need to explain too much. Avoid fixating on a clever example. Consider its benefits and its deficits. Try out alternatives before deciding, particularly alternatives that are clear but not clever. If possible, seek the opinions of others.

Once I select an example, I strip out most of its complexity. I avoid side issues, caveats, and details that do not contribute to the story. Be prepared to rewrite your examples several times. When revising, delete details that are not vital to your readers. Remember, the purpose of an example is to explain something that is complex. An example as complex as the idea it's supposed to explain is not helpful.

Use Multiple Examples

In the late 1980s, my research team and I had to explain problem-oriented policing. We had definitions and other abstract descriptions, but we felt that they were inadequate. We needed vivid examples. So we told stories. We wrote three extensive case studies and many short ones (Eck & Spelman, 1987). We know these stories worked because others repeated them in their writing.

Seldom will you find a single example that adequately communicates your idea. There are three reasons for this. A single example may not sufficiently capture the variety of people, things, or events your idea covers. You need several examples showing the qualitative differences. Or, a single example may not communicate the varied applications of your idea. You need several examples of the same thing in different circumstances. Or, a single example may not appeal to your range of readers. You need diverse examples, so that every reader connects with at least one example.

Though several examples are usually better than one, several poor examples are not better than one good example. Do not choose quantity over quality. Each example should show a different aspect of your core idea.

Examples Are Seldom Evidence

Examples are seldom evidence. They illustrate, like a drawing. Suppose you have surveyed many people, collecting much data. The evidence comes from your analysis of the data. Still, quotes from people you interviewed might help your readers understand your analytical findings. Their purpose is to help the reader understand the evidence.

Examples are evidence when you claim that something exists. In my doctoral dissertation, I asserted that there were such people as "place managers." I used, as examples, bartenders, landlords, store clerks, life guards, and others who operate places. These examples give evidence that "place managers" exist. However, the examples were not evidence that place managers are common, behave the way I described, or had the effects I imagined.

With that exception, use examples to illustrate your evidence but do not assert that the examples are anything more than illustrations.

Use Counterexamples

An example clarifies and reinforces your point. A counterexample challenges it. Consider the idea that dogs come when you call them, followed by several examples of actual dogs returning to their owners when called. A dog that did not come back is a counterexample. Counterexamples do several things. First, they show fairness; you are trying to be objective. Second, counterexamples illustrate the limitations of your ideas. Puppies rarely return when called. Dogs that have been abused may not return either.

Imagine you are reporting on a training program for youth. Your data shows that the youth in the program did better than other youth. You have statistical analysis results to show this. You should also provide an example of a real young person and describe how he succeeded. Three such examples would be better. But what about the youth who went through the program and failed? Examples of these youths are counterexamples. These may help your readers understand the limits to the program.

Use Anti-Examples

All ideas have boundaries. An idea expresses something, but it does not explain other things. You need to make those boundaries clear, even when they are foggy. One way is to pick examples on the idea's side of the boundary and examples on the other side. I call these anti-examples because they illustrate what you are not talking about.

When creating the CHEERS chart, we imagined how readers might misinterpret each criterion. Then we selected examples that showed what each criterion was not. Anti-examples shout, "My idea has nothing to do with things like this, or this, or even this." To choose good anti-examples, you need to know how your reader may become confused.

So what is the difference between counter and anti-examples? Anti-examples describe things you are not discussing. In contrast, counterexamples describe things you are talking about but differ from the mainstream. Consider the youth training program again. Examples illustrate youths who were successful and counterexamples illustrate youths who went through the program but failed. Anti-examples are stories of youth ineligible for the program.

If we were defining mammals, part of that definition would be that mammals give birth to live young. Examples could be a fox, dolphin, and bat. An anti-example could be a crow. It too is warm-blooded and shares characteristics with the bat. So a crow helps draw a line between mammals and birds. A counterexample might be our dear friend, the platypus; it's an egg-laying mammal. Though peculiar by mammalian standards, it is still a mammal (unlike crows). The counterexample helps readers avoid mistaken exclusions (e.g., believing platypuses are not mammals), but the anti-example helps readers avoid mistaken inclusions (e.g., crows).

Stick to the Truth

Except for some names (see below), ground each example in truth. For simple examples (like the recurring platypus), this is not too difficult. However, if you are telling a story as an example, then check your facts carefully. If you did not experience or witness the story but are citing someone else's tale, then you should check their sources.

In Oscar Wilde's "The Importance of Being Ernest," the lead character states, "The truth is rarely pure and never simple." And this is the problem with real examples. Life is complex so real examples can overwhelm readers with the complexity and hide the point you are trying to make. Sometimes the only real examples you have are obscure and foreign to your readers. To make them compelling, you would have to take a detour into the background of the example. On other occasions, there are no real examples. You will run into this problem if you are making a conjecture about a future outcome, something that might happen but has not yet happened. And examples are static; you cannot alter significant facts and play "what if games." Hypothetical examples address these problems. So let's look at them.

Consider Hypothetical Examples

A hypothetical example is a story that could be true, but isn't. Any time you have to describe something that may or may not occur (e.g., some future event), you can use a hypothetical example to illustrate it. A hypothetical example often begins with, "suppose," or "imagine," or "let's assume."

Are real examples superior to hypothetical examples? Like many things, it depends. Real examples give the appearance of being true, and therefore may be more persuasive. If readers doubt that the thing you are describing could occur, then a real example is necessary. Nothing else will convince.

Real examples are messy. In the 1980s, I wrote a research guide for police (Eck, 1984). When I began, I looked for actual applications of the research principles I was describing. Every example had exceptions, complexities, errors, caveats, and undocumented assertions. To use these examples, I would have to take readers on side trips to explain why the example's researchers did the odd things they did. My solution was to make things up. I created realistic but simple problems. I invented hypothetical examples that fit the world of my readers (police) and communicated research principles.

Another advantage of hypothetical examples is that you can experiment with them. To illustrate the importance of a particular element, you can repeat the example with variations. If things are this way, we see these sorts of outcomes. However, when things change, we see other outcomes. It is harder to experiment with the actual world this way.

There is no single right answer to whether to use real or hypothetical examples. Sometimes real examples are what you need. If you are describing something very odd—something your readers may feel is not credible—then you need a real example. Sometimes you have real examples that fit your needs exactly. At other times, you do not have a succinct, real example. Then hypothetical examples will be better. In either case, stick to the truth as much as possible.

Be Careful with Names in Examples

With real examples, you may describe actual people in actual settings doing actual things. Should you give fictitious names to those people? Should you disguise the location? Should you alter descriptions of actions?

Some organizations have rules that govern this. Universities have human subjects rules to protect research subjects. Laws prevent the disclosure of the names of juveniles and medical patients. Libel laws prevent slandering. Always follow these rules.

These do not cover all circumstances, and sometimes they are too lax. I supplement these with my own rules for situations where organizational rules do not apply or are ambiguous. My first basic rule is to minimize harm to people. Second, I won't use a real name unless doing so helps readers. Ideally, the person's name is already in the public record (e.g., the author of an article or named in a news account). And my third rule is to use real names when I am certain they did what I am claiming they did. If someone tells me a story I want to use as an example, I get permission to use it and to use their name. If I witnessed the events, I consider using their names if the story reflects well on them. I ask them if naming them is OK. For example, I checked with my friend, Tom Brady, before I outed him and his cigar habit in Chapter 1. As you may recall, I noted he gave up cigars in 1988. I added that detail to my story at his request.

Mostly, I do not use people's real names. Sometimes I use fictitious names that only a 19th-century parent would give to their child (e.g., Hortense, Sophronia, Ichabod, or Mortimer). If the gender of the person is unimportant to the story, I create a pseudonym that any gender might use (e.g., Pat or Leslie). And I tell my readers the names are fictitious: "In late April, a few years ago, a person I will call Cular Blatterwort, called the police to report a platypus eating tomatoes. This was not the first time Blatterwort reported the tomato-poaching platypus, but it would be the last ..."

I have focused on names but we should consider other identifying characteristics that might divulge who you are discussing in your example. The safest approach is to provide as little identifying information as possible. If, for example, the person's gender is irrelevant to the example, write the example in a gender-neutral manner.

Examples are powerful ways to reach your reader. They can clarify what abstract definitions and descriptions cannot. They can create powerful sticky images that your readers will have difficulty forgetting. Use them wisely. But as powerful as examples can be, analogies may have even greater powers.

Analogies

There are two situations where an analogy may be useful. First, the thing you describe is foreign to your readers, but your readers know its analog well. The analog should behave, in meaningful ways, like the thing you want your readers to understand.

Consider my earlier example: the bridge over the Quagmire of Confusion. I had to describe the gap between what a reader understands and what the writer understands. The gap is an abstract idea. However, from experience, I know how it feels to struggle with a written abstraction without the aid of examples. It is frustrating, at a minimum. So I used a swamp as an analog. Falling into a bog is a dirty, stinky experience. I guessed that almost all of my readers had encountered a swamp or had read stories about people having unhappy experiences with wetlands. I could have selected, as an analog, a missing piece of software code. Some of my readers might have had a gut feeling for this analog. To many readers, however, it would have been as abstract as the concept I was explaining.

Another reason to use an analogy is that more is known about the analog than the concept you are explaining. Another branch of science has studied something that behaves much like the thing you are describing. Your readers may be just as unfamiliar with the analog as they are with the item you are discussing—however, it's easier for you to explain the analog. Jennifer Light (2009) describes the use of analogy in an early theory of cities by sociologists Ernest Burgess and Robert Park. Burgess and Park drew an analogy between nature's ecology and cities' operations (recall Hawley in the previous chapter). Biologists had studied the progression of grasses on Lake Michigan's sand dunes: one species of grass may invade another species' territory. These biologists used a theory of succession of grass species. Burgess and Park took this as an analog to cities. Instead of grasses, they treated neighborhoods as being natural areas for various ethnic groups. One group would move into a neighborhood dominated by another, analogous to a grass species moving into a different species' territory (Light, 2009).

There is an analogy between how fast people suffering heart attacks call an ambulance and the speed at which crime victims call the police. Crime victimization is not the same as a heart attack, but they have something in common: they are both emergencies in which victims often delay seeking help (Claessona et al., 2014; Holborn et al., 2004; Leslie et al., 2000). This analogy may prompt crime researchers and policy makers to examine medical emergency research.

Shopping can be a useful analogy to how criminals find targets. This is the core of Patricia and Paul Brantingham's (1981) offender search theory.

Analogies are common in science. Analogies prompt insight. Some have argued that analogies are fundamental to all human understanding, communication, and creativity (Lakoff & Johnson, 1980).

Look for ways the analogy does not fit. Do not just look for ways to make the analogy fit. Before using an analogy, make a pros and cons list. List all the ways the analog fits your topic. Then list all the ways it does not. Ask yourself how the analogy breaks apart. Could it tumble readers into the Quagmire of Confusion? Could the analogy offend people? There is no point in sending readers into a tizzy over an analogy. Choose a different one.

Be careful when drawing analogies from fields that you have not studied. If you just saw something about cosmology on the internet analogous to the idea you are describing, it might be best to leave it be. That is, unless you are prepared to dig deep into cosmology.

Some analogies are tasty. Take the "self-licking ice cream cone." Simon Worden (1992) used this phrase in an article describing the National Aeronautics and Space Administration. He was making a point about a public organization producing benefits for its administrators but only secondarily serving its purpose.

The self-licking ice cream cone exemplifies the virtues of a wonderful analogy: short, memorable, original, and vivid. When I chanced upon Worden's analogy, I saw self-licking ice cream cones everywhere.

Later, British soldiers in Iraq substituted lollipop for ice cream:

> The British force existed not to protect the Iraqi population of the city: it existed largely, indeed almost exclusively, to protect itself. This was not lost on many of the soldiers, who coined a phrase for this approach: we were, it was said, "a self-licking lollipop."
>
> (Ledwidge, 2011: 30)

Metaphors and Similes

It is hard to draw a line between analogies and their siblings, metaphors and similes. For practical purposes, the terms "analogy" and "metaphor" are interchangeable: they serve the same purpose. However, there is a clear distinction between similes and metaphors.

In a simile, you compare two seemingly different things using the words "like" or "as." If you wrote "The bandit fled like a bird on the wing," you are using a simile to compare a bandit to a bird. If you wrote "The bandit flew down the street," you are using a metaphor comparing the bandit's speed to flying.

Because these two short forms of analogies differ by just a few tiny words, I will not belabor the difference. But one difference is of modest importance. When you write a simile, you label it with "like," "as," or "than" so your reader knows that it is figurative. When you use a metaphor, you do not mark it. You risk your readers taking you at your word. You may mean to be figurative, but you cannot predict how your readers will interpret it.

Here is a simile from one of my favorite crime fiction writers, George V. Higgins. The person talking is describing entering a cellar: "it was darker'n a carload of assholes in there" (Higgins, 1982: 54). More than the lack of light in the space, the simile conveys the speaker's dislike of being in that space. The simile is marked by a contraction of "than" in "darker'n." If the speaker had said, "it was a carload of assholes in there" then we would have a metaphor. A reader might conclude that the speaker found himself among people he disliked.

The self-licking ice cream cone is an absurd idea, so there is little risk that a reader will take it literally. However, for other metaphors the risk is greater. For that reason, you need to use metaphors with care.

Consider James Q. Wilson and George Kelling's Broken Windows metaphor:

> Social psychologists and police officers tend to agree that if a window in a building is broken and is left unrepaired, all the rest of the windows will soon be broken. This is as true in nice neighborhoods as in rundown ones. Window-breaking does not necessarily occur on a large scale because some areas are inhabited by determined window-breakers whereas others are populated by window-lovers; rather, one unrepaired broken window is a signal that no one cares, and so breaking more windows costs nothing. (It has always been fun.)
>
> (Wilson & Kelling, 1982: 32)

The metaphor is powerful because we all know what a broken window looks like. And we have all experienced the dread of wandering amongst derelict buildings. By using it as a metaphor, Wilson and Kelling gave their readers a clear visual and emotional image of their vague term "incivilities."

I chose this example of a metaphor because the Broken Windows theory of police is controversial. This example illustrates how the right metaphor can capture people's minds and drive policy. That is not a reason to avoid metaphors. It is a warning that you need to be careful with metaphors.

Use similes and metaphors that your readers can understand. Broken windows worked as a metaphor because readers immediately understood the connection. Self-licking ice cream cones—though impossible—are also easily understood. What if your metaphor or simile is not understood? Consider this hypothetical example.

Suppose I am writing about the history of racial oppression of African Americans in the United States and I write this, "The long fetch of history created the segregation we see today." Few of my readers will get my meaning. Many will fall into the quagmire if they imagine a dog retrieving a stick. How does a dog returning a stick fit with the rest of the sentence?

It doesn't. "Fetch" has a different meaning in my metaphor than it does in common English. If my readers are meteorologists, oceanographers, or sailors, they might get the sense. They would know that "fetch" is the distance wind blows over water. The fetch is important because the longer the fetch, the larger the waves (e.g., a 50 mph wind blowing over a pond will raise ripples but over hundreds of miles of ocean it will generate large waves).

My misplaced metaphor is clever: it suggests that the longer the history, the more severe the racial oppression. Still, whether you agree or disagree with this idea, "fetch" is not the way to express it. It does not fit my audience.

Clichés

Many clichés are overused metaphors or similes. If a tornado strikes a town, someone will say to a reporter, "It looks like a war zone." If an academic compares two theories, they will title their paper "A Tale of Two Theories." If you have heard a simile or metaphor before, it's probably a cliché. Do not use it. But you can adapt it. Stephen King, in his book, *On Writing* (2000) (see *Further Reading*), repurposed the cliché "kiss of death" into "the smooch of death."

Exercise 10.3

Find a cliché. Create an original twist on it. The twist should give it a new life: change the direction of its meaning or apply it to something different than was originally intended. You can make this into a game with friends. The purpose of this exercise is to have fun while enhancing your cliché detector and practicing twisting them. Note how difficult it is to create a good twist.

Clichés signal to your reader that you are a follower, unoriginal. If an expression is trending on social media, just made popular in a movie or song, or all over the news, avoid using it in your writing. Save it for drinking at the bar with friends, staff meetings, and other settings where there is no permanent record of your blandness. If you can twist it, King style, so it fits into your story, then give the twist a try. In my experience, this is far more difficult that it seems. Most of my twists fail. Still, it is fun, and sometimes, rarely, I succeed.

Mixed Metaphors

A mixed metaphor is a mashup. When a writer uses two or more metaphors in the same sentence or paragraph, he can create one. Often the mashed up metaphors are clichés. "I will burn that bridge when I cross it." This mixed metaphor fuses the time-worn expressions, "Do not burn your bridges behind you," and "We will cross that bridge when we come to it." Imagine standing on the bridge while setting it alight. It could be worse. Here is a triple mash-up: "I will burn that bridge over troubled water when I cross it."

The originator of the next mixed metaphor was speaking to a reporter.

"Everybody goes into the Trump relationship woodchipper," said Trump's former White House communications director Anthony Scaramucci, who had his own falling-out with the president. "You either come out on the other side with your dignity and your personal story intact or you're reformed as Trump compost and you're fertilizer under his shoe. You have to make a decision and it happens to everyone."

(Markay et al., 2020)

The metaphor references the villain in the movie Fargo who forced a body into a wood chipper. This famous scene is grotesque, funny, and original. But nothing goes into a wood chipper and comes out intact. That is the point of putting something into a wood chipper; to turn it into chips. Wood chippers do not make compost or fertilizer; they make chips. In this quote, compost and fertilizer are parts of different metaphors. If Scaramucci had said, "Everyone goes into the Trump compost heap" then the metaphor would be consistent, not mixed.

There is an exception. If you want to be funny, then create a memorable mixed metaphor to drive home a point. The key is to mix with obvious intent, originality, and a wink. You want your readers to laugh with you, not at you (cliché).

It is best to avoid mixed metaphors. This is relatively easy. Follow these rules. First, avoid clichés. Second, use one metaphor at a time. If you feel the urge to use two, and you cannot resist, put an enormous gap between them. After your first metaphor, write several paragraphs with no metaphors. Then switch to a new topic. Now you can introduce the second metaphor. Third, ask someone to read your passages and look for unintentional goofs.

When Not to Use Analogies, Similes, and Metaphors

These ways of making comparisons help when you are writing something that is general: when explaining a theory or interpreting the meaning of facts. They are not appropriate when you have facts that you need to convey. If you are a police officer writing a crime report, do not use analogies, similes, or metaphors. In particular, do not use George V. Higgins's simile when describing the search of a building.

Final Words

Writing with sweet clarity only goes so far. Sometimes clear writing is not enough to make a complex topic understandable. Examples and analogies help make vague ideas clear. Counterexamples and anti-examples can help your readers see the boundaries around your ideas. Multiple examples help show the various ways your ideas can play out. Analogies help your readers transfer their understanding to your unfamiliar idea. They are controlled fictions that reveal important features.

You should use all the imagery I described in this chapter, but beware of their dangers. When you find a great example or analogy you fall under its sway. It alters your view of the world. At the same time your well-chosen example is highlighting particular features of your idea, it may be hiding other features. Examples and analogies can insist that your idea has more validity than it deserves. A poorly chosen example or analogy can also make your ideas seem weaker.

Consider broken windows in Broken Windows theory. It is both an example of disorder and a metaphor for urban decay. What if the authors of this theory had chosen "dog shit" as their central example and metaphor? We have all stepped in this type of disorder. Could the authors have convincingly argued that crime increases in neighborhoods when people do not clean up after their pooches? Would any police chief have justified crackdowns using a dog shit metaphor?

With a good image comes great power and responsibility. You can use the image to brand your readers' minds. Based on this image, readers may do good, or do bad. Beware: the first person infected by an enticing example or metaphor is the writer.

Examples and analogies have special roles at the beginning and end of your document. By introducing a potent image—with an example or analogy—you guide your readers. I address this in the next two chapters.

11 Beginnings

Comments on Beginnings

Most times, the way isn't clear, but you want to start anyway. It is in starting with the first step that other steps become clearer.

Israelmore Ayivor

There are two fatal errors that keep great projects from coming to life: 1) Not finishing; 2) Not starting.

Buddha Gautama

A Chicken and Egg Problem

What is the most important thing in writing? "To make somebody read it," asserts former *Guardian* editor, Tim Radford (2011). This is because no one has to read what you wrote. Well, almost no one. We who teach must read your papers. If writing for instructors has been your only writing experience, you may not have considered that almost no one wants to read your work.

To convert possible readers to actual readers, you have to convince them, fast. You do not have ten pages, or even three. Here is what you have: the title, perhaps an abstract, and the first couple of paragraphs. You may have a gem in your conclusions, but your readers will never see it if you have no hook. As you will see, examples and metaphors make excellent hooks.

This chapter examines those things readers encounter first: titles, abstracts, and opening paragraphs. Here is the paradox: readers encounter them first but you write them last. In the next chapter, "Endings," I tell you to write the ending mindful of your beginning. How can you do this? Simple. Go back and forth between the start and the finish, but make the last revisions to the beginning.

So why did I put Beginnings before Endings? It was a hard decision. I decided that you probably would find this order more appealing, less jarring than the alternative. As you read this chapter, keep in mind that you may draft your beginning early, but you will finish it last.

Enough with the introductory stuff. Here is what the rest of this chapter contains. First, I discuss the purposes of beginnings. Then I examine titles and the ways you can approach them. Much of what I have to say about the titles of documents applies to section headings. Third, I will consider abstracts. These are short summaries required in some documents. After abstracts, I turn to the first sentences and paragraphs. These are key to hooking your readers.

DOI: 10.4324/9781003167532-14

Next, I look at stories. The story must be simple so readers understand it. In the sixth section, I describe "The Promise." Your promise to your readers is that you will help them with a problem about which they care. The seventh section describes two ways to give your readers a sense of what will come after the beginning: the route they will take from beginning to the end. The last section gives a generic checklist for creating a beginning.

Purposes of Beginnings

Think of fishing: pole, line with a hook, bait, and a net. To land a fish, you must accomplish four tasks. First, attract it. To do that, select the right place and the right jiggle on the line. Second, tempt the fish to bite. To do that, use the right bait. Third, hang on to your fish. To do that, use a barbed hook and keep tension on the line. Fourth, land it. To do that, use a net.

How do you attract readers? You create a distinctive title and you put that title where the readers you want will see it. How do you tempt readers? You write a beginning that makes readers believe they will gain from reading your work: helping them solve one of their problems or giving them something useful. How do you hold the reader? You keep on topic, using short active sentences and common words, striving for sweet clarity throughout your document. How do you land the reader? You end your writing well. In summary, the beginning attracts and tempts. The middle holds. The ending lands. Unlike fishing, your reader should be better off at the end. But we will get to endings in the next chapter.

When crafting your beginning, consider both logical and emotional bait. The title and first passages should tell your readers about your topic. People will not look at your document unless they believe you are writing about something that interests them. But that is not enough. You must convince them that they have a problem you will help them solve. In short, you want your potential reader to think, "I must read this."

Consider this book. My title tells you it is about writing. But that is not sufficient. My first paragraph suggests a problem: your writing is not clear. And I provide a solution: read this book. This is the *logical function* of the beginning. Appeal to the head.

Second, a good beginning has an *emotional function*. It sparks curiosity, joy, anticipation, concern, or hope. Give readers more than the naked facts. I chose the opening lines of this book because many students are anxious about their writing. I also know that most students want to improve some part of the world. I implied, "You have a problem. You want to improve the world, but to do this you must write clearly. You know you do not write clearly. So you need to learn how. This book will get you started." By playing on existing anxieties and providing a promise of relief, I appealed to the gut.

All of your readers are busy and distracted. You need to attract their attention and convince them that reading your stuff is more important than the other things vying for their time. Usually, appealing to logic is necessary but insufficient. You need to engage their emotions, too.

Perhaps you think this is crass and commercial. Is it pandering? Maybe, but not reaching out to your potential readers is self-centered and self-defeating. If you do not show potential readers that your work can help them, they will not read your work. You need to do this fast because your potential readers do not have the time or interest to pander to you. If you want fish, you must attract and tempt them; they will not jump into your lap on their own initiative.

Titles

The first thing your readers see is the title. You need to get the title right, so do not fall in love with your first, ever-so-clever, title. Give your writing a temporary name, a "working title." Now play with alternative titles. Here are some considerations.

A good title specifies the topic of the report, paper, book, or article. That is its logical function. It also should spark interest. This is its emotional function. It should be clear and interesting. That is my theory. How well does it do in practice?

Let's look at four titles addressing the same topic, but from four very different sources.

If you are writing for an organization, it will have something to say about the title. Read the titles of earlier reports to learn what kinds of titles are acceptable. Your organization may only want dull titles. The US Government Accountability Office (GAO) has a long, proud history of dull titles, because it seeks neutrality in government policy debates and it has a specific audience: members of Congress and their staffs.

Here is an example:

> Criminal Alien Statistics: Information on Incarcerations, Arrests, Convictions, Costs, and Removals
>
> (Government Accountability Office, 2018)

This title describes the content of the report. If you are a national policy maker whose interests involve immigrants and crime, then this title is sufficient.

If you have full control over the title then you probably will want to use one that attracts attention. This is particularly the case if your potential readers may overlook you. The next two titles come from national advocacy groups: one that bends left and one that bends right.

Here is the title of a webpage from the Southern Poverty Law Center, addressing the same topic as the GAO report:

> Trump Is Lying about Immigrant Crime—and the Research Proves It
>
> (Southern Poverty Law Center, 2017)

It tells prospective readers what the essay is about, and with words like "lying" and "proves" it addresses the emotional function.

Here is a title from a conservative writer for the Heritage Foundation, also on the topic of immigrants and crime:

> Crimes by Illegal Immigrants Widespread across U.S.–Sanctuaries Shouldn't Shield Them
> (Heritage Foundation, 2019)

Here too the title achieves its logical end emotional functions. The words "illegal," "widespread," "sanctuaries," and "shield" appeal to the emotions while describing the content.

Finally, here is an example of an academic journal title on immigration and crime:

> Is Immigration Responsible for the Crime Drop? An Assessment of the Influence of Immigration on Changes in Violent Crime between 1990 and 2000
> (Wadsworth, 2010)

The title reveals the topic. Presenting a question appeals to curiosity. Among academics, curiosity is a strong emotion (or should be).

A title does not stand by itself. Readers will interpret it in the context of who publishes it. The reputation of the GAO signals possible readers that the contents will be dense in fact and neutral. The reputations of the two advocacy groups color how potential readers will interpret their titles. Academic papers are harder to pin down. Academic social scientists often strive for neutrality (like the GAO) but they sometimes drive a particular policy (unlike the GAO). Academic pontificators often function more like advocacy groups. Your choice of a title should reflect your understanding of your readers and the context in which they will read your title.

Here are a few titles I like. I will start with two examples I helped create.

> When Is a Bologna Sandwich Better Than Sex? A Defense of Small-N Case Study Evaluations
> (Eck, 2006)

I choose this title because I wanted it to stand apart from the titles in the journal's table of contents. The title comes from a joke my father told me. The joke serves as an analogy throughout the paper. Several friends have put the article on their courses' reading lists. Mission accomplished.

> Putting a Price on Justice: How to Incentivize the Downsizing of Prison Populations
> (Jonson et al., 2015)

We chose this title because of the irony of "putting a price on justice." We claim that the lack of a price causes the excessive use of prisons. We knew this title might spark curiosity, discomfort, and perhaps anger, by putting conservative principles in service of a liberal cause, reducing prison populations.

> Where Is Latisha's Law? Black Invisibility in the Social Construction of Victimhood
> (Kulig & Cullen, 2017)

When I asked the second author how he and Teressa Kulig chose this title, he said, "Virtually all laws named for victims are named after white victims, often young and female. We chose the name 'Latisha' to represent the unacknowledged victims because it is a name given mostly to African American females. We also considered its alliteration with 'laws'."

The Darwin Awards: Sex Differences in Idiotic Behaviour

(Lendrem et al., 2014)

I do not know why these authors choose that title, but it grabbed my attention. I read the piece! The title did its job.

Look at the construction of these four examples. The authors of the first three lead with the emotional function. After a colon, they appeal to the logical function. The authors of the fourth example mix the logical and emotional messages by using "Idiotic" in the second part.

Titles need not be funny. But even if solemn, they do not have to be boring. You still should combine gut and head appeal. Consider these two titles. Which would you choose if you could read only one?

Building on the Foundation of General Strain Theory: Specifying the Types of Strain Most Likely to Lead to Crime and Delinquency

(Agnew, 2001)

Girls' Crime and Woman's Place: Toward a Feminist Model of Female Delinquency

(Chesney-Lind, 1989)

The first is boring. It gives me the impression that the paper will be typically academic and tedious. The second title juxtaposes girls and woman/crime and place. It is not humorous, but it is catchy. It suggests that the paper could interest me.

Consider this example:

Counter-Carceral Acoustemologies: Sound, Permeability and Feminist Protest at the Prison Boundary

(Russell & Carlton, 2020)

It appeals neither to the head nor to the gut. I have no idea what this paper is about: it fails the logic function. The gobbledygook words gave me emotional nausea. Just as people will stare at a dead dog in the road, terrible titles spark curiosity. I tried reading it.

Exercise 11.1

Look at the readings your instructors assigned you. Place the titles in three categories: those that made you want to read the piece, those that screamed "boring" or were repulsive in other ways, and those that you did not react to in either way. What are the common characteristics of the titles in each list? What makes the repulsive titles repulsive and the attractive titles attractive? Try retitling the one in the repulsive and neutral lists to make them attractive. Be sure that your new title reflects the content.

The same principles for choosing document titles also apply to interior section titles. The title for each section carries the reader forward. Each section heading should signal the purpose of what follows. Appealing to the gut is less important, but doing so can be helpful.

Abstracts

Abstracts entice readers or repel them. An abstract is a brief summary of a paper. The ideal abstract tells the reader what the paper is about, how you have studied the problem, and what you concluded. Despite being useful for readers, many written documents do not have abstracts.

From the abstract, a reader should be able to determine if the paper is of interest and what they will learn. Great abstracts not only accomplish these goals but also entice readers to read on.

Unlike movie trailers, an abstract should have spoilers. A movie trailer tries to entice you to buy a ticket without giving away the ending. In an abstract you should give away the ending. Your readers' time is limited. Give them your findings. By reinforcing the conclusions, the abstract helps your reader recall your most important points. If some readers stop reading after reading your spoiler, then allow them to stop. If the abstract is interesting, readers are more likely to tackle the full paper.

Here are example abstracts from three titles I discussed earlier.

Putting a Price on Justice: How to Incentivize the Downsizing of Prison Populations

We argue that the proximate reason the United States overuses prisons is that for local prosecutors and judges, sending offenders to prison is "free"; the state pays. By completely subsidizing prison use, states incentivize local overuse of prisons. State prisons in the United States are common pool resources, so options to managing common pool resources used in fisheries and environmental protection may have applications to corrections. We propose, for this purpose, seven options: six involve pricing systems and each having several variants. Each approach, in its own way, puts a price on justice. We also outline other changes in correctional and sentencing practices policy makers need to make to implement these approaches. We anticipate potential consequences, good and bad, of incentivizing justice. Finally, we fully expect our proposals to incur the ire of some political idealists on the right and the left. Nevertheless, for policy makers who are concerned about practical solutions to the grave injustices and high costs of mass incarcerations, our portfolio of options should be useful.

(Jonson et al., 2015: 452)

The Darwin Awards: Sex Differences in Idiotic Behaviour

Sex differences in risk seeking behaviour, emergency hospital admissions, and mortality are well documented. However, little is known about sex differences in idiotic risk taking behaviour. This paper reviews the data on winners of the Darwin Award over a 20 year period (1995–2014). Winners of the Darwin Award must eliminate themselves from the gene pool in such an idiotic manner that their action ensures one less idiot will survive. This paper reports a marked sex difference in Darwin Award winners: males are significantly more likely to receive the award than females ($P < 0.0001$). We discuss some of the reasons for this difference.

(Lendrem et al., 2014: g7094)

Here is an example of a poorly written abstract. It fulfills all the requirements of an abstract, yet it does not invite the reader. The central reason is that it has many of the problems we saw in earlier chapters. It is the antithesis of sweet clarity.

It is proffered rather frequently that co-offending is the dominate form of criminal offending among juveniles because of the enhanced salience of peer pressure during adolescence, and that this enhanced propensity to co-offend is pivotal for understanding the age-crime curve. Using National Incident-Based Reporting System (NIBRS) data for 2002, the authors conduct an analysis of 466,311 criminal arrests drawn from seven states. Their findings indicate that co-offending patterns by age are not noteworthy in elucidating why participation in illegal activities rises in adolescence, peaks in early adulthood, and then declines thereafter. Once co-offending is differentiated from solo offending, with solo offending representing the bulk of criminal activity among all age groups, including juveniles, a curvilinear relationship remains between age and solo-offending and between age and co-offending. These nonlinear associations are not conditioned by an offender's sex, race, or by offense type. The authors also analyzed co-offending crimes reported to police. In many types of crimes, offenders and victims come into contact, thus allowing for the estimation of the perpetrator's age notwithstanding whether an arrest was made. The findings generated in this supplemental analysis are similar to those produced using the arrest data. The results of this study have consequential theoretical implications not only because they cast doubt on the assertion that differences in co-offending levels between juveniles and adults account for the age-crime curve, but they also contravene the widely held belief that most juvenile offenses are perpetrated in the company of others rather than by individuals acting alone. Based on the new data reported here it appears that group offending is merely incidental in circumstance and thus of little etiological significance.

(Stolzenberg & D'Alessio, 2008: 65)

The abstract contains 272 words in ten sentences. The mean sentence length is 27.2 words. Two of the ten sentences are in the passive voice: beyond my limit of endurance. Its Flesch-Kincaid Grade Level is 18.3: requires readers with six years of education beyond high school. In short, it is unnecessarily difficult. You do not want a yawn to be your readers' emotional response. Here is my revised version:

Some researchers claim that juveniles are more likely to offend with others than alone. Co-offending, they assert, is due to peer pressure during adolescence. Therefore, co-offending is pivotal for understanding the age-crime curve. Using National Incident-Based Reporting System (NIBRS) data for 2002, we analyzed 466,311 criminal arrests from seven states. We find that co-offending does not explain why participation in illegal activities rises in adolescence. It peaks in early adulthood, and then declines. Solo offending dominates all age groups, including juveniles. Once we separated co-offending from solo offending, we find a curvilinear relationship between age and solo offending and between age and co-offending. Neither an offender's sex nor race influenced these associations. The offense type did not influence the associations either. We also analyzed co-offending in crimes reported to police for offenses where offenders and victims come into contact. Our reported crime findings are like those using the arrest data. Our results cast doubt on the assertion that differences in co-offending levels between juveniles and adults account for the age-crime curve. They challenge widely held beliefs that most juveniles commit most offenses in the company of others. Based on our research, group offending is incidental and does little to explain juvenile involvement in crime.

I replaced proffered, contravene, and etiological, and other million-dollar words with common words. I shortened sentences and rearranged some clauses. I removed a sentence on methods. Instead of referring to "the authors" I use "we" or "our." I replaced all passive voice with active voice.

The revised abstract has fewer words (204) in more sentences (15). Thus, the average sentence is shorter (13.6 words). It has no passive voice. Finally, its Flesch-Kincaid Grade Level is six points less than the original (12.0). A high school graduate can understand it.

Executive Summaries

Many documents have executive summaries. An executive summary is a long summary—several pages compared to the few paragraphs typical of an abstract—which a reader can use instead of examining the entire report. They are called "executive" summaries because they are for leaders who have limited time and patience to read the entire report. Occasionally, they are substitutes for the full report. The *Kansas City Preventive Patrol Experiment*'s full report went on for many hundreds of pages. Its executive summary is about 30 pages. I never met a person who read the entire report, other than the authors. For an executive summary, use the same outline as your document and write summaries of each chapter or section. Connect these summaries with transitions so readers' attention flows from beginning to end. Your goal is to provide your reader with a solid idea of the content of the report, but without the details. If you have done your job well, the full report becomes an appendix to the executive summary. If your agency wants an executive summary, look at examples of them in earlier reports from your agency. For shorter pieces, such as journal articles, the abstract serves the same function as an executive summary.

I began this section by noting that many nonfiction documents do not have abstracts. Even if you face no requirement to write one, consider doing so. Crafting an abstract helps you sharpen your understanding of your work. It forces you to clarify what is essential and to separate this from what is just interesting and useful. Then, if your boss corners you and blurts, "I have no time to read your report. What's it say?" you will have a ready answer.

Openings: First Sentences and Paragraphs

I did not appreciate the value of opening sentences until I read an article in the *New Yorker* by Calvin Trillin. Trillin was extolling the virtues of strong opening lines, and his favorite was one by a *Miami Herald* crime reporter, Edna Buchanan. Her winning first sentence was, "The corpse had a familiar face." This sentence is a great beginning because the reader wants to know more. The line was so good that Buchanan published a book with that title, which was adapted to a TV series.

One of my favorite opening lines comes from Stephen King's novel, *The Gunslinger*:

The man in black fled across the desert, and the gunslinger followed.

(King, 2017: 1)

Who is the man in black? Who is the gunslinger? Why is he following? Who is the good guy?

You do not have to be an award-winning journalist or novelist to come up with great first lines. Here is one from an article in the Association for Gravestone Studies newsletter:

> Al Capone did not rest in peace. After a debilitating battle with syphilis that resulted in dementia, history's most famous mobster died of a stroke on January 25, 1947, at age 48. He was buried in Chicago's Mount Olivet Cemetery. But his story does not stop there.
>
> (Broutman, 2018: 2)

In what way did Capone not rest in peace? What story could there be of Capone after he was buried?

Now, read this example.

> Ecology is commonly defined as the study of the relation of organisms to their environment. While this is useful as a generic statement, it begs for amplification.
>
> (Hawley, 1986: 1)

Did it excite your curiosity? Are you begging for amplification? I was begging for the opposite of amplification. After two sentences, I knew if I read further my mind would drift to the origins of dust bunnies, why mosquitoes buzz, the need to restock the toilet paper supply, the invention of catsup, and other critical topics.

Only someone with a commitment to human ecology would find this opening interesting. The preface to the book starts with an even more stultifying sentence, "For some years I have speculated on the feasibility of a unified theory of human ecology" (Hawley, 1986: vii). How many readers care about his lifelong search for a unified theory? Hawley's hook has all the utility of a rusty nail tied to the end a piece of string: no fish would come close to it.

If Hawley made human ecology boring, could someone make human waste interesting? Here is the first paragraph of a report on sanitation systems:

> Investing in sanitation and hygiene is about not only saving human lives and dignity; it is the foundation for investing in human development, especially in poor urban and peri-urban areas. However, one of the main bottlenecks encountered the world over, is the limited knowledge and awareness about more appropriate and sustainable systems and technologies that keep project costs affordable and acceptable.
>
> (Tilley et al., 2008: 3)

The authors of this paragraph tell us that shit is important and why. Comparing these two openings, I would rather read about human crap than human ecology.

This is how W.E.B. Du Bois opens his *The Souls of Black Folk*:

> Herein lie buried many things which if read with patience may show the strange meaning of being black in the dawning of the Twentieth Century.
>
> (Du Bois, 1903: 1)

I like the phrase, "the strange meaning of being black." It suggests occult knowledge, which we can learn if we read on.

Here is a recent writer beginning his book with W.E.B. Du Bois:

> While W.E.B. Du Bois was studying philosophy at the University of Berlin in the final decade of the nineteenth century, he believed—as do many Americans even today—that racial

troubles in the United States were both the most serious in the world and utterly unique. As he later recalled, "Race problems at the time were to me purely problems of color, and principally of slavery in the United States and near-slavery in Africa." Much to his surprise, a fellow student, a Pole from Kraków scoffed at the narrowness of his view: "You know nothing, really nothing, about real race problems."

(Duneier, 2016: 3)

The author, Mitchell Duneier, connects his readers' early 21st-century experiences with Du Bois's experiences 100 years earlier. He implies the question, why did Du Bois (a black man from the United States) know nothing about real race problems (according to his white Polish friend)? Duneier appeals to curiosity.

Here is another example of a good start:

Imagine a world where distance has died, where globalization and high-tech wonder have rendered place irrelevant, where the internet, Blackberries, and planes are the coin of the global realm, not local differences. From the North End of Boston to the North Beach of San Francisco, imagine cities where neighborhood difference is an anachronism, a victim of "placelessness."

(Sampson, 2012: 3)

Sampson not only asks us to conjure this world in our imagination, he provokes us to ask, "Where will this lead?" We know that he is going to contrast our vision with something else, but what?

Jane Jacobs opens her famous book, *The Death and Life of Great American Cities* with a fight.

This book is an attack on current city planning and rebuilding. It is also, and mostly, an attempt to introduce new principles of city planning and rebuilding, different and even opposite from those now taught in everything from schools of architecture and planning to the Sunday supplements and women's magazines. My attack is not based on quibbles about rebuilding methods or hairsplitting about fashions in design. It is an attack, rather, on the principles and aims that have shaped modern, orthodox city planning and rebuilding.

(Jacobs, 1961: 13)

The boldness of her statement tells us that Jacobs is not going to play footsie, shillyshally, pre-varicate, or pull punches. She will thrash planners, but how? The reader wants to see Jacobs kick butt, but what is wrong with city planning and rebuilding? Her book does not disappoint. While clobbering the standard thinking of her time, she builds an alternative view of cities. If you pick a fight in your first sentence then you must fight in your subsequent paragraphs.

In each of the good beginnings, the authors created a conflict or tension that makes the reader curious to discover its resolution. Examples and metaphors can do this too.

Stories

A story can be an example or a metaphor. The story must be simple so readers understand it. Here are the first two paragraphs and the beginning of a third, from a paper I helped write.

In January 2006, a college student we call Heather Smith was home visiting her family during a holiday break. On a rainy day during her visit, she was driving a Chevrolet Cavalier eastbound around a sharp curve when she skidded over the center line and struck a tractor trailer, head on. Her car spun and wedged itself underneath the trailer of the truck. Heather was trapped in the car for almost 30 minutes before rescue personnel were able to extract her. She died at the hospital that afternoon. She had been wearing a seatbelt.

To the Cincinnati Police Officers who worked the two blocks of road where Heather died, the curve was known as the "kill zone". Heather Smith was the third person to die in the kill zone in the previous two years, and the seventh person to be involved in a life threatening injury crash in those two blocks. This paper explains how officials in Cincinnati concentrated their efforts to ensure Heather would be the last serious injury or death on this small stretch of road. Our review of crash outcome analyses presented in this paper subsequently indicates Heather was indeed the last such fatality on this curve; in addition, police no longer call it the kill zone today. The story of how the kill zone became safer is a small but significant piece of the much larger story we tell about how police policies focusing on harm reduction have the capacity to significantly reduce life threatening vehicle crashes.

Heather Smith is one of almost forty thousand people who died annually in the U.S. in traffic crashes on average over the last five years. Police devote considerable resources to traffic related problems ...

(Corsaro et al., 2012: 502)

The example gives a human face to the statistical body of the paper. Our first paragraph focuses on Heather. The second paragraph switches to the police reaction. Although the police were highly analytical, we wanted to show that their humanity drove their work as much as the numbers. The beginning of the third paragraph connects the death of Ms. Smith to a much bigger problem. We wanted to suggest that the police actions we describe have general application. The emotional hook is dominant in this opening, but a logic hook stands at its side. In the next chapter, I will return to Heather.

Not all stories are true. Jean-Louis Van Gelder begins his paper on decision-making by summarizing a story from Homer's *Odyssea*.

In Homer's classic tale, Greek hero Odysseus upon returning home after the Trojan War passes the island of the Sirens with his ship. The Sirens are known to lure passing sailors to their island with their enchanting songs only to have them shipwreck on its treacherous rocks. No one, it is said, is able to resist their temptation. Having been warned of their dangers, Odysseus instructs his men to put beeswax in their ears and orders them to tie him to the mast of the ship and under no conditions untie him during the journey. The song of the Sirens turns out to be as seductive as foretold and Odysseus begs and threatens his men to be released of his fetters, only to be bound tighter to the mast by them. This way the ship safety navigates past the island and steers free of the destructive seduction of the Sirens. The lessons of this famous tale are manifold and, as I will argue in this chapter, highly pertinent to our understanding of criminal decision processes.

(Van Gelder, 2018: 31)

Van Gelder uses this ancient tale to challenge our understanding of criminal decision-making. Van Gelder briefly reminds us of the story's important facts and then tells us he will explain why this ancient tale still is relevant to criminologists.

Here is an example by Bill Spelman. His topic is prisons but his metaphor is dance. It describes the extra effort women must make, relative to their male dance partners. Bill wants to focus on doing things backwards.

> The late Ann Richards once remarked that "Ginger Rogers did everything Fred Astaire did, except backwards in high heels." Ginger's feat was doubtless more difficult than Fred's, but some problems are easier to solve backwards than forwards. Backward induction—reasoning from the end state back in time toward the beginning state—is the classic means of solving problems of dynamic programming (Merton 1973) and sequential game theory (Hart 2002). More generally, working backward is often offered to beginning math students as a simple approach to try in otherwise-complex problems (e.g., Kessler 2005).
>
> The effect of prisons on crime may be such a problem. Certainly it has proven difficult to work directly. Studies conducted in the last decade have produced effects that vary by almost two orders of magnitude ...
>
> (Spelman, 2013: 644)

Here is another example from Jane Jacobs. This comes from a magazine article that predates her famous book.

> This year is going to be a critical one for the future of the city. All over the country civic leaders and planners are preparing a series of redevelopment projects that will set the character of the center of our cities for generations to come. Great tracts, many blocks wide, are being razed; only a few cities have their new downtown projects already under construction; but almost every big city is getting ready to build, and the plans will soon be set.
>
> What will the projects look like? They will be spacious, parklike, and uncrowded. They will feature long green vistas. They will be stable and symmetrical and orderly. They will be clean, impressive, and monumental. They will have all the attributes of a well kept, dignified cemetery.
>
> (Jacobs, 1958)

Her first sentence tells us something important will happen. She builds expectations. Then she tells us that the results of all this work will be boring. Together, these two paragraphs create surprise and a question. Why is all this work going to lead to boredom? She does not tell the reader what she is going to say, but she lets the reader know that it will be something interesting.

Sometimes a direct statement works well. In the next example, Todd Clear tells his readers what his paper is about in the very first line. He has no story, but he tells us that he has a solution to an important problem.

> This article presents a private-sector model for "justice reinvestment" in criminal justice. The model has as its central aim to move funds from the institutional corrections budget into the socioeconomic infrastructure of high-incarceration communities in ways that develop the capacity of those communities to become better places for people to live, work, and raise their families. This development is accomplished by creating strategic reductions in the number of people incarcerated, with the savings distributed to targeted private-sector initiatives.
>
> (Clear, 2011: 585)

This technique is direct, clear, and does not waste words. If your readers will understand what you are discussing without a preamble, then consider this approach. Its limitations are that it may not work well if your readers do not understand the importance of your topic. In such cases, you will need to set the stage before introducing your topic.

Four Ways to Begin

Matt Shipman claims there are four ways to begin a science article (Shipman, 2013).

Create a mystery—begin with a sentence or paragraph that makes your reader want to find out what happened: either the cause or the consequence. The Al Capone grave example does this. So does W.E.B. Du Bois with his "strange meaning of being black."

Connect to a person—lead with a human who has a problem like the one you will discuss in your paper. This should be a specific person, not an abstract concept. This person could be you. The Heather Smith car crash example does this. Mitchell Duneier does this with his story of W.E.B. Du Bois.

Appeal to the reader—start with a problem that the reader is likely to have experienced. Talk directly to the reader. The opening of this chapter is an example of a direct appeal.

Hook to a recent event—establish immediate relevance to what is occurring now. Jane Jacobs does this with her "This year is going to be a critical ..." So does Todd Clear.

I have provided several examples of useful introductions. You might better appreciate their utility if you consider a poor beginning. This inauspicious start comes from a chapter in a book on zoning.

> The values and concerns that motivate reformers often bear little resemblance to the legislative measures that result, or appear to result, from their efforts. In a society in which land is primarily a commodity—highly valued and actively traded—it should come as no surprise that measures intended to influence its development and use, whatever their ostensible purpose, should function, in practice, to protect and promote the interest of those who trade in and develop land. Nor should it seem unusual that such measures are employed to reinforce long-standing patterns and practices of racial discrimination and segregations. Zoning is an acknowledged example of such measures.
>
> What follows sets forth the hypothesis that zoning, in addition to its well-recognized use as an exclusionary mechanism, also has been frequently employed in ways that have undermined the character, quality, and stability of black residential areas; that zoning not only has been used to erect barriers to escape from the concentrated confinement of the inner city, it has been used to permit—even promote—the intrusion into black neighborhoods of disruptive incompatible uses that have diminished the quality and undermined the stability of those neighborhoods. For reasons explained later, I refer to this practice as expulsive zoning.
>
> (Rabin, 1989: 101-102)

There are many problems here: sentence length, needless words, and irrelevant passages. An even bigger problem is that the first paragraph does not help us understand the second paragraph. Sadly, the author, Yale Rabin, is making an important point: governments have used land use zoning to destroy black neighborhoods. He should not make his readers work hard to understand his accusation. Here is my rewrite of Rabin's beginning.

> This paper examines governments' use of zoning to undermine the character, quality, and stability of black residential areas. Historians, legal scholars, and researchers have documented that governments have used zoning to confine blacks to inner-city neighborhoods, and to keep them from leaving. This is called "restrictive zoning." I contend that local governments also have used zoning to permit—even promote—the intrusion of disruptive incompatible uses into black neighborhoods. These intrusions have diminished the quality and undermined the stability of those neighborhoods. I call this use of zoning "expulsive zoning."

I made two significant changes. First, I eliminated the first paragraph. It seems to be more relevant at the end of the article than the beginning. He did not need to introduce zoning; his chapter is part of a book on that topic. Second, I broke up the lengthy sentence in the second paragraph. It contained too many ideas so I gave each their own sentence. I dropped his phrase "For reasons explained later." Everything in this paragraph "will be explained later." A reader expects points raised at the beginning to "be explained later."

Problems and Promises

Remember that "mission statement," or proposal, I suggested you create, back in Chapter 5? Here is where you put it to use.

You are writing because you (or your supervisor) believe something is not perfect with the world. This imperfection is the principal motivating force behind your writing and is the principal reason anyone would want to read your work. Your promise to the reader is that you will help them make headway against this problem. You are arguing for a particular solution. Or, you are arguing against a common solution that makes things worse. Or, you are explaining techniques and processes that readers should use to improve their job performance. Or, you are arguing for a new way of thinking that is more useful for fighting the problem than the existing way. Regardless, in the absence of a problem, you have nothing to say. And, to your reader, without a promise that your work helps address this problem, you are useless.

Look at Clear's and Rabin's paragraphs. Both imply a problem their writing addresses. Clear's problem is that governments imprison too many people and this is disrupting communities. Rabin's problem is that governments use zoning to thwart the aspirations of African Americans and this disrupts communities.

The two authors also make promises. Clear suggests a solution for his problem. Rabin promises a way of thinking about zoning laws that might lead to fair treatment of people.

You do not have to put your problem statement and promise at the very beginning, like Clear and Rabin did. Often, starting with something to entice the reader, like Spelman's dance metaphor, is helpful. However, do not put off the problem and promise for long. Soon, readers will ask themselves, "What is this thing all about?"

Promises take many forms. Here are four common ones:

- This paper is about ... (your promise is that you will describe this thing).
- This article challenges ... (your promise is that you will challenge something).
- This report answers the question ... (your promise is that you will give answers).
- This monograph shows you how to achieve ... (your promise is that you will show these things).

You do not have to use these exact words. However, a reader should be able to summarize your promise with words like these. Imagine a reader summarizing your report to her supervisor, who wants to know what you wrote about. Give this reader a script she can use, in one, two, or three sentences. Do not make her life difficult.

Overviews

Once you have hooked your reader with the title and opening paragraph, and you have described the purpose of your document with the abstract and promise, finish your beginning with an overview. An overview is important for any document more than three pages. There are two types of overviews, one for arguments and one for documents. For a short document, use the first. For a long document, with several sections, use both.

The overview of your argument is a short summary of the logic and evidence leading from facts to conclusion. It is a form of abstract, but focuses on the logic of your argument. Here is a general example of an overview of your argument:

> In this document, I make the following argument. Most people believe X. However, evidence from A, B, and C contradicts this. Based on this evidence, Y seems more plausible. If Y is more plausible than X, then we should be doing something different. I suggest some different things to do.

In the next chapter, I tell you to put a concluding summary at the end of your document. Write the end first. Once you have written a concluding summary, create a revised version of that summary for the beginning.

The overview of your document is an annotated outline. The beginning of this chapter, and most other chapters in this book, contains such an overview. Its basic format is something like this:

> This document contains __ sections. Section one addresses this. Section two describes that. Section three presents something. And so on, until the final section concludes with some more things.

It is neither complex nor exciting. Its purpose is to give your readers a roadmap so they are not surprised. If your document is particularly long, readers can use it to skip to the sections about which they are most interested.

I have described these two overviews separately because they have different purposes. The first focuses on the logic structure but does not tell where in your document the reader can find the bits of your argument. The second describes where your reader can find things, but does not focus on the logic structure.

You may be asking, "Why can't I combine them?" You can, if your document has the same order as the logic structure. However, as I discussed in the chapter on order, many orders are not simple linear paths: one thing leading to another to another to another to an ending. For complex orders, keeping these two overviews separate may be the simplest approach, even though it will create some redundancy.

I create rough drafts of these overviews early in my writing. Then I revise them as my document changes. Here is the one problem I encounter. If I say in my beginning overview "This report has six parts," then my final draft must have exactly six parts. If I say that section three discusses topic W, then that is exactly what that section should discuss. This sounds obvious, but I have mistakenly overlooked this point in the past. It is embarrassing. I have found this mistake in students' papers, published reports, journal articles, and other documents. Yes, it's obvious, but it's easy to overlook.

The End of the Beginning

To help you remember, Table 11.1 is a table summarizing how to begin a document. I offer it as a combined checklist and outline. For each part, consider the logic and the emotional functions. These will vary by part. The overview of the document may be light on the emotional function, whereas the opening might be emotionally heavy and logic light.

You made a promise at the beginning of the document and showed how you were going to deliver that promise. As my daughter's primary school teachers were fond of saying, "What you have promised you must perform." It's a line from the fairy tale, "The Frog Prince." And just like the Princess, who must allow the frog to share her pillow, the fulfillment of your promise is the central part of your document. Your conclusion should remind your reader of that promise and show how you delivered on your obligation. Thus, your beginning connects to your end. I turn to endings in the next chapter.

Table 11.1 The Beginning

Parts	Is It Required?	Comments
Title	Yes	Have you ever seen a serious document without a title?
Abstract	Depends	A requirement for academic writing and some government documents.
Opening	Strongly suggested	Can be combined with problem and promises.
Problem & Promises	Yes	Connect it to the ending.
Argument Overview	Strongly suggested	May be integrated into the overview of the document.
Document Overview	Strongly suggested	Not necessary for very short documents.

12 Endings

The Beginning of Endings

Endings are inevitable. Good endings are not. In fact, creating a good ending is far more difficult than crafting a strong beginning. It is a struggle to avoid fading away.

Your endings should be original, interesting, and memorable. Why did you write the document if you did not have something new to offer about something important? How can you influence thinking or action if your readers cannot remember your message?

The four sections of this chapter are to help you create endings. After this introduction, I discuss the purposes of endings: recap, alert, direct, arouse, and recall. Next, I describe ways you can end things: a period, a question mark, or an exclamation point. Loops are my third topic: connecting ends to beginnings. As you might expect, a chapter on endings must end. So I have an ending, too.

Elements of Endings

After a long and difficult writing project, you may view the ending as a relief. You are pushing up against a deadline. You are tired of the project so you are tempted to wrap things up in the quickest possible way. Please take a breath, gather some energy, and end well. And remember, your ending should be the second to last thing you complete. The last thing you finish is your beginning.

If you recall my advice from the previous chapter on beginnings, I suggested you create a draft ending before writing your beginning. Return to your "mission statement." Look at it again. Did you accomplish your mission? Can you provide a quick summary? That quick summary is the first draft of your ending.

DOI: 10.4324/9781003167532-15

Endings are made of multiple elements. Five elements, to be precise. Depending on your topic and what you want to achieve, you may emphasize one element more than the others. Nevertheless, you will need to touch each. To help you remember them, I gave them the acronym RADAR for Recap, Alert, Direct, Arouse, and Recall.

Recap

If you have read a murder mystery, or seen one on television, then you know what will happen at the end. The detective will explain how she deduced who did the killing, and why. That's a Recap. After your long train of evidence and logic, you need to create a compact summary of your argument. That is one function of the ending: to pull things together in a summary.

With your mission statement as a guide, you state the reason for producing this document, the goals you had, and the goals you achieved. Your Recap tells an abridged version of the story in your main report. If you write it well, you can reuse it, with minor modifications, as the abstract or the overview in your introduction.

Sometimes, a set of bullet points or even a table works well. In 2014, a community organization asked me to review a police department's problem-solving capabilities. I wrote a report with 16 recommendations (Eck, 2014). In the conclusions, I summarized them in a table like Table 12.1. I grouped the recommendations by topic and marked who is primarily responsible for carrying out each recommendation.

There is no celestial law for a Recap's format. If you think a diagram will serve your readers, then use a diagram.

Alert

If you have written skillfully, your report tells a good story; one that your readers believe. In fact, they may not be able to imagine an alternative story. But you know the holes in your argument. Honesty requires you to issue a warning.

You must Alert readers to the gaps in your story, those places where your story relies on tissue-thin evidence from dubious sources and assumptions resting on even weaker evidence. You need to Alert your readers to the limits of your evidence, logic, and assumptions.

You need to think deeply about how you could be wrong. You must provide caveats: limitations for your readers to assess. You need to tell your readers about the *possibility* of errors. I emphasize "possibility." If the errors were inevitable, your story is a lie you should not have told. If the errors are impossible, you do not need to issue a warning. You are, therefore, describing errors in a twilight Goldilocks zone of uncertainty.

Even if you believe the possibility of being wrong is small, you need to issue an Alert. You may explain why you think the possibility is slight. You may explain how the limitation might be true but inconsequential. And you may explain that more research is necessary. But back your explanations with logic and evidence. In short, avoid over and understating the limitations.

Direct

You have told a great story and alerted readers to its limitations. Now you need to answer the question, *"So what?"* Remember, you are producing consequential writing: writing that improves people's lives. You are directing your readers to take or avoid particular actions.

Table 12.1 Summary of Recommendations

	Primary Responsibility for Acting		
	Police	Community	City
1. Make CPOP more visible	X		X
a) Publicize problem-solving efforts	x		
b) Create CPOP annual report	x		x
2. Make CPOP more accountable	X		
a) Reintegrate problem solving within STARS*	x		
b) Improve Problem Solving Tracking System	x		
c) Update data elements within the Problem Solving Tracking System	x		
d) Conduct rigorous evaluations of problem-solving efforts	x		
3. Make partnerships a critical element	X	X	X
a) Improve community involvement	x	x	
b) Engage non-resident stakeholders	x	x	x
c) Coproduce solutions	x	x	x
4. Educate with CPOP		X	
a) Educate the public		x	
b) Involve youth in problem solving		x	
5. Learn from experience	X	X	X
a) Create lessons from problem-solving experiences	x	x	
b) Create a problem place strategy	x	x	x
6. Sustain CPOP leadership in the CPD	X	X	X
a) Strengthen the Chief's Scholars Program	x		
b) Assure new police understand and can undertake problem solving*	x		
c) Assure new leaders value problem solving		x	x

* Efforts known to be under way.

When you wrote your "mission statement" you should have addressed the tangible benefits of your writing. You should have made some notes for your beginning section describing the directions you will give. Now you will answer the *so what* question with a set of recommended directions.

In academia, we call the *so what* answer "implications." We have three types: implications for theory, implications for research, and implications for policy. The first tells readers if your work supports or undermines a theory, or if it suggests alterations to the theory. The second tells readers how they should change their methods of research. The third tells readers what actions people and organizations should take to address a problem. Or it warns readers to avoid some actions.

If you are writing outside academia, you may believe that your readers do not care about theory and research implications. However, if you care about how they think about the problem, you care about theory. And if you care about knowledge gaps that might need filling, you care about research. So even if you are not writing for academics, you need to consider theory and research implications.

I sense you asking, "How can I write about implications if I have just warned my readers about my story's limitations?" The answer is, use the tiny word "if." You might write something like this: "My review of police training on the use of force suggests ____. If the limitations I have just recounted are not substantial, then the following policies make sense ..." If your readers believe the limitations are substantial, they can ignore your recommendations. That is their choice so respect it. If they view the limitations as minor, then they will want to know what to do. Your statements after the "if" provide that guidance.

For any social problem, there are multiple solutions. Most of them won't work. So the question you must ask yourself is this: how do my recommendations stack up against the alternatives, including doing nothing? Your directions should make a comparison. You must not only answer "So what?" You must answer "*Why this instead of that?*"

When you use the Direct element you appeal to the head. It is an overt analytical statement. The next element goes to the gut.

Arouse

The fourth element is to Arouse. You have made a rational argument for a particular direction. Your readers now know what you want them to do. Your next challenge is to Arouse them. You appeal to urgency, fear, love, fairness, or justice to motivate your readers to change. You have told them what can be done, given your argument. Now you motivate them to act.

Sometimes the change you want to bring about is an outlook on life. Steven Pinker (2011: 695–696), for example, ends his *The Better Angels of Our Nature* with a message of hope: despite what we might believe, the facts are that humans have reduced violence over the millennia. Jane Jacobs (1961: 447–448) ends her *Death and Life of Great American Cities* by noting that cities appear to have many problems, but cities have great capacity to solve these problems. Neither of these authors is advocating that their readers take some new tangible action. Rather they are saying, "Chill. Things are far better than you think."

If you are writing about the suffering of victims, racial oppression, unfair administration of justice, gender-based discrimination, the costs of bureaucracies, the intrusion of government into the lives of citizens, or a host of other topics, then a sensible appeal to a reader's midsection may be necessary.

The arousal element is optional. In some circumstances, it is inappropriate. Imagine your supervisor has asked you to summarize the differences between two ways of rehabilitating offenders and told you not to advocate for either side. Your supervisor will give your report to a committee who will use it in their deliberations. Here, you should not make an emotional appeal for change. The committee has that job.

Some readers may resent a heavy-handed emotional appeal. I sympathize with such readers. For me, a little arousal goes a long way. If you think many of your readers are like me, then you should understate your inspirational message. If your analytically based directions are convincing, then a simple reminder of what is at stake may be sufficient. But, if your readers want a table-thumping or teary-eyed ending, then give it to them (staying within the facts).

Recall

The last element is to help your readers remember what you said long after they've stopped reading. If you are writing a report for an organization or group, you want them to Recall your report long enough to act on it. If you are writing an academic journal article, you want your readers to remember your piece and use your ideas later. If you are writing a blog, newspaper editorial, or anything for a general audience, you want your readers to ponder your ideas and do something differently.

This is your last chance to plant your ideas in your readers' minds. You want them to Recall your ideas weeks, months, and years later. If you end up with a quiet muddle, you lose that opportunity. A good ending aids this. Consider the one, two, or three things you want your readers to Recall long after they have stopped reading. Not more than three; it is hard enough to get people to remember one thing. It might be a conclusion or it might be an implication or it might be part of your arousing message. Therefore, when you are addressing the first four elements, consider how you will aid Recall.

You can address the RADAR elements in any order. The acronym is a palindrome, and the elements overlap. Arousal and Recap can assist Recall. Direct is assisted by Alert and Recall. Still, last words count so emphasize Recall at the end. You should emphasize the elements that best serve your readers' needs. To show how you can vary the emphasis, I turn to three ways to end.

Ways of Ending

If you search the internet for how to end stories, you will find plenty of advice. Much of it is for fiction writing. There is less advice for nonfiction writing of the sort you and I are discussing. What to do?

This bothered me for weeks until a friend told us he had seen a moose. My wife and I like watching moose, so he gave us directions to its likely hangout. Armed with a camera, and following our friend's directions, we found the moose lair, moose tracks, and fresh moose turds. But we missed the moose! Where was it? On the way home, we stopped at a diner. At the counter, I complained to my wife of my difficulties with endings. She stated that there are only three types of endings: periods, question marks, and exclamation points. We had no moose, but I had a useful typology of endings.

To be clear, she was not referring to the punctuation at the very end of the last sentence. She was referring to the tone of the last paragraphs. The last sentence of the last paragraph can end with any punctuation mark.

Period Endings.

These endings present your findings as strong conclusions. Period endings give a clear, direct statement of the lesson you want your readers to take with them after they finished reading. This is the most common ending. Often, period endings are used when new research strengthens old conclusions. If writing a fictional murder mystery, a period ending tells your reader that all the evidence confirms the butler (or some other character in the story) did it. Period.

A period ending Recaps your arguments and offers some Alerts describing limitations to your work. You Direct readers to firm implications, although you may decide not to Arouse them. Downplaying arousal does not mean your results are inconsequential. Quite the opposite, your results land your readers on solid ground. You remind readers of the problem you set out to address, the promises you made them, and then show how you fulfilled those promises. You address Recall by making this ending memorable.

Imagine you have examined a new program in a nearby police agency to determine if your police agency should use it. A period ending to your report Recaps your review and Directs your readers to adopt it or not. Period endings convey confirmation rather than surprise. If you have a surprise, then use an exclamation point ending (below).

Question Mark Endings?

These endings tell your readers to think further. Not because they are confused by your writing, but because there is an important question they need to contemplate. Since almost all non-fiction writing raises questions of some form, reserve the question mark ending for those circumstances where you want readers to ponder the question more than recall an answer. If this were a murder mystery, then the story ends with considerable doubt as to the guilt of the suspect or even whether a murder occurred at all.

This ending uses one or more questions. It is of the form, "Given what I just reported, would the following choices make sense? If we select option A ... If we select option B ..." You do not advocate for any option. You just describe the utility and problems with each.

Let's return to your report on a program in a nearby police agency. Given that you have looked at a single example of this program, and there are no strong studies evaluating the program, you may feel you cannot provide a recommendation. Instead of directing your readers to act, end with a set of critical questions that your agency's leaders can ask to help them make decisions.

Research articles often end this way when evidence is weak, contradictory, or controversial. If you do not have the authority to advocate, regardless of the state of the evidence, this is a good way to end.

Your Recap is a set of statements, but you Alert, Direct, and Arouse through questions. Make the questions memorable, to satisfy the Recall element.

Exclamation Point Endings!

These endings are like period endings, but exclamation point endings should surprise. They suggest, "We did not see that coming," or "Contrary to what we expected ..." or "Despite common wisdom ..." Use these sparingly since most conclusions are not surprising. Or, they suggest you are certain of your conclusions and alternative conclusions must not be considered. If your lesson is not startling or there is reasonable room for doubt, use a period style ending. If this were a murder mystery, then a conclusion that the death was accidental or a suicide warrant an exclamation point.

Suppose you were asked to review the actions of police agencies with regard to protests and marches. Your conclusions will be used by senior commanders, or at least be seriously considered. If you find that some crowd control practices provoke disorder, then you should issue a clear warning: do not do these things!

Several years ago, I co-authored a paper with two colleagues, YongJei Lee and Nick Corsaro, on police force size and crime. We reviewed all the research on this topic we could dig up. After a thorough analysis, we concluded that the studies showed that changing the size of a police force would have no detectable impact on crime. One reason is that cities seldom hire enough new police to make much of a difference in crime. We ended our article in two sentences:

> Here we break with the traditional way of concluding a research paper. We anticipate little benefit to pursuing this line of inquiry, and suggest that it is time to end it.
>
> (Lee et al., 2016: 447)

Do not do any more studies on the impact of police force size on city crime. The end offers direction to researchers: find something else to do. It signals an implication for local government leaders: do not expect crime to decline if you hire more officers. Earlier we provided Alerts and showed why these might not be great concerns. The ending does not Arouse: if you fail to heed our advice your work may be useless. We reminded readers of the stereotypical endings of academic research in the hope this would aid Recall.

You do not need to use a literal exclamation point; a period at the end of a strong statement is sufficient. You can also end with an exclamation point disguised as a question mark. To do this you need to have a clear preference among alternatives. You want your readers to take your preferred course of action, but you do not want to sound dogmatic. Therefore, list the alternatives and ask questions about each. The answers to these questions should clearly single out your choice. You can either give these answers or assume your readers can figure things out for themselves. Your preferred choice should be last. This is less dogmatic than stating, "Do X, because A, B, and C suck." However, you may be dishonest if you do not put all the available facts on the table.

Ways and Elements

As I implied, the way you end shapes the emphasis you place on each element. All three ways to end emphasize Recap and Recall. However, period, question mark, and exclamation point endings vary in their emphasis on Alert, Direct, and Arouse.

Alerts are particularly important for ending with a period or exclamation point. When you end with a period, you are summarizing your conclusions. Although you may not be calling for specific actions, readers still need to know the limits of your conclusions. With exclamation point endings, you are calling for a specific action, so it is even more critical to Alert your readers of the limitations of your story. Why are Alerts less important for question mark endings? This is because you are asking your readers to explore. Your questions emphasize the ambiguity of the available options. Thus warnings, though needed, are not as important.

A period ending may emphasize a recommendation, but question mark endings do not. So some period endings emphasize directions and others do not. Question mark endings do not emphasize direction. Exclamation point endings Direct, so you need to emphasize this element.

Exercise 12.1

Reexamine a few books and articles you read for other purposes. How did the author end: periods, question mark, or exclamation point? What elements of the ending—Recap, Alert, Direct, Arouse, or Recall—did the authors emphasize?

With the period ending, the strength of the Arouse element depends on the strengths of the results. An emotional appeal for changes in thinking is needed for question mark endings. You do not provide a specific direction, but you are challenging your readers to view the world differently. For exclamation point endings, arousal can be important. If you are pointing to a single unambiguous conclusion and ruling out alternatives, then arousal may be needed. If you have an exclamation point ending because of a surprise, then arousal may not be appropriate. Your readers need to consider the unexpected conclusion.

Looping

Endings should connect to the beginning. In the beginning, you stated a problem. And you made a promise that you would accomplish something in the pages that follow. Did you do that? How should we view the problem at the end? What actions against the problem should we take? Your ending reminds readers of why they picked up your document. It helps them understand what they know now that they did not understand then.

Trish Hall has an example of looping in her book, *Writing to Persuade*. She begins the chapter called "Don't Argue" with a story of a dinner party. Two guests are arguing over whether the government should allow people to purchase soft drinks with food stamps. She writes:

> I couldn't question the integrity or good will of either of them. But as their voices got louder and they just kept arguing, I retreated, heading to the kitchen to wash dishes. Even by the sink, I could still hear them. They went on for at least 15 minutes, which felt endless to me.
> (Hall, 2019: 102)

In that chapter, Hall goes on to explain that a writer trying to persuade others should not argue. Instead, the writer should show respect for the opposing viewpoint so others will respect the writer's views. At the very end of the chapter, Hall notes: "I left the party with my mind unchanged. The dishes, however, were done early" (Hall, 2019: 108).

Hall's beginning introduced her topic with a story. She then uses the story to bring the reader into a larger discussion over the futility of forceful arguments. She gives other examples and cites research. In the end, she returns to her original story and drives home her argument against arguing. The story connecting the beginning and end of the chapter makes her lesson memorable.

Exercise 12.2

Reexamine a few books and articles you read for other purposes. Did the authors loop their ending to the beginning? How?

Here is another example of a loop, from the conclusion of Jessica Trounstine's study of local governments' creation of segregated communities.

> This book began with a quote by Ta-Nehisi Coates (2015), a brilliant, lyrical theorist of race and racism. The quote describes the intimacy of the linkage between the punishing fear, violence, and failing schools that Coates experienced as a black child growing up in west Baltimore, and the tangible successes of white Americans. Coates explains that the "violence that undergirded the country so flagrantly on display during Black History Month [commemorating the civil rights movement] and the intimate violence of [the street] were not unrelated. And this violence was not magical, but was of a piece and by design" (p.34). What is clear is that if we do nothing about this design, politics will continue to polarize, and inequality in wealth, education, safety, and well-being will continue to worsen. Much is a stake.
>
> (Trounstine, 2019: 214-215. Trounstine is quoting Ta-Nehisi Coates, 2015: 34)

This is Trounstine's very last paragraph. She explicitly calls her readers' attention to the very first words of her book. She clearly wants her readers to think about things differently, so she ends with arousal. This appeal contrasts sharply with the interior of her book, which is a logically organized set of statistical analyses.

My last example of looping comes from a piece I introduced in the previous chapter. There I showed you the opening story in a paper on traffic crash reduction. The end of the paper loops back to this story.

> Thus a focus on vehicle crashes is not completely separated from a focus on crime; and neither is the attention of vehicle crash prevention separate from the focus of crime prevention. That the police are largely responsible for addressing both sets of problems creates research opportunities for academics who are routinely involved with policing. They should do more to take advantage of this set of circumstances. Judging from the current literature, however, it appears that the criminal justice interest in vehicle crashes, when it occurs, is largely accidental.
>
> To summarize, we found consistent evidence to suggest CARS was linked with a moderately significant reduction in vehicle crashes. We therefore conclude it was no accident that Heather Smith was the last to die in the kill zone. A law enforcement approach targets rule violations (e.g., speeding and impaired driving) regardless of where or when it occurs. In addition, a law enforcement approach targets drivers. In contrast, an analytical approach places drivers in the context of road and traffic conditions. Consequently, it can target not only drivers, but roadway and traffic conditions as well. Finally, the success of a law enforcement approach is measured by citations issued, and other police actions. The success of an analytical approach is measured by the reduction in vehicle related harms (e.g., crashes, injuries, and deaths). If harms do not decline, then the police actions need to be altered, regardless of the number of such actions.

Heather Smith was the last to die in the kill zone because the Cincinnati Police set out to make sure that the circumstances that led to her death were eliminated. It did not need to be this way: the police could have simply issued more tickets along this stretch of roads, or simply written her death off as an accident. The elimination of the kill zone, therefore, was a choice. Given that vehicle crashes produce more deaths than homicides, and impose significant monetary and emotional harms on the public, police and researchers alike should place greater attention on creating effective methods for analyzing these problems, developing effective solutions, and measuring harm reduction.

(Corsaro et al., 2012: 512)

We created two loops connecting the beginning to the end. One involves the use of the word "accident." We use the word "accident" in each paragraph, and this connects to our title, "Not by Accident." We reinforce this loop in the last paragraph by stating that eliminating the kill zone was "a choice." The second loop involves Heather Smith. Her story began our paper. It also ends with it. We remind readers that there are people involved and our readers can do something to save them: arousal.

Examples and metaphors can be very helpful for creating endings that loop back to the beginning. In a long document, you can remind readers of the story or metaphor throughout. They can serve as a thread binding your ideas into a whole.

The Ending of Endings

I have discussed the five elements of an ending (RADAR). You need to Recap your findings in short summary. You need to Alert your readers of reasonable ways you could be wrong. You need to Direct your readers to implications from your findings. You need to Arouse your readers to action. And you need to help your readers Recall your message. I have also discussed three ways to achieve these elements, drawing on the metaphor of how to end a sentence. I showed how each way emphasizes different elements. Finally, I advocated for looping your ending to your beginning. At a minimum, you should restate the problem and how you have made progress in tackling it.

Is a formula for ending all nonfiction documents presumptuous? Probably. My suggestions are just that; suggestions. If you are clever, you may find other elements and a fourth or fifth way to end. You might even discover that for some writing, you should not loop. My formula will get you going and serve you reasonably well. As you gain experience, look for, and use alternatives. Remember, the goal is not to follow a recipe, but to write with sweet clarity.

If my discussion of how to create endings is useful, then consider this outline to structure your endings:

1. Summarize what you have argued in the body of your document.
2. Give a brief, honest discussion of potential failings with your conclusions.
3. List the implications for actions, assuming the reader is willing to overlook the potential failings.
4. Plead for these to be put into action by appealing to something your readers care about.
5. Find some memorable way to wrap up that helps your reader Recall your work.

The emphasis you place on each of these points will depend on your topic and your readers. So you may omit items three and four. If you do, please do not end with a warning, the Alert. Instead, end with item five. You can enhance each of these five points with looping. So after you draft your ending, go back to your draft beginning and revise it to foreshadow the ending.

You are writing to motivate change in the world. Even if it is a very small change, every ending is an opportunity to influence your readers. Do not throw this opportunity away.

Part IV When Words Are Not Enough

13 Tables

Comments on Tables

A picture is worth a thousand words.

Unknown

Numbers have an important story to tell. They rely on you to give them a voice.

Stephen Few

If you don't have a seat at the table, you are probably on the menu.

Elizabeth Warren

Setting a Table

I have encouraged you to write with sweet clarity using words, sentences, and paragraphs. But that is only part of the story. Sweet clarity is just as crucial when creating the exhibits accompanying your text: tables, graphs, and diagrams. It is odd that so few writing books mention these vital forms of communication. So it is no surprise there is a separate set of books on visual information that barely touches on writing. Much professional writing involves creating and explaining tables of numbers, graphs and charts, and diagrams of processes. You need to know how to bring these tools into your work with the same attention to clarity you give to your writing. Fortunately, many of the same principles that apply to writing with words apply to writing with exhibits.

What Is a Table?

If a picture is worth a thousand words, how many words is a table worth? Many of the things tables can do, a written passage can do too. So why use tables? Answer: tables may be able to do things better. Compare the following written description to the table that follows.

Tables are excellent at portraying statistical evidence. If you have many numbers your readers need to view, then a table is far superior to a long passage enumerating all the numbers. Tables are far superior to written text at showing relationships in data. If you want to show a correlation or the lack of it, a table is your choice. But tables have a limitation. Because labels

DOI: 10.4324/9781003167532-17

Table 13.1 Tables Have Advantages over Writing

	Writing	**Table**
Showing statistical evidence	Poor	Good
Showing relationships	Poor	Good
Explaining and defining	Good	Poor

in tables must squeeze into small areas, tables are not good ways to define terms and explain details. I have summarized all of this in Table 13.1.

There is no clear winner. The table is better at describing the bottom line result but is vague about the meaning of row and column headings. The written passage could stand alone but is not as clear as the table. Rather than assuming tables and writing compete, let's proceed by agreeing they are members of the same team.

Now would be a good time to define what I mean by a table. A table is two or more lists displayed at right angles so that the intersection between the row list and the column list form cells containing information. You can see this in Table 13.1. The list showing ways to communicate has two elements: Writing and Table. It runs across the top row. The list showing tasks has three elements and runs down the side column. This table has six cells, where the columns and rows intersect. I have placed my judgments in each cell. Later I will show a table with three lists.

When analyzing data, you will produce several tables. You are exploring the data and trying to deduce the story. Nothing in this chapter applies to these tables. They are your first draft tables seen only by you and your co-authors. Once you begin writing, you must revise these tables. You will not revise the facts, but the formatting of the facts. The new tables are for your readers and must be consistent with your text. These tables are the ones I am discussing here.

This chapter addresses four topics. First, I will show how to make tables clear. The principles for writing with sweet clarity also apply to tables. Remove everything that fails to aid the story. Organize table elements so the table's story pops out. I focus on tables with numbers. Second, I suggest three styles for table titles. These are the same styles I mentioned for ending a document. The third section examines tables without numbers (like Table 13.1). In the next-to-last section, I describe how to integrate tables and your written passages. If tables and text are on the same team, they should communicate and enhance each other's work. The concluding section reminds you not to revise tables separately from revisions in text. Revise them together to assure consistency.

Tables without Borders

A table should tell a story: tiny or big. It might have a single lesson or several. You want your readers to comprehend that story quickly. To do that, you need to remove all distractions and provide clear directions. In earlier chapters, I showed how complex writing could be simplified to make it clearer. I will do the same thing here, but with tables.

Let's look at a good example of a bad table. I'll explain why it is unclear and full of distractions. Then I'll show you how to declutter it and enhance its clarity. The table comes from one of my first professional writing assignments (Eck, 1979: 32). My original table was not as bad as Table 13.2. But it was not much better.

To understand how Table 13.2 fails, I need to explain its purpose. I was working for an organization of police executives. The executives wanted to improve criminal investigations of burglary. They thought predicting the outcome of burglary investigations would help solve crimes.

Table 13.2 Percent Predicted Cleared versus Percent Actually Cleared

ACTUAL OUTCOME	PREDICTED OUTCOME		
	Not cleared by arrest	Cleared by arrest	Total
Cleared by arrest	420 (5.6%)	295 (3.9%)	715 (9.5%)
Not cleared by arrest	6170 (82.0%)	638 (8.5%)	6808 (90.5%)
Total	6590 (87.6%)	933 (12.4%)	7523 (100.0%)

Note: "Cleared" is police jargon for solved. There are a number of ways police clear cases, so "cleared by arrest," means the police identified and arrested one or more suspects.

Earlier research in California suggested predictions were possible and accurate. My boss asked me to replicate this research in many police agencies. The question I was to answer was, "How accurate are burglary investigation outcome predictions?" Twenty-six agencies agreed to participate. Each sent me data on 500 solved and unsolved cases. Table 13.2 reports the results for 15 agencies (I analyzed the data from the other 11 agencies separately because these agencies used a different investigative process than the 15). Although my audience was police chiefs, I suspected I was writing for the captains, lieutenants, and sergeants who would receive the report from their chiefs. I was not writing for academics, although I suspected a few might read my report. Now that you know the purpose of the table, and my readers, let's look at the table.

What makes this table bad? The short answer is that it is difficult for readers to quickly grasp its story because the table is disorderly and cluttered. How easy is it for you to understand this table's story? You can dig out the answer, but you have to work harder than is necessary.

Let's tackle the order problem first. Notice that "predicted outcome" has two types, not cleared and cleared (in that order). In contrast, "actual outcome" has cleared and not cleared, the reverse order. An accurate prediction is one where the prediction matches the actual. To calculate accuracy, readers must add the percent in the second cell of the left column to the percent in the middle column's top cell (to get an accuracy rate of 85.9 percent). Their eyes must go from the bottom left to the upper right. But in western cultures, we usually read from the top left and go down or right. This problem is not insurmountable, but it requires readers to waste effort on inessential issues.

Another problem is the emphasis the table places on the number of cases relative to the percent of cases. To answer the question, the reader needs to examine the percents. These are all in parentheses. Parentheses indicate that what they contain is of less importance (this is true in writing sentences, too; parentheses suggest, "You can skip this"). The table shows the number of cases first and in a dominant position. But these are not the most important numbers.

Let's look at a table with these order problems addressed (I will tackle the other issues in a moment). We are now looking at Table 13.3. I switched the columns and raised the percents' importance by putting them first. I subordinated the numbers by placing them inside parentheses below the percent and giving them a smaller font. All of this helps focus the reader's attention on the figures that matter most.

Table 13.3 is much like the table in my original report. Although these changes improve the clarity of the table, I could have done better. The table is still too cluttered. Lines are the main culprits. Before we get rid of them, let's attend to the purpose we want them to serve. We want

Table 13.3 Percent Predicted Cleared versus Percent Actually Cleared

ACTUAL OUTCOME	PREDICTED OUTCOME		
	Cleared by arrest	Not cleared by arrest	Total
Cleared by arrest	3.9% (295)	5.6% (420)	9.5% (715)
Not cleared by arrest	8.5% (638)	82.0% (6170)	90.5% (6808)
Total	12.4% (933)	87.6% (6590)	100.0% (7523)

Note: "Cleared" is police jargon for solved. There are a number of ways police clear cases, so "cleared by arrest," means the police identified and arrested one or more suspects.

Table 13.4 Percent Predicted Cleared versus Percent Actually Cleared

ACTUAL OUTCOME	PREDICTED OUTCOME		
	% Cleared by arrest	% Not cleared by arrest	Total
% cleared by arrest	3.9% (295)	5.6% (420)	9.5% (715)
% Not cleared by arrest	8.5% (638)	82.0% (6170)	90.5% (6808)
Total	12.4% (933)	87.6% (6590)	100.0% (7523)

Note: "Cleared" is police jargon for solved. There are a number of ways police clear cases, so "cleared by arrest," means the police identified and arrested one or more suspects.

the lines to make the cells distinct, so a reader's eyes travel down columns and across rows instead of bounding about. And we want lines to direct readers' attention to the essential parts of the table: those that tell the story. Unfortunately, lines often fail at these tasks. So we cannot just delete lines. We need to find other methods to aid readers.

Table 13.4 is much better than my original. Instead of lines, I now use shading and white space to guide readers' eyes. The advantage of adding extra space between rows and columns (rather than using lines) is that readers see the figures that matter, but do not notice the space. The shading in Table 13.4 draws attention to the middle four cells where the story resides. I could have also removed the exterior border.

I will make a final set of changes: retitle the table to connect it to the table's story; and change the row and column headings to make them more intuitive. This will allow me to remove the footnote. I will remove redundant symbols. I will excise all the numbers in parentheses, saving one. And I will restrict shading. The result is Table 13.5.

Here are the reasons for the changes. The title answers the readers' question, and the percents explain the reasoning. There are fewer words and symbols to get in the way of comprehension. I removed "outcome" on the assumption that the main text of the report would explain that. Instead of using the police jargon, "cleared," I made the outcomes the "arrest" and "no arrest" of a suspect.

Table 13.5 Burglary Investigation Outcome Prediction Is 85.9 Percent Accurate

	PREDICTED		
ACTUAL	% Arrest	% No arrest	Total
% Arrest	3.9	5.6	9.5
% No Arrest	8.5	82.0	90.5
Total	12.4	87.6	100.0%
			(7523)

The numbers in parentheses do not serve a purpose, except to show how many cases each percent reflects. The number of cases are not part of the main story. It is a side issue of interest to a few readers. So I give the total number of burglary cases in the lower right cell. Those readers interested in knowing the number in each cell can calculate these numbers. Whether you do this depends on what your readers expect. In a social science journal, retaining these numbers might be a good idea. There will be a large proportion of readers who want to see them. For other audiences they may get in the way.

Most of the percent signs are redundant. The title signals that we are talking in the language of percent. The column and row headings also signal this, as does 100 percent at the bottom right. With the raw numbers removed, there is less chance for confusion in the center of the table where the story gets told.

To emphasize the main story, I shaded the two cells whose contents sum to the accuracy rate. This change draws the readers' eyes to the main diagonal of the table. If I had wanted to tell the story of prediction errors, I would have given the table a different title and shaded the two cells in the off-diagonal (8.5 and 5.6).

Finally, I removed the border lines. They are minor distractions so who needs them?

The result is a simple table that answers a question. When accompanied by written paragraphs, a reader should have little trouble understanding it.

How simple should you make tables? As simple as possible without losing important information. Important information is information that (a) tells the story, like the two shaded numbers in Table 13.5, (b) helps verify your claims, like the column and row totals and the number of cases in parentheses, and (c) helps readers interpret the table's content, like the labels for rows and columns. Like all writing, it's a judgment call.

When you draft a table, you might start with something like Table 13.1 or 13.2. This is your first draft. You needed those details to conduct your statistical analysis, but not all of them should be in your table. Remove the details that distract from your story. Look at several versions, including a version that is as simple as you can imagine. If possible, ask someone to give you their opinion and explain why they prefer one version over others. Most people leave too much stuff in their tables, so err toward removing things.

I hope the changes I have shown illustrate the usefulness of eliminating extra words and symbols and selecting clear labels. Nevertheless, let's look at a three-dimensional table.

Imagine you are studying three types of facilities: apartment buildings, bars, and convenience stores. You want to know how crime varies by facility. Further, you are examining these three facilities in two neighborhoods. You have three dimensions—facility, neighborhood, and crime—and you are stuck with a two-dimensional page or computer screen.

Table 13.6 Percent of Places with Repeat Crimes by Neighborhood

Places with	Neighborhood A				Neighborhood B				A+B
	Apartment bldgs.	Bars	Convenience stores	Total	Apartment buildings	Bars	Convenience stores	Total	
No crime	83% (30)	60% (6)	50% (4)	74% (40)	76% (16)	67% (4)	100% (1)	75% (21)	74% (61)
One crime	14% (5)	30% (3)	38% (3)	20% (11)	14% (3)	0% (0)	0% (0)	11% (3)	17% (14)
Two or more crimes	3% (1)	10% (1)	12% (1)	6% (3)	10% (2)	33% (2)	0% (0)	14% (4)	9% (7)
Total	100% (36)	100% (10)	100% (8)	100% (54)	100% (21)	100% (6)	100% (1)	100% (28)	100% (82)

Table 13.7 Most Places Have No Crime, But a Few Places Have a Lot

	Neighborhood A			Neighborhood B		
	Apartment buildings	Bars	Convenience stores	Apartment buildings	Bars	Convenience stores
No crime	83 (30)	60 (6)	50 (4)	76 (16)	67 (4)	100 (1)
One crime	14 (5)	30 (3)	38 (3)	14 (3)	0 (0)	0 (0)
Two or more crimes	3 (1)	10 (1)	12 (1)	10 (2)	33 (2)	0 (0)
Total 100%	(36)	(10)	(8)	(21)	(6)	(1)

Table 13.6 is a first draft of your results. You should be able to see several problems with this version. As distracting as lines and extra symbols were in the simpler tables above, they are even more so here. The other problem is that the row totals (three of them) make it challenging to find the story. What is the story this table tells?

Table 13.7 is a cleaned up version of the same table. I removed the row totals and the lines, including the border. White space takes their place. I used shading to draw attention to the parts of the table with the central information and used a white space to separate neighborhood A from B. I left the numbers in parentheses because they seem to be part of the story, but I made them smaller.

The title gives a thumbnail version of the story. The text accompanying the table would provide more detail, including caveats. It would say something like:

> Table 13.7 shows most facilities have no crime, regardless of neighborhood or facility type. Very few places have two or more crimes, regardless of neighborhood or facility type. Neighborhood B has a larger percent of facilities with multiple crimes, compared to neighborhood A. However, we need to be cautious about such a conclusion given the low number of places.

Just as you tell a story with your written paragraphs, you are telling a story with your tables. So what you choose to remove or leave in the table depends on the story. Table 13.7 allows easy comparison of facilities within neighborhoods. This table makes sense if the main story is about facilities and neighborhoods are a sidelight. If neighborhood-to-neighborhood comparison is important to the story, a different table is needed. To compare the same facility in different neighborhoods forces readers' eyes to compare widely separated cells and ignore cells in between.

Always put the things you want readers to compare as close together as possible.

Suppose the story you tell hinges on facility comparisons across different neighborhoods (e.g., bars in A, to bars in B). And also suppose that of the three facility types, apartments are the most critical to the story. In that case, Table 13.8 is a better version than earlier tables. The cells we want the reader to compare are next to each other. The table highlights apartments. And the bold numbers focus on evidence of concentration of crime in apartments.

Remember those row totals I discarded? Suppose they were important because you needed to compare neighborhoods. Table 13.9 brings them back and allows a quick comparison of all crimes in the neighborhoods, regardless of location. I imagine this table accompanying

Table 13.8 Crime Is Concentrated in a Few Facilities, Regardless of Neighborhood

Neighborhood	Apartment Buildings		Bars		Convenience Stores	
	A	B	A	B	A	B
No crime	83 (30)	76 (16)	60 (6)	67 (4)	50 (4)	100 (1)
One crime	14 (5)	14 (3)	30 (3)	0 (0)	38 (3)	0 (0)
Two or more crimes	**3** (1)	**10** (2)	10 (1)	33 (2)	12 (1)	0 (0)
Total 100%	(36)	(21)	(10)	(6)	(8)	(1)

Table 13.9 Crime Is Slightly More Concentrated in Neighborhood B

	A	B
No crime	74 (40)	75 (21)
One crime	20 (11)	11 (3)
Two or more crimes	**6** (3)	**14** (4)
Total 100%	(54)	(28)

Table 13.8, not replacing it. I picked a dramatic title. If other evidence (e.g., statistical tests) showed that neighborhoods were not different, I would select a title consistent with these facts.

There are two core lessons. First, eliminate distractions. Distractions often include lines, symbols, and redundant data. Second, organize your table to assist your reader to discover the story. This often involves arranging columns and rows to facilitate comparisons and the use of differential shading and bolding to direct readers' eyes to the important pieces of information. It sometimes means you should create several tables rather than try to pack everything into a single table. What you eliminate or add depends on the story you are telling, the data you are showing, and the readers to whom you are telling your story.

Exercise 13.1

Examine tables of data in published works. What do you like and dislike about them? How can these be improved? Revise several.

Three Styles for Table Titles

In the examples above, I changed the titles of tables as I cleaned them. But I did not explain my choices. All tables have titles. When considering titles to tables, I decide first on their style. Do

I want to describe the data with the table? Do I want to raise a question? Do I want to reveal the lesson from the story? Just as in endings, you can use three styles: period, question mark, and exclamation point. The period ending describes the content. It conveys a neutral tone and gives readers no advice on how to interpret the table. The question style stimulates inquiry by highlighting uncertainty or demanding a look beyond the obvious. The exclamation style summarizes the story the table tells. It reveals a lesson readers should draw from the data. Reexamine the titles to the tables we discussed above.

- **Period.** Tables 13.2, 13.3, 13.4, and 13.6 use this style: e.g., Percent Predicted Cleared versus Percent Actually Cleared. The title restates the row and column headings: a reason I prefer not to use this style.
- **Question?** I could have retitled Table 13.7: "Is 85.9% Percent Accuracy the Important Criterion?" The title challenges readers to consider something they may overlook.
- **Exclamation!** Tables 13.5, 13.7, 13.8, and 13.9 use this style: e.g., Burglary Investigation Outcome Prediction Is 85.9 Percent Accurate. The title states one lesson from the table's data, the conclusion most relevant to the story I am telling.

Often, several lessons or questions compete for the chance to appear in the title. Pick one. Choose the single lesson or question most important to your story.

The style you choose depends on your readers and what you are trying to achieve. Academic journals tend toward period titles. A consultant report to a community group or government agency might communicate better with an exclamation. If the table is at the beginning of a document, the question style might be a good way of introducing the paper's purpose. I gravitate to exclamation style titles, but often I curtail my urge depending on my audience.

Tables without Numbers

Tables are just as useful for communicating a story without numbers as they are for communicating a story with numbers. Remember the table about burglary investigation outcome prediction? There is a general story we can tell in a table without numbers. It applies to any situation where you are dealing with a process that produces one of two outcomes, which I call A and not A. For example, someone predicts the outcome (A or not A): a doctor uses a medical test to predict if you have a disease; a pollster predicts the outcome of a forthcoming election; a financial advisor picks a stock she thinks will increase in value in the next year; a gambler picks the winner of tomorrow's race. We then compare their predictions to what actually occurs (A or not A): did you get the disease, did the pollster call the election right; did the stock go up in value; did the horse win?

These, and numerous other predictions, have the same underlying logic as predicting burglary investigations outcomes. Table 13.10 shows that logic without using any numbers.

Table 13.10 Prediction Accuracy and Errors

Occurs	Predict	
	A	Not A
A	Accurate	Error–False negative
Not A	Error–False positive	Accurate

Table 13.11 Classification of Police Problems

Environments	Behaviors					
	Predatory	Consensual	Conflicts	Incivilities	Endangerment	Misuse of police
Residential	Home invasion robbery	Drug sales houses	Child abuse by boy friends	Student party houses	Fireworks displays on apartment balconies	Elderly people reporting space aliens
Recreational	Theft from vehicles in an amusement park parking area	Drug sales in nightclubs	Fights in bars	Couples having sex on a public beach	Drownings at public pools	Calls to police about African Americans using a picnic area
Offices	Theft of purses from office workers	Workplace shootings	Vandalism of offices by protesters			
Retail	Store robberies			Vandalism to businesses		Excessive shoplifting reports
Industrial		Purchasing stolen metal	Strike related violence		Unintentional deaths in factories	
Agricultural	Propane theft for meth production	Illicit marijuana farms			Suicide by older single male farmers	False reports of cow tipping
Educational	Band instrument theft from high schools	Drug sales on college campuses	Fights at a high school bus boarding area	Graffiti on churches	Students being struck by vehicles in front of middle school	False reporting of student violence threats
Human Service	Attacks on social workers	Methadone diversion	Fights among clinic clients			
Public Way	Street robberies		Road rage attacks	Defacement of road signs	Suicide jumpers from a bridge	
Transport	Pickpocketing at bus terminal			Panhandlers at bus stops		
Open / Transitional	Theft of metal from unused factory	Homeless use of abandoned buildings		Toppling tombstones in an abandoned rural cemetery	Drownings in abandoned quarries	

Source: Based on Clarke and Eck (2016). Also see Eck and Clarke (2003).

If I knew in 1979 what I know today, I would have placed Table 13.12 in my report before the numerical table. This table could have communicated the general principles needed to interpret the table containing numbers. I would have used the same style—format, shading, bold, lines—in both tables.

Two-by-two tables are very useful, but so are larger tables. Table 13.11 is example of an 11-by-6 numberless table. Ronald Clarke and I created it to classify police problems (Clarke & Eck, 2016). We started by creating two lists. The first describes the behavior of the people involved in the problem. The second list contains the types of environments where these behaviors occur. Our goal was to describe a map of possible police problems: showing their diversity and common features. That is what Table 13.11 does.

The cells contain examples explained in the text (the empty cells indicate that I could not think of an example, even though such problems may exist). The text surrounding the original table defined the row and column labels and interprets the table.

As this table is quite large, there was not enough room to use white space to separate rows. Therefore, I shaded every other row. Row shading directs the readers' eyes across the table without having to use grid lines. If I had shaded the columns, I would direct readers' eyes down the page. In this example, it probably does not matter which I used, although I find the horizontal shading more appealing. You should experiment with various shadings. If your table will be displayed in color, then consider a light color that is easy on your readers' eyes (blue or green). Do not use a dark color in the background because your text will be hard to read unless you make the text a light color.

A table like this has advantages and disadvantages. The principal advantage is that you can communicate considerable information in a relatively small space. Writing a narrative describing the same information takes several tedious pages. The principal disadvantage is that readers will have to spend some time scrutinizing the table. Compensating for the density of information is the fact that it's easier to find things in a table than in a block of text.

Not all tables get published. Often, when I am writing, I start by composing a table with words. This helps me organize my thoughts. Once I have a table that makes sense to me, I write a description of it. Sometimes that description can stand on its own; readers will not need a table. Then, the table does not make it to my final draft. In other circumstances the table assists readers. Then I keep it.

Exercise 13.2

Look for written descriptions of ideas, particularly ideas that classify topics. Can you draw a table that accurately reflects the idea?

Writing with Tables

We are considering tables as part of writing, not stand-alone exhibits. Therefore, we need to consider how your word narrative works with your tables. Very few tables are self-explanatory. Consider Table 13.11. I have not defined the row and column headings. I am sure you are puzzling over what we meant by several of these categories. In our original article, we provided definitions. We also discussed several examples. We did not explain every detail. We tried to hit a balance between saying little or nothing about the table and repeating the information in the table.

What is in this Goldilocks zone? Four things. (1) The purpose of the table: the question that the table tries to answer. (2) Background information readers need to correctly interpret the table: definitions, for example. (3) The story told by the table: lessons you want the reader to learn from the table. (4) Cautions: limitations to the story that readers might not realize.

Like a pitcher and catcher in baseball, written explanations and tables work together but have distinct roles. The tables cannot be fully understood without the written narrative and the narrative cannot be fully understood without the tables. A reader should learn from both. Placing tables within their corresponding text helps readers.

Here is a hypothetical example of text referencing a table (not shown). I annotated this example, with bracketed comments, to label the function of each sentence.

> Table 45 examines whether education is associated with people's attitudes toward the police [the purpose of the table]. The attitudinal information comes from the survey I described earlier [background information]. Lower numbers reflect attitudes that are more negative and higher numbers reflect positive attitudes [background information]. As you can see, as education rises, the percent of people expressing the most positive attitudes increases [the table's story]. There is one exception, however ... [a caution].

Unfortunately, few tables get placed in the best locations particularly if you have multiple tables and figures competing for space. You will notice misplacement in this book; my tables are close to where they belong, but sometimes they are separated from their text. Readers need to switch back and forth between the table and its text. This extra effort can inhibit readers' quick understanding. There is no perfect solution. But you need to do two simple things: make explicit reference to each table within your text and put tables as close to their text as possible.

Clearing the Tables

The same principles of sweet clarity apply to tables as to written passages. This means eliminating anything that is not useful for telling a story: extraneous lines, symbols, and flourishes. It also means attending to readers' needs through organization and selective use of directions.

Another similarity is the need to edit and revise tables. Your first draft of a table is not the table you want others to see. This is especially true of anything your computer draws based upon factory-set defaults. It's your shitty first draft table. You will have to revise it. Just like writing, you will have to make many judgment calls. As you revise a table, check the text surrounding it. You may have to revise that too. Similarly, if you are editing written work that references tables, revise the tables to make them consistent with their texts. Use the same words in your text as you use in tables. For example, if you are studying marijuana sales locations, do not call them dispensaries in the text and pot shops in the tables. Pick one term and stick with it.

Tables have great value for organizing numbers and ideas, but they have limitations. In many circumstances, it is easier for readers to interpret graphical images than tables. If you find that you are struggling to eliminate table clutter, then consider the possibility that you should use a different type of exhibit.

In the next two chapters, I describe how to create simple and clear figures. First, I describe figures for portraying statistical data. I call these figures "graphs." By now, it should come as no surprise to you that the same core principles of sweet clarity we apply to text and tables apply to graphs. The chapter that follows graphs examines another type of figure I call "diagrams." Diagrams portray ideas describing relationships or processes and may contain little or no statistical data.

14 Graphs

Picture Stories Told by Numbers

Tables help readers understand simple stories. Tables provide less help as stories become more complex. They can block readers' understanding. It is time to turn to figures. Figures can help readers comprehend complex stories, even stories words cannot tell. I love figures so much I have two chapters describing them.

This chapter examines figures depicting numbers. I call such figures "graphs." They tell stories from numerical information. We have all seen bar charts. They are examples of graphs.

The next chapter delves into pictures of processes and relationships not built on numbers, e.g., family tree or organization chart. I call these types of figures "diagrams." Do not let my distinction between graphs and diagrams get you too excited. Both are figures and I distinguish them here for practical purposes.

The principles we discussed for writing passages and creating tables with sweet clarity apply to figures too: graphs as well as diagrams. Keep your reader in mind. Tell an honest story. Make graphs your readers can interpret with ease. Simple graphs, with which your readers are familiar, will be your basic tools. They will serve most of your graphing needs. When you must innovate, avoid all decorative flourishes that do not help your readers understand the graph's story.

Imagine your doorbell rings. You open the door. There stands a uniformed delivery person holding a large box emblazoned with your name. What treasure could this box contain? You take the box and open it on the kitchen table. Inside, you discover wrapping encasing another box. Opening the second box you find more wrapping and a smaller box. Within that box, you discover still more wrapping and a tiny box. Inside you find a bubble-wrapped elegant metal case containing earbuds. The earbuds are your precious content. Everything else is packaging.

DOI: 10.4324/9781003167532-18

I distinguish between content and packaging. But you cannot understand the content without groping around: exploring your data. In the last chapter, I made a distinction between tables you used to explore data and tables you used to communicate to readers. The same applies to graphs. This chapter examines communication graphs: those your readers see. The first graphs you explore, with the curtains drawn, the doors bolted, and the lights low, are not my concern. But when a graph ventures into the world, you must make sure it's packaged so people can understand its content. All graphs need some packaging, but how much?

Three sections follow. The first discusses the basic principles of graph construction. The second section compares bad and good graphs to show how simple graphs work better than ornamented graphs. I close the chapter with a brief set of rules for integrating graphs into your larger text.

Layers of a Graph

Graphs have three layers. Think of a stage play. A play's top layer consists of key actors. Their conflicts, compromises, and collaborations tell the story. You pay to see their movement, gestures, and dialogue. Without these actors, you would not buy a ticket. However, they cannot tell their story without others. The play's bottom layer embraces set designers, stage managers, lighting technicians, costume creators, riggers, carpenters, sound designers, and a host of others we seldom see on stage. Between scenes, we may see prop runners, dressed in black, move the scenery. But on stage, they never interact with the actors. The middle layer contains minor characters, some never speaking, helping the key actors tell the story. If two key actors in the play are arguing at a café, the minor character serves them coffee and crumpets.

A graph's top layer tells the story, with the unobtrusive assistance of the middle layer, all supported by an almost invisible bottom layer. I show this in Figure 14.1. Let's start at the bottom, jump to the top, and conclude with the middle.

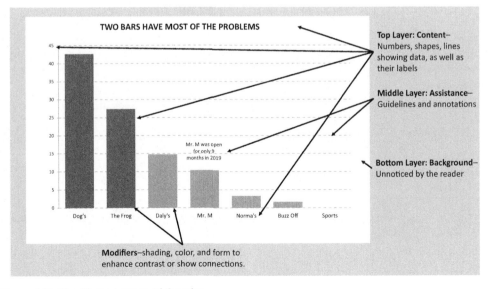

Figure 14.1 The Three Layers of Graphs

The bottom layer contains the background. In most printed texts, the paper colors the background. You do not want to draw attention to it, despite its importance. Keep the background muted if not invisible. It does its job best when readers overlook it, just like stagehands.

The top layer of your figure contains your content and forms the heart of the graph's story. The title is a prominent element in this layer. Bars and lines, along with their labels, reveal the data's message. If you removed the top, the rest becomes gibberish. Make the top stand out from the background to draw readers' attention to the story.

Presentation Backgrounds

In a presentation, consider a dark background color. You might be tempted to use the same background you use in your report. Think again. Written and oral presentations are different means for communicating information. That which works well for one rarely works well for the others.

Between these layers live the things that help readers interpret the top layer. Things like grid lines, explanations, and other aids. Aids should stand out from the bottom layer while not competing with the top layer. Middle layer items do their job best when they direct readers' minds to the top layer. Like a play's minor players, they should never compete for attention with the lead actors. In fact, if you can tell the story without the middle layer, do so.

Modifiers are tools used to alter each layer by adjusting shading, color, and shape. In a bar chart, for example, you usually make all the bars the same shape, color, and shade. However, you may want one category of things to stand out because of its importance to the story. Then, give it a different color or shade. Modifiers must aid readers without dominating readers' attention. If a reader's first reaction to a graph is "Oh, what a delightful shade of gray" or "My, that is ugly," then you have gone too far. For this reason, never use 3D effects; more on this later.

To summarize, here are the basic principles of clear graph design:

*   Keep the bottom layer quiet. Your readers should not notice it.
*   Focus readers' attention on the top layer. This is where you tell the story of your data.
*   Use the middle layer to assist the top layer. Everything here plays a subordinate role to the top layer.
*   Use modifiers of layers to help drive the story without becoming the story.

Next, let's look at some basic graphs.

Four Graphs for Most Occasions

If you play with software for analyzing data, you will find an overwhelming selection of graphs, each with many variations. There is a growing corpus of books (see *Further Reading*) on visual information containing more graph types than you could draw in a lifetime. If you search online, you can find many more. I will not attempt to make sense of this cornucopia of visual displays. Instead, I will show a very few types of graphs, ones you will probably use most frequently, and how to make them clear. You can adapt these principles of clarity to any other graphs that you may learn later. All of them, for example, will have a top, middle, and bottom layer.

How to Select a Basic Graph

Answers to two questions point to the graph you need. Will you describe one variable or compare two or more variables? Is your data lumpy or smooth?

Describe One or Compare Several? Suppose I have 100 addresses, and I want to tell a story of a single variable: the number of crimes at each address. I need to *describe* the address with the most crime, the least, and so on. Describing data is one of the most common forms of analysis because it is the most basic. Any form of data analysis begins with describing.

What Is a Variable?

You learned about variables in a statistics course. But you forgot. I won't tell anyone. A variable describes something. For example, height describes people, trees, buildings, and rocket flight. People come in different heights: height varies. In a graph showing how many people have different heights, the number of people and their heights are variables. Together they show the distribution of heights within a group of people.

Once you describe, you may want to *compare*. Suppose I have two neighborhoods with 100 addresses each, and I have the number of crimes at each address. How does the distribution of crime among addresses in neighborhood A compare to the distribution of crime among addresses in neighborhood B? Are the worst crime places in the neighborhoods equally bad? Are the safest places in the neighborhoods equally safe?

Lumpy Data or Smooth? Officially, I should restate the question, are your data discrete or continuous? But let's not get too wrapped up in jargon. Lumpy (discrete) data describes categories. If you have data describing land use, your lumpy data's categories might be homes, stores, banks, restaurants, bars, and so forth. Often such types lack a natural order. It does not matter which comes first: bars, homes, banks, stores, or restaurants.

Some lumpy data has order. A survey asking people to describe the clarity of writing examples could employ the categories: clear as a bell, clear enough, somewhat foggy, murky, and it's easier to see through molasses at midnight without a flashlight. The data is lumpy, but the lumps line up good to bad. There is, however, no way to classify writing as one-third of the way between murky and molasses. People answering the question must select the category closest to their opinion.

Smooth (continuous) data has order without lumps. Variables can possess fractional values, like the Flesch-Kincaid Grade Level score, for example. Other examples of continuous variables include income, age, time, and distance. Smooth data comes as counts, degrees, fractions, proportions, or percents of things.

For lumpy data, use bars. For smooth data, use lines. When describing, use one set of bars or a single line. When comparing, use two or more sets of bars or multiple lines. Remember, this rule of thumb is not a court-enforceable edict. You will find exceptions. Start with the guidance illustrated in Figure 14.2 and adjust as your needs dictate.

Let's now look at how writers create bad graphs and what you can do to make sure you do not.

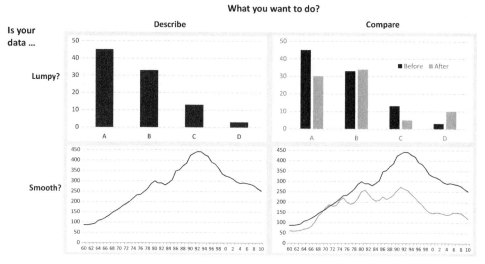

Figure 14.2 Four Basic Graphs

Bad, Ugly, and Good Graphs

Don't Use Pie Charts

I must challenge one foul thing right away, pie charts. A rare moment when a pie chart is ideal might come your way, but don't bet on it. I am still looking. Nevertheless, pie charts provide a valuable lesson in producing better graphs: graphs with sweet clarity.

William Playfair, in 1801, invented pie charts (Tufte, 1983). Fortunately, he also invented many other more useful graphs. So do not judge him harshly. We all make mistakes. Pies depict lumpy data. They show the part's (wedges) contributions to the whole (circle). This is a modest benefit. Many other ways to do this are available, including writing, "All the lumps added together equal 100 percent."

Not only do pie charts lack great value, they also impose costs on readers. According to research, readers have more trouble interpreting pie charts than many other charts, like the common bar chart (Cleveland & McGill, 1984). Why?

Interpreting a bar chart requires your reader to compare the relative heights of the bars. Comparing bar heights is easy; the reader's eye scans across the graph.

A pie chart forces your reader to estimate the area of segments making up a circle and compare them. Comparing circle slices is a harder task because it requires assessing the angles of lines radiating from the pie's center. If a reader has an intuitive grasp of geometry, a pie chart may be OK. Not everyone does. Just as long words require more energy from your reader than short words, pie wedges take more energy to understand than bars.

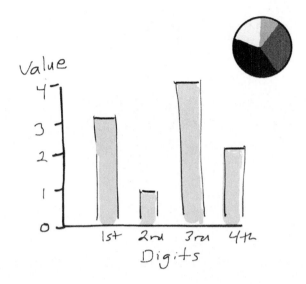

Table 14.1 Calls for Police from Bars in Mt. Fog

Bars in Mt. Fog	Calls to Police	% of All Bar Calls
Buzz Off	3	1.6
Daly's	27	14.8
Dog's	78	42.6
Mr. M	19	10.4
Norma's	6	3.3
Sports	0	0.0
The Frog	50	27.3
Total	183	100.0

You can provide grid lines across a bar chart so your reader can compare the heights of bars far apart. You cannot do this with a pie chart. Readers will have difficulty comparing two pie wedges not next to each other. And when two slices have similar volumes, your readers cannot reliably pick the biggest slice. When sharing a pizza, have you ever accidentally misjudged a slice only to have someone else grab the larger one? If so, you understand the problem with pie charts.

The problem gets worse as the number of slices increases. The more categories you have, the greater the challenge for your readers. This is not the case with bar charts; they can help readers even if they have many categories of similar heights.

Suppose I had the hypothetical data shown in Table 14.1: bars in the town of Mt. Fog and the number of police calls to each in a year. I could use Table 14.1 to present the data, but readers will grasp the story faster if I use a graph.

Let's pretend I decide to create a pie chart, like Figure 14.3. The bottom layer is the page, the top layer is the pie, and the middle layer is the key on the right. Can you differentiate among the shades of grey? Can you connect the pie wedges to the key? Color might help you, but your eyes still must flit from wedge to key, repeatedly. The more categories in a pie chart, the more flitting. And what if a category has nothing in it, like Sports? You can find Sports in the key

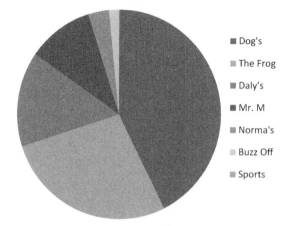

Figure 14.3 Pie Chart: Calls to the Police from Eight Bars

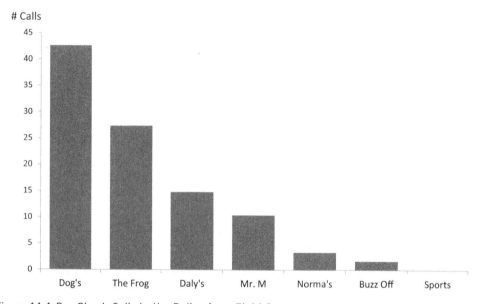

Figure 14.4 Bar Chart: Calls to the Police from Eight Bars

(middle layer) but not in the pie (top layer). Though part of the story, the pie chart eliminated this character.

Now consider the same data displayed in a bar chart (Figure 14.4). Again, the bottom layer is the page; the top layer comprises the bars. The middle layer comprises the axis lines. Do your eyes have to go back and forth between a key and the bars? No. Each bar has a clear label. Can you quickly determine the ranking of each bar? Yes. I organized the bars from most calls to the least for this purpose. Did I leave Sports out of the story? No. The graph contains Sports. I do not need a key. I do not need color. I need a better title, however. This bar chart has little packaging, and that packaging enhances rather than distracts from the substance.

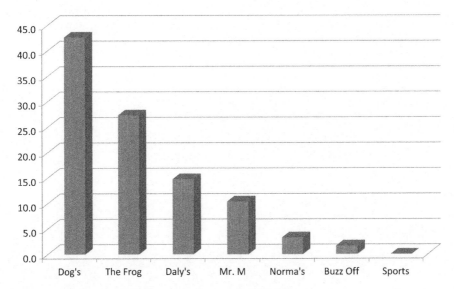

Figure 14.5 3D Bar Chart: Calls to the Police from Eight Bars

I hope I have persuaded you to have no public relationships with pie charts (what you do in the privacy of your home is your business). Let's look at something else you should never do in public.

Never Add Fake Dimensions

Consider this example of a 3D bar chart (Figure 14.5). The data has two real dimensions: the list of bars (horizontal axis) and the proportion of calls (vertical axis). The fake thickness added to the top layer contributes nothing to the story. Instead of assisting the top layer, the fake third dimension increases readers' difficulty judging the bars' relative heights. I cannot imagine any legitimate reason for adding a fake dimension. If you want to confuse readers, hide something from them, or misdirect their attention, then a fraudulent dimension may be useful.

Keep Things Simple

As bad as the previous graph is, worse graphs show up frequently. I wish I could claim that I had seen nothing like Figure 14.6, but I have. Look at the bottom and middle layers. A distracting box surrounds the bottom layer and contributes nothing. The middle layer's shaded backdrop dominates the graph. The value labels for the vertical axis are duplicated in the middle layer. The grid lines compete for readers' attention. In the top layer, the graph lays at an odd angle, distorting the bars and making interpretation difficult. Fake 3D graphs make readers work harder than necessary to dig out the story.

I have identified some ways to make bad graphs. Now I will illustrate how to make good ones. I will start with the bar graph in Figure 14.7. It is simple, with few distractions. I eliminated the vertical axis line and substituted light grey dashed lines to show the bars' heights. Although a

Calls

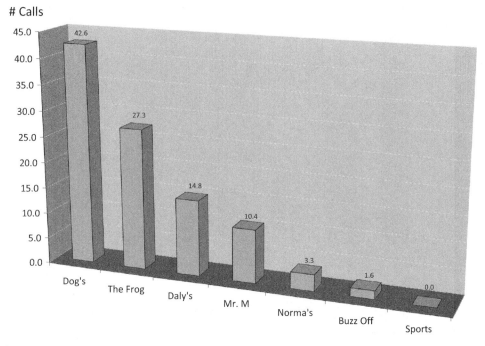

Figure 14.6 A Terrible Graph: Calls to the Police from Eight Bars

Calls

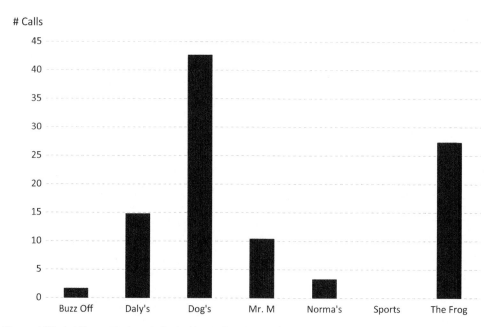

Figure 14.7 Arbitrary Order: Calls to the Police from Eight Bars

vast improvement over the previous examples, we can do better. The bars are in an arbitrary order. The readers' eyes have to jump around to make comparisons.

Figure 14.8 places the bars in increasing order of calls. Now, readers can rapidly understand the relative importance of each bar. I could have used the reverse order: most to least. The

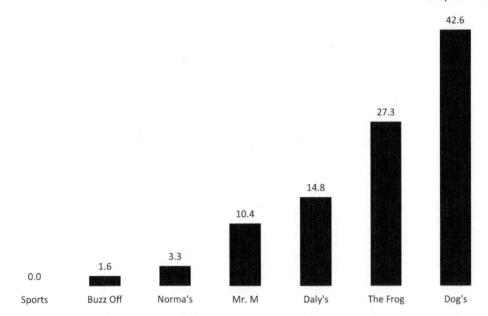

Figure 14.8 Useful Order: Calls to the Police from Eight Bars

choice depends on how I want to tell the story. The order influences the text surrounding the graph. Readers of English scan left to right. Therefore, if I use this graph, my explanatory text should start with Sports. Figure 14.8 answers the question, which bar is the safest and puts Sports at the front of the story. If I want to answer the question, which bar has the most crime, I should reverse the order and begin with Dog's.

There is a lesson here for editing. When revising your text, revise all tables, graphs, and diagrams to maintain consistency.

Figure 14.8 eliminates the middle layer. Rather than use a vertical axis with labels and grid lines, I placed value labels above each bar. Placing value labels over bars helps readers when they need an exact number and when the graph has few bars. When there are many bars, there is no room for legible labels. If the exact number is unimportant, for example, the reader only needs to know the general difference, use a vertical axis with values evenly placed along it. Grid lines help readers when they need to compare the heights of bars far apart on the graph. Grid lines are most helpful when there are more than three bars. These lines are middle layer elements; make them a shade lighter than the bars (e.g., with black bars, use grey grid lines).

So far, the examples involve data description. To compare two or more variables, we need three dimensions of data. Real dimensions, not fake ones. Imagine the police in Mt. Fog decided to reduce calls from bars. They create a program to do this. Pretend you are a consultant and Mt. Fog city government is paying you to evaluate the policy. You will need to compare calls in the year before the police implemented their policy to calls in the year after.

Figure 14.9 portrays the results. The three dimensions are drinking places, the number of calls, and time (before and after the program began). The key, a middle layer element, explains the third dimension. The key sits in an unoccupied part of the graph: not taking up valuable space, not competing for attention, but visible. The drinking places march from most calls to least before the program. Each drinking place has two bars: black for number of calls before and grey for number of calls after. The total category shows the overall impact.

Figure 14.9 A Bar Chart with Three Variables

The story is obvious; the policy worked. Most of the drop in calls came from three drinking places. The three lowest-call drinking places show little or no reduction. Frog's is an anomaly.

Here is another editing point. If you were the consultant, before you wrote the first draft of the text explaining the policy's impact, your graph might look very different from Figure 14.9. Revising the first version would help you grasp the story in the data. Always assume the first few graphs you produce are inappropriate for your final document. Revise them until you understand the story and keep revising them while writing.

Often we array labels along the horizontal axis. All the above graphs use this form. However, too many vertical bars can hinder readers' comprehension. Consider Figure 14.10, constructed using upward bars. I organized the 26 labels from least to most frequent. The lack of space forced me to use small fonts and array labels on diagonals. Readers will have difficulty with such an arrangement.

In contrast, look at Figure 14.11. I projected the bars sideways by putting the labels on the vertical axis. Readers will have less trouble understanding these labels. Sideways bar charts help readers the most when there are many categories or when the labels are long.

Charts with Smooth Data

Let's turn to graphs of smooth data and look at some bad and good ways of doing this. For smooth data, use lines rather than bars. Why? Bars impress upon the reader the lumpy nature of the data, but lines imply continuity. Many things are continuous, but I will use time in these examples. A time series shows changes in something over weeks, months, years, or decades. Typically, that something gets measured regularly: every week, month, year, or decade.

Some writers make time series graphs too complicated. Assume I am graphing the effort devoted to a crime control policy (e.g., money or person-hours spent) and the outcome of effort (e.g., crime levels). I want to answer the question "Does more effort yield better outcomes?" Figure 14.12 should help answer that question. Does it? By now you can see Figure 14.12's many faults:

- A fraudulent third dimension creating ribbons rather than lines.
- The disorienting rotation of the chart image.
- The shadow box the 3D effect makes.
- The useless box surrounding the key.
- The cramped area of the graph because the key is taking up useful space.
- The dark grid lines that compete for your attention.

So, regardless of what story the data tell, this chart impedes readers' understanding. It's like reading a bed-time story to a child while your mouth is filled with marbles. It might be a helluva story, but who would know?

Figure 14.13 depicts a reasonable graph for the same data. I removed the 3D effect and all of the problems it creates. I eliminated the key. I relegated the grid lines to the background by using dashed grey lines.

The data lines in Figure 14.13 cross each other repeatedly. So I placed the labels where it is obvious which line they refer to. An alternative is to use a key. But as a reader, most keys slow me up. So as a writer I prefer to label the lines. If I cannot apply unambiguous labels on the lines,

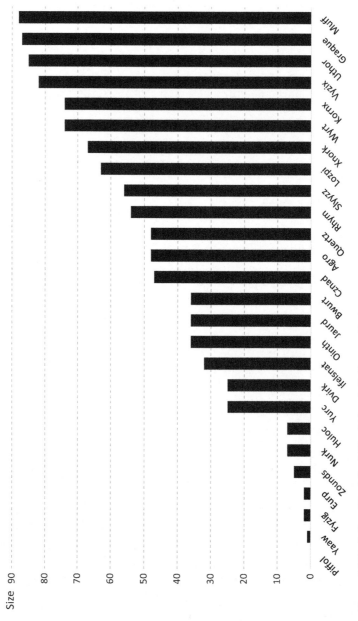

Figure 14.10 A Bar Chart that Would Look Better on End

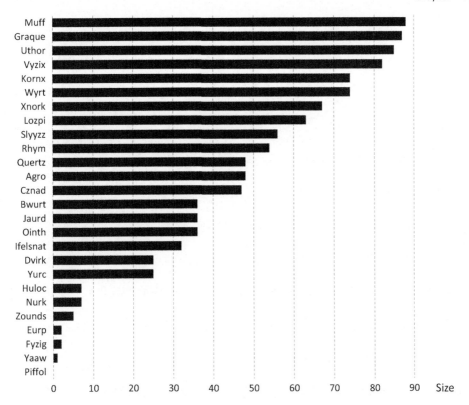

Figure 14.11 A Bar Chart Flipped to Make Labels Easier to Read

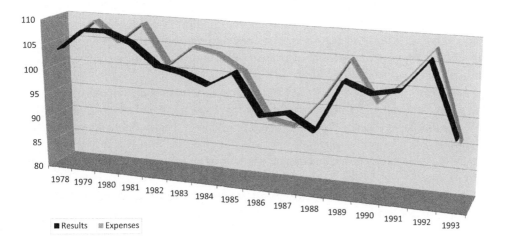

Figure 14.12 A Terrible Time Series Graph

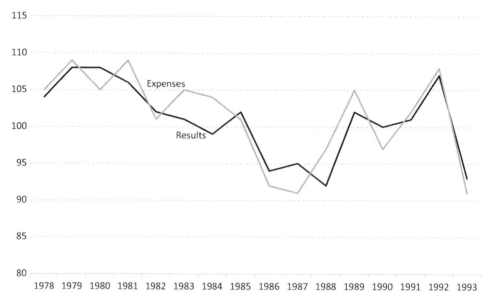

Figure 14.13 An Improved Time Series Graph

I will put a key in an unused space in the graph. In this example, I would place it in the lower left or upper middle of the chart.

Researchers often use time series charts when evaluating programs. Assume that the program I am examining starts at a specific time, like in Figure 14.14. The vertical line shows the switch. To the left of the line, the policy has not begun. To the right of the line, the policy is active. If the program did not start at a specific time but was phased in over an interval, I could have used a grey band rather than a line. Whether a line or band, a vertical band invites the reader to compare the crime trend before the policy to the crime trend after.

Always show the switch. Without it, your readers must jump from the graph to the text and back to uncover the story. If your report has many details and several dates, readers may become confused. So respect your readers by marking the beginning of the program on the graph. You do not have to mark the switch with a vertical line. There are other options. You could give the background to the off period a grey shade.

A word about the dots and squares on the lines: they are reminders the data is reported in evenly spaced intervals, although we can think of the data as smooth. If this reminder is not essential to the story, eliminate these modifications to lines, as I did in Figure 14.13. I added them to Figure 14.14.

Figure 14.14 has three dimensions of data: years, crimes, and policy. So the top layer of the graph contains the vertical line. Excel, the software I used, does not automatically add vertical lines; I had to do that myself. You need to be the master of your tools and not let them master you. If the software does not do the job, you should either find a work-around or use different software.

You can show more than three dimensions in a graph. But every new one threatens the graph's clarity, so you must work harder to tell the story. Consider Figure 14.15 with its four dimensions: time (horizontal axis); crime (vertical axis); crime type (different lines); and economic recessions (grey stripes). The rates of homicide are vastly different from the rates of

Figure 14.14 A Time Series Graph Showing a Policy Switch

aggravated assault and robbery, however. If I plot all three crimes using the same vertical scale, we would see little or no change in homicide; its trend would appear flat.

To reveal the story, I needed my readers to be able to make multiple comparisons. I plotted homicide using a smaller scale on the vertical axis. I let the two charts share the time axis and placed it between the two graphs to provide a visual break. I explained the stripes in a key on the far right. I differentiated among the crimes by altering line shade and width. I used the title to tell the story. At the bottom, I gave a caveat about recessions and revealed the sources for the data.

Exercise 14.1

Examine graphs you discover in materials you are reading. Imagine how you can improve them by removing elements or changing the shading, shape, and position of features.

Graphs and Text Must Work in Harmony

Like composing sentences and paragraphs, you can construct graphs in many ways. Regardless of how you choose to portray data visually, remember sweet clarity. Aim for simple graphs, readers can easily interpret.

When I am writing an article or report describing data, I produce my graphs first and then use them as the report's outline. Writing supplements the graphs, rather than the other way around. However, whether you start with graphs or start with words, your text must work with your graphs, and vice versa. Each graph must serve a purpose. Never use a graph as decoration.

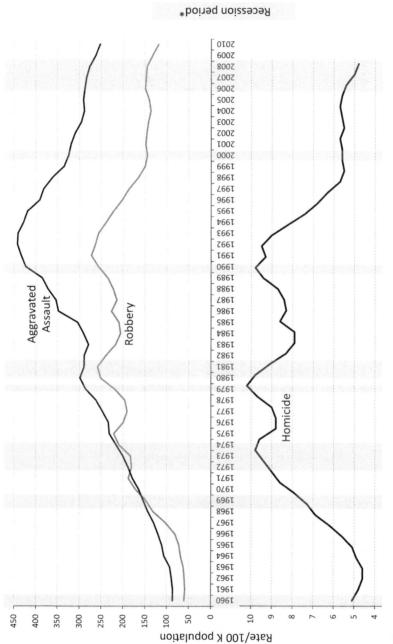

Figure 14.15 Economic Recessions Do Not Seem to Influence Violence

Note: The National Bureau of Economic Research (NBER) uses a restricted definition so periods of recession are probably shorter than periods of high unemployment.

Source: Crime data from the FBI Uniform Crime Reports. Recession data from NBER through Wikipedia, http://en.wikipedia.org/wiki/List_of_recessions_in_the_United_States.

If a reader can understand the story without the graph, then remove it from your final document or put the graph in an appendix. If the graph is necessary, then you need to introduce it within the text. Otherwise, it's like inviting a stranger to a party but not introducing her to your friends: it's rude.

The text accompanying a graph should tell your readers three things. First, state the question the graph answers. Readers should not be confused over the purpose of a graph. Second, tell readers the graph's answer to the question. Readers should understand the graph's story. Third, explain those features of the graph critical to readers' understanding of the story. This includes oddities and limitations, particularly when they conflict with the story. But the text should not repeat all the details of the graph. Text and graph are complements, not substitutes, for each other.

As with tables, you have three choices for a graph's title: period, exclamation point, or question mark styles. A period style describes the data you are showing. Consider Figure 14.15. Using this style, I could have given it the title, "Violent Crime Rates and Economic Recessions: 1960–2019." Instead, I summarized the story using an exclamation point style. If I had wanted to focus on unknowns or uncertainty, I would have used a question mark style, like "Do Recessions Increase Violent Crime?" All three choices work in the right context, but make sure the title fits the text surrounding the graph. To help your readers, aim for a consistent style across graphs. Arbitrary and unexplained shifts in styles will impede your readers' abilities to understand your story.

Any text within a graph should mimic the text accompanying the graph. Labels on a graph should use the same nouns and verbs as you use in the text. If you use "firearm" in your written explanation, then use "firearms" in the graph (not "guns" or other synonyms). If you use a set of gender terms in your explanation, use the same words in the graph.

This chapter does not scratch the surface of graphs. In *Further Reading*, I recommend several books on the visual display of data. If you routinely write with data, then you should explore the variety of graphs available to address the variety of problems data visualization creates.

15 Diagrams

Comments on Diagrams

Make big plans; aim high in hope and work, remembering that a noble, logical diagram once recorded will not die.

Attributed to Daniel Burnham

The greatest value of a picture is when it forces us to notice what we never expected to see.

John W. Tukey

Whenever I am infuriated I revenge myself with a new diagram.

Florence Nightingale

Drawing Is Thinking

Often, I think better if I draw the idea and then write about it. Typically, if I cannot draw an idea, I do not understand it. Some of my drawings worm their way into my final document. Drawings also help my readers. I know this because authors around the globe have used several of my diagrams repeatedly. Many of your readers will understand a clear diagram faster than clear text. Others will benefit from both. And if you are not used to drawing pictures of your ideas, you should try diagramming to help you clarify your thoughts.

Diagrams show relationships among ideas or concepts. They are theoretical, in contrast to data-intensive graphs. Diagrams often show decisions or processes creating change. Diagrams help explain things difficult to explain in words. They form pictures of abstract notions.

I distinguish diagrams from graphs because they serve different purposes. Also, the techniques for drawing diagrams differ from those used to create graphs. And the distinction justifies two bite size chapters instead of one monster chapter. You may not find anyone else making this distinction, so do not treat it as fundamental. In your final document, you will probably label both graphs and diagrams as "figures."

I use diagrams in three ways. Some I use to summarize an argument. These I place after paragraphs describing my ideas. Alternatively, I begin with a diagram and then summarize it in the text. In this case, the diagram is my argument and my text is the supplement. The third way I use diagrams is to organize my thoughts before writing. These diagrams may not make it to

DOI: 10.4324/9781003167532-19

my final document. They are thinking aids. Until my last draft, I seldom know how I will use the diagram. They move around, come and go, as I revise and edit.

In the next section I address why you should use diagrams. Then I summarize lessons I have learned about making useful diagrams. The largest section provides examples of some simple diagrams. Countless diagram types exist, so this is just a taste. I have a short discussion of diagrams with fictitious data, hypothetical graphs. Then I turn to layering. Sometimes a diagram is too complex for readers. So I explain how to build a diagram, layer by layer, to overcome this problem. I conclude by discussing how to integrate your diagrams and text.

Why Use Diagrams?

A good diagram can reveal things hard to pick out of written text. You could write that two concepts have symmetry, for example, but the diagram shows symmetry. Did this example help you? Maybe a little, or not at all. It is entirely in words. I should have used a diagram.

Because diagrams can reveal things words have trouble showing, I often draw diagrams then write. I see relationships I might have overlooked. This is the reason many professions employ diagrams: computer flow charts, electrical diagrams, production process illustrations, architectural drawings, network charts, and many others. Even grammarians use diagrams to portray sentence structures. A diagram illustrates an idea, or set of ideas. A picture may be worth a whole lot of words, but a good diagram is worth more.

Cartoon-like, a diagram simplifies reality. Do not include every detail you can imagine. Draw attention to a few important ideas and their relationships. The cartoon shows a distorted but recognizable image of a figure. The cartoonist leaves out features common to most people but highlights particular features: hair, ears, nose, lips, and so forth. Movies do the same thing. A movie of an actual event will show many fewer characters than the number who actually participated in the event. Nevertheless, the audience gets a realistic idea of those events. Like your first written draft, your first diagram may contain too much detail and many distractions. It can confuse you and will certainly confuse your readers. You must edit and revise.

Difficulty with diagraming tells me something is wrong and I should alter my thinking. Ugly diagrams force me to rearrange my ideas, find new facts, question old facts, and develop a stronger set of ideas. Drawing diagrams is a thinking tool, first. Readers never see my early diagrams; they are first drafts. Only later do I use them as a tool to explain ideas to readers.

Diagrams appeal to readers who learn from pictures. I like diagrams for that reason. I tend to think in images, so when an author is courteous enough to provide a diagram, I appreciate it. I will ponder their diagram first, read their text, and then reconsider their diagram. Authors who try to present complex ideas only in text are showing a bias for one particular way of learning. These authors put visual thinkers, like me, at a distinct disadvantage.

Finally, diagrams can travel farther than words. At least two diagrams I helped create are used across the globe, several others have traveled only in North America. The ideas they contain would not have traveled so far had I just used words. The spread of infographics and memes on the internet illustrates the power of diagrams for getting complex ideas across to thousands, if not millions, of people.

Too many types of diagrams exist for me to describe them all, or even a significant fraction. So what follows is an idiosyncratic collection of diagrams that I have found useful. I want you to appreciate the importance of diagrams and to create your own, rather than give you a set portfolio you can adapt to your purposes.

An Approach to Drawing Diagrams

I start my diagrams on paper. Often scrap paper: napkins, conference handouts, meeting agendas, and other discards. You can do this anywhere: stuck in traffic; in your dentist's waiting room; viewing boring training videos. I like academic meetings. I pretend to take notes on handouts while my fingers sketch something outside the room. I tried drawing apps. They were not as fast and easy as a pen and paper. I have diagramed in dirt, on scraps of lumber, and on dust-covered car windows. I can be as bad at drawing as I want. I can knock off variations of a diagram to explore alternatives.

Once I have a crude idea of what my diagram should look like, I redraw it in PowerPoint. There is nothing special about PowerPoint, there are other software packages. But it's handy, reasonably simple, and I know how to use it. In PowerPoint, I start with a blank slide with a white background. Then I use the drawing tools to make arrows, boxes, and other shapes. I use text boxes to label features and annotate. If I am making the diagram for a presentation, I use a few colors. If the diagram is for a written document that I will publish, I use blacks and greys. I check for contrast to make sure a reader can easily discern the different elements.

I center the image on the page, aiming for balance. Imagine a diagram's pixels having weight. I try to make the left and right sides equally heavy; I do not want my diagram to look like it wants to tilt. Attending to balance and other aesthetic features sometimes reveals ways I can improve the ideas I am drawing. Also, diagrams with balance, symmetry, and flow help readers more than ugly diagrams. I have noticed, readers reproduce and disseminate them more often than my ugly diagrams.

I try to direct my readers' eyes. I ask: where do I want the reader to begin? Where do I want them to end? The top left or top center is often the best starting point. Most readers' eyes go to the top first. Readers move their eyes from left to right, from top to bottom, or clockwise. So I try to arrange elements of the diagram from top to bottom, left to right, or clockwise. If I cannot do this, then I signal the direction I want my readers' eyes to follow. Arrows help.

As I draw, I draft text describing the diagram. I write my first draft inside PowerPoint's comment box. It's easier than leaping from PowerPoint to Word and back. Later, I copy the notes to my writing document and integrate them into the flow of my text.

A diagram that is obvious to its maker may be obscure to everyone else. So test its utility before you settle on a design. In the middle of the 1990s, I worked for a regional drug enforcement organization made up of investigators from local, state, and federal agencies. I headed the evaluation section and had the task of analyzing the efforts of the various enforcement groups. My team developed a set of templates for graphs and diagrams and then asked members of the enforcement teams if the images were understandable. Based on their remarks, we revised the templates for our reports. Having my primary readers down the hall is a luxury I no longer have, but I still ask people to provide comments on draft diagrams and graphs. Often they catch something I overlooked.

These are the basic points. In the next section, I give a number of examples of different types of diagrams. Like writing, diagraming takes practice. So if you are not used to making diagrams, jump in and start practicing.

Simple Diagrams

My first example shows the evolution of a diagram and illustrates how thinking can draw diagrams and how drawing can influence thinking. Years ago, while researching problem-oriented policing a colleague, Bill Spelman, suggested Routine Activity Theory would help us. He found the theory in an academic journal. Cutting through the article's sociological discourse, Bill sketched the article with a diagram like Figure 15.1.

Once I saw his diagram, I saw Bill's point. To help police solve problems we could suggest they pay attention not only to offenders but to targets and locations where the crimes occurred. Now, three decades later, many police fully understand the trifecta of Targets, Places and Offenders. In the late 1980s they didn't. Bill's diagram is one reason for this change. Further, this diagram helps more than police. On occasion, I work with community groups on crime and disorder issues. For many community members, Figure 15.1 reinforces something they have demanded for years: governments should fight crime using tactics but rely less on arrests. This simple diagram shows two other compatible ways of dealing with crime: focus on what is taken or attacked, and attend to how places repel or facilitate crime.

I find Bill's triangular summary of Routine Activity Theory appealing because it captures elements of the theory using a simple geometry, and because the number three has special significance in western folklore. Neither geometry nor folklore are logical reasons for using the triangle, although they do help readers remember it. It turns out, however, that attention to non-logical attributes like symmetry has value, as I will explain.

Years after we started using the crime triangle to train police, I was conducting research on illicit drug sales locations. I tried to use the triangle to help me understand how addresses with illicit drug sales operations differed from their neighbors where no drugs were sold, but ran into a problem. I had Offenders: those dealing the drugs. I had Targets: those buying the drugs. These two people needed to meet at a Place. I was studying these addresses. The original Routine Activity Theory focused on Guardians who protected Targets (Cohen & Felson, 1979). I have put these people in Figure 15.2. Marcus Felson, one of the creators of Routine Activity Theory, suggested there are people who try to keep offenders out of trouble (Felson, 1986). He called them Handlers. I have placed them in Figure 15.2 as well.

Figure 15.2 looks clunky. Out of balance, the figure points to the need to identify someone who cares about Places, like Guardians care for Targets and Handlers for Offenders. The diagram's

Figure 15.1 Routine Activity Theory Imagined as a Triangle

Figure 15.2 Unbalanced Crime Triangle

Figure 15.3 Revised Routine Activity Theory Accounting for Place Managers

ugliness demanded I find these people. I interviewed police who dealt with drug-dealing places. They suggested that property owners and their employees were the people I sought. I took their advice and introduced Managers (Figure 15.3).

This experience taught me diagrams can solve problems words cannot. Nothing in social science requires an explanation to be symmetrical or balanced. Still, my irrational search for symmetry and balance helped me find something I had not considered. The search uncovered an idea research validated in the years following. Not all diagrams will lead you to new ideas. My point here is that they can. And simple diagrams reveal more than complex ones.

The crime triangle just shows the elements of a theory. You could replace it with a table with three rows and two columns (Felson, 1995). The reason for using a diagram instead of a table is the diagram makes it intuitive and memorable, much like graphs communicate better than tables.

Path Diagrams

Researchers use path diagrams to show what is causing what. Figure 15.4 depicts a path diagram of Broken Windows theory. A path diagram comprises three elements. Words express concepts, like disorder. Arrows show causal relations between concepts. The concept at the tail of the arrow causes the concept at the point. The double-headed arrow tells us that informal

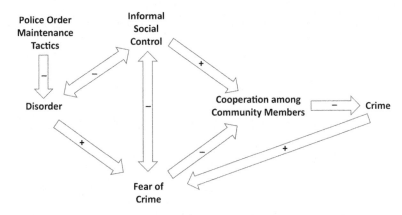

Figure 15.4 A Path Diagram of Broken Windows Theory
Source: Based on Green & Taylor (1988), and Weisburd et al. (2015).

social control and fear cause each other. If there is no arrow between two concepts then neither directly causes the other. Disorder, for example, does not have a direct impact on crime; it influences crime indirectly. Arrows from disorder, to fear, to cooperation, to crime create a path.

Signs (positive and negative) describe the nature of the relationships. In the example, disorder has a positive influence on fear of crime, meaning the more disorder in a neighborhood, the more neighborhood residents fear crime. The less disorder, the less fear. Combining signs and arrows, you can determine the results of increasing disorder, assuming the theory is true.

When drawing this diagram, I tried to keep it simple. I eliminated boxes around the names of concepts, for example. I considered using thinner solid arrows instead of hollow ones. If I had used thin arrows, I would have had to place the signs next to them. I chose hollow arrows to make it more clear which signs went with each arrow. When drawing complex path diagrams, with more arrows and some crossing others, I use thin arrows. The diagram starts at the upper left and flows to the right.

Figure 15.4 shows how concepts could influence each other. It is not a statement of fact. Each arrow is a visual image of a guess, a hypothesis. With the appropriate data and statistical techniques, you could put numbers next to each arrow to show whether you have validated or refuted that guess.

Figure 15.5 illustrates a path diagram with data. I based it on research conducted by Daniel Oppenheimer (2006). Oppenheimer wanted to know how word length influences readers, so he ran an experiment. This figure reports the results.

In the experiment, Oppenheimer gave his research subjects a written passage from a student's graduate school application. Oppenheimer experimentally varied word length. Some subjects received the passage as originally written. Others received the passage with the original nouns, verbs, and adjectives replaced by synonyms that were longer. Oppenheimer asked his subjects to rate their difficulty of understanding the passage, and to judge whether the applicant should be admitted to graduate school.

Oppenheimer showed his results with a path diagram, which I have simplified. Numbers following "R" show negative or positive correlations. Numbers following "P" indicate statistical significance. The positive correlation between word length and difficulty of understanding shows the longer the words in the passage, the more difficulty subjects had understanding the

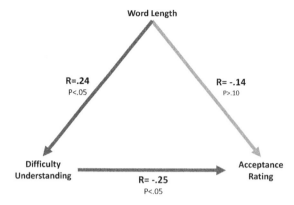

Figure 15.5 Word Length Impedes Comprehension
Source: Revised from Oppenheimer (2006).

passage. This finding is statistically significant at a .05 level. The other two arrows show nega-tive correlations. Difficulty of understanding reduces the acceptance rating subjects give the writing. Further, word length alone reduces acceptance ratings, although this correlation is not significant. The figure tells us long words undermine the intent of authors.

The diagram begins at the top and flows down. Because I want to display the numerical findings, I made the numbers more prominent than the arrows. I emphasize the correlations relative to significance by making the font bold and larger for correlations than for significance. The arrow for the insignificant finding I show in grey instead of black.

Figure 15.5 illustrates why you should not take my distinction between diagrams and graphs too seriously. Figure 15.5 has characteristics of both: abstract concepts and numbers. Some authors place a diagram early in their document to describe their theory. After they discuss data, the authors reprise the diagram with numbers. Your goal is to tell a clear truthful story. Be creative.

Flow Charts

Flow charts depict processes. They are frequently used in computer programing and systems analysis. You can use them to describe any process. For any single process there are many ways to draw its flow chart.

In the late 1980s, my research team was looking for a way to tell police how to solve problems. To create it, we modified a standard sequence used by many professions. After a lot of dis-cussion, we came up with the SARA process: Scanning identifies problems; Analysis dissects problems; Response creates solutions; Assessment determines if the solution worked (Eck & Spelman, 1987).

We drew the SARA process like Diagram 1 (in the upper left) of Figure 15.6. We wanted to demonstrate that it was sequential. We also wanted to illustrate feedback. We drew the straight arrows because in 1987 we did not have software to draw curves. Some academics suggested the SARA process was too linear. They overlooked the feedback.

So, in the mid-2000s, I redrew the diagram, and added three more arrows (Diagram 2 in Figure 15.6). I hoped the curved arrows would convey the idea problem solving is somewhat loose, or freewheeling, rather than linear.

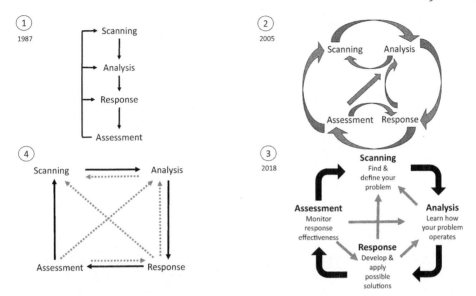

Figure 15.6 Four Versions of the Same Flow Chart

Over a decade later, I redrew it again (Diagram 3) for a community training course. This new design retains the clockwise flow. But rather than simply naming each stage, the titles explain actions at each stage.

In the last panel of Figure 15.6 (Diagram 4), I show the second version drawn with straight arrows. The changes are both substantive (adding arrows) and style (for example, straight instead of curved arrows). This version makes the clockwise movement along the outside contrast with the counter clockwise movement in the inside. Many of my changes are of this sort: they do not change the meaning, but they do streamline, balance, and simplify the diagram.

As these alternatives show, you can depict a process in many ways. The diagrams on the right are supposed to convey an organic process while those on the left seem mechanical.

Other problem-solving diagrams exist. I showed an example earlier, but show it again in Figure 15.7. I did make a few style changes. Flip back to Figure 6.2 and decide which version you prefer. Both figures show branching. You can use branching flowcharts to show all manner of processes. The limitation is that each decision can have only a few choices: more than three and the chart can become a mess.

Process charts are useful for showing the steps required to commit a crime. Superficially, they look like path diagrams. However, the arrows imply one step follows another: a step does not necessarily cause another step. Like flow charts, they show how one thing leads to another. Tamara Herold, created this simple process chart (Figure 15.8) to illustrate how student party riots progress (Madensen & Eck, 2006). She built it upon an earlier diagram created by Clark McPhail to describe crowds (McPhail, 1991). McPhail included three stages in his original diagram: assembling, assembled, and dispersing. Herold divided assembling into three stages. Initial planning occurs months before the drinking party and included organizers' choices to hold an outdoor drinking event. Preassembly preparation occurs within days of the event and includes acquiring alcohol and sending out announcements. The assembly process occurs hours before the event and involves students coming to the event. The assembled gathering occurs

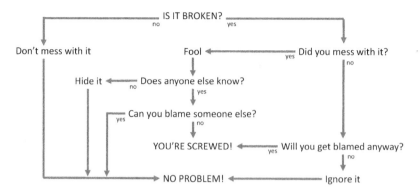

Figure 15.7 A General Problem-Solving Flow Chart

Figure 15.8 A Process Model of Gatherings
Source: Redrawn from Madensen & Eck (2006).

when most attendees party on the street. The circumstances are prepped for a riot, which may or may not happen. The last stage begins when students leave the area. It may involve property destruction far from the gathering. In our guide to police on how to deal with such riots, we listed actions they could take at each of the five stages to reduce the chances of rioting and damage.

Organization Charts

You are probably familiar with organization charts. They usually show how different units within an organization (such as a business, police agency, military command, or a criminal enterprise) are connected to each other. At the top is the organizational leadership. Directly below are the major units, and below them are subunits clustered to the major units. Lines show which units report to other units. Sometimes dashed lines show alternative reporting arrangements among units. These types of charts are so common that you can find software that will draw them for you.

You can apply the principles of organization charts to other things than organizations. In Figure 15.9, Tamara Herold and I organized a set of related concepts concerning places (Madensen & Eck, 2013). Crime researchers use the term "place" in at least three different ways. Many people use it as a synonym for area, neighborhood, or region. Several of my colleagues use it to mean a street segment: both sides of a street block from corner to corner. Tamara and I use it to indicate a particular address, building, or other facility (e.g., parking lot, park, or plaza). Rather than get into a silly fight over which usage is best, Tamara and I decided to use a diagram to show how various places are related and to give each a particular label. Further, we wanted to differentiate among address places used for crime purposes.

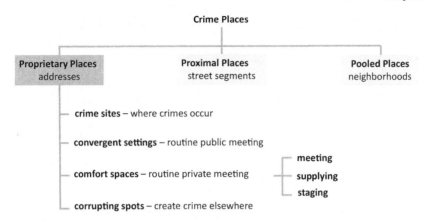

Figure 15.9 An Organization Chart Describing a Set of Definitions
Source: Revised from Madensen & Eck (2013).

The original text accompanying this figure (not shown here) explained the labels and various subcategories. For example, a crime site is a form of proprietary place. A proprietary place is a small location that has an owner and a specific function (a convenience store, apartment building, or bar, for example). It differs from a proximal place in that proximal places contain multiple proprietary places facing a street. In addition, it differs from a pooled place in that a pooled place will contain a great many proximal places on many streets. Typically, neither proximal nor pooled places have a single owner or single function. Comfort spaces are another type of proprietary place. However, offenders avoid committing reportable crimes at these locations since they want to use these as locations to stash weapons, cash, or drugs, to use them to stage crimes elsewhere, or to just meet and hang out. In short, the figure serves as a glossary with a set of relationships among the terms.

Figure 15.9 is the same as Figure 6.1, but I made a small change. I surrounded text with shaded boxes to draw attention to proprietary places: the core of the story I am telling.

Hypothetical Graphs

In the previous chapter, I discussed graphs: figures representing numbers. However, sometimes we want a graph of an ideal or typical relationship without statistics. My first example shows such a generalization, the crime involvement of places. Regardless of the type of place, crime always follows the same pattern (Wilcox & Eck, 2011). The horizontal axis lists sites from the place with the most crime to the places with no crime. The vertical axis plots the proportion of crimes at each place. On the far left is the small proportion of places with most of the crime. A very large proportion of places with no crime reside on the right. Between are a modest proportion of sites with a little crime.

To illustrate this curve's universality, we listed all the types of places where research shows this curve applies. We found no exceptions to this curve, so we called it a "law." This diagram, Figure 15.10, helped us compress a large literature into a few pages.

In 1990, Lawrence Sherman described a theory of police crackdowns. Sherman (1990) noted that often offenders delay coming back immediately after a crackdown has ended. As a result,

Figure 15.10 A Diagram Summarizing Multiple Studies
Source: Updated and revised from Wilcox & Eck (2011).

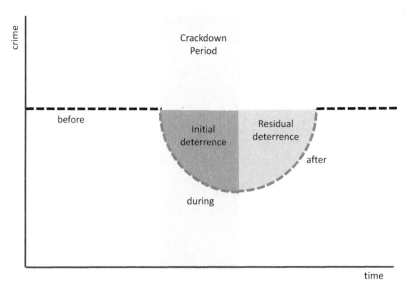

Figure 15.11 Sherman's Police Crackdown Theory
Source: Based on Sherman (1990).

the police can prevent crime both during and for a short time after the crackdown. He called this bonus "residual deterrence." Although he used no diagrams, he could have. Figure 15.11 describes crackdowns and residual deterrence. The horizontal axis depicts time. The vertical axis depicts crime. The crackdown lowers crime immediately. Then the police end their crackdown, but crime does not bounce back right away. Residual deterrence is a bonus reduction after the crackdown ends. That is Sherman's theory in a picture.

The point of diagrams is to give a vivid description of a theory by removing details. The diagram presents a caricature of the real world: one that captures its essential elements, not every detail. Once readers understand a theory, they can test it in the messy actual world. If a reader does not understand the theory, they cannot use or test it.

Layering

The best diagrams show complex ideas simply. However, sometimes your idea is too complicated for a single diagram. Then you should consider two or more diagrams of increasing complexity. You introduce the most basic ideas in the first diagram. The second adds a few new ideas. The third adds more, and so on. Your reader receives your ideas in small doses rather than in a large lump. I call this layering; each diagram lays down new ideas on the preceding diagram.

I used layering earlier when I described the development of the crime triangle. Figure 15.1 showed the three key elements. Figure 15.2 added two more elements. Figure 15.3 added another element and completed a second triangle. And here is Figure 15.12, which adds yet another layer of ideas.

Figure 15.12 An Example of the Last Stage in Layering
Source: Revised from Sampson et al. (2009).

In the mid-2000s, a friend suggested other actors who guide Guardians, Handlers, and Managers. They provide incentives for Guardians to guard possible Targets, for Handlers to redirect likely Offenders, and for place Managers to manage their potential crime Places. Rana Sampson, who trained police in problem solving, gave many examples of such people and institutions. And she showed how police officials made use of these influencers to improve guardianship, handling, and managing. Since Guardians, Handlers, and Managers are controllers we called this diverse collection of influencers "Super Controllers" (Sampson et al., 2009). In short, Super Controllers control controllers.

We used a diagram like Figure 15.12 to illustrate the nested relationship. Offender and Target convergence at a Place creates a situation ripe for crime. However, controllers (Guardians, Handlers, and Managers) can thwart crime. Super Controllers give incentives to controllers to prevent crime. Here are some examples of Super Controllers: regulators, such as state liquor control agencies who monitor bars; financial institutions, such as insurance companies who stand to lose money if there is too much serious crime at a place; the press, who can embarrass people and organizations who facilitate crime; courts, who can enforce civil laws; and business associates who can informally pressure a store's owner to reduce trouble around his place.

Because you have seen Figures 15.1, 15.2, and 15.3, Figure 15.12 is simple. But imagine if I had used Figure 15.12 to explain how all seven concepts interact to suppress or create crime. You probably would have to expend much more effort to understand the ideas.

I learned layering from an article published in the 1980s by Patricia and Paul Brantingham (1981). I was thumbing through their book, backwards. So I saw their last diagram first. It was daunting; my stomach clenched. Fortunately, I read the article from the beginning. The Brantinghams' first diagram was simple. Then, in many following diagrams, the two authors added layers of new ideas. Each diagram was more complex than its predecessor, but each step was simple. When I reached the daunting last diagram I understood it instantly. Layering is like providing a staircase from the ground floor, where your reader starts, to another floor, where you want your reader to end. Your reader does not have to make superhero leaps.

The principal problem with layering is space for several figures. But sometimes you can put a series of diagrams in a single figure. Consider Figure 15.13. It describes the idea that at the core of each social science is a type of exchange. The core exchanges differ by whether they are organized (economics and political science) or unorganized (sociology and criminology), and by whether they are voluntary (economics and sociology) or involuntary (political science and criminology). Psychology is the outlier. Each box could be a separate figure surrounded by explanatory text. Combining them in a single figure saves space and makes it easier for readers to compare the cartoons (drawn by my daughter).

Diagrams and Text

Just like tables and graphs, any diagram you present to readers must coordinate with your text. You should *not* have:

- Orphans. If you have a diagram, the text must point to it. If it's not worth mentioning, remove the diagram.
- Synonyms. The technical terms you use in the diagram should appear in the text. If the diagram says "weasels," then it's weasels, not varmints, in the text.

Figure 15.13 Exchange Is the Core of Social Science, Mostly
Source: By Emily Eck (2011).

- Duplication. The text should not be a complete recounting of the diagram. And the diagram should not attempt to account for every detail you write.

  Here are the things you *should* have:

- The text should inform the reader of the purpose of the diagram. It should summarize its story. And it should explain any quirks that might impede readers' understanding.

- Your written explanation of the diagram should mimic the order within the diagram. If the diagram starts the reader in the upper left corner, then the text explaining the diagram should begin with the same corner.
- As your written explanation moves through the diagram, make sure your readers know you have moved from one part to another. If you think your readers will lose their way, consider labeling parts of the diagram. If you label parts of your diagram, then refer to the labels in the text. Do not ignore them or invent new labels in the text.
- When you revise your diagram, change your text. And when you revise the text, revise any associated diagrams.
- If you draw a prominent element in your diagram that you do not explain in the text, ask yourself if you can eliminate the element from the diagram.
- Remove decorations. If a square box makes your point, do not use a cube. Anything you place in the diagram should serve a purpose.

You do not have to include diagrams in your document. Their greatest aid may be to you, the writer. Diagrams are thinking tools. You can use them before you write, while you organize your thoughts, and while writing. If a diagram helps you organize your ideas and clarifies your written words, you may not need it in your document. I often find I believe my idea is complex. Then I diagram the thing. Several revisions of the diagram later, my changes have removed much of the complexity. Then I have something words can explain without a diagram. This is why I mentioned diagrams many chapters earlier when discussing organization (Chapter 6).

Exercise 15.2

Find a reading in which the author describes an idea but does not use a diagram. Then create a diagram that reflects that idea. If that is difficult, consider two or more competing diagrams that could reflect the idea. What type(s) of diagrams did you use? Why? Did you think of questions about the idea, while drawing the diagram, that had not occurred to you before? Why?

Some of the lack of sweet clarity in writing is due to the way authors write. They have a clear idea but express it poorly. However, some of the muddle is caused by authors whose ideas are not very clear. There is no surefire cure for this. Nevertheless, pictures of ideas (diagrams) can help reveal ideas that words fail to disclose. Writers who do not, or cannot, create diagrams may labor under a disadvantage. So practice creating diagrams and explaining them.

Part V   Rewriting and Revising

16 Editing

Cleaning Up Your Mess

Whether you are Hemingway-drunk or Gaga-irresponsible, you need to clean up your mess. It's time to edit and revise. Be prepared to do this three, four, or more times before you have a sober, responsible draft that shines with sweet clarity. If you do not, unfortunate things happen.

A friend sent me the e-mail example below. I removed the words revealing the university. The words in bold were in the original document.

> Dear ___ Students, Faculty and Staff,
>
> The Department of _____ is seeking your input regarding perceptions of crime and safety in the areas on and around the _____ campuses. Your feedback is important to guide our Safety Initiative and police reform efforts.
>
> Later today, you will receive an email invitation from _____ to participate in a web-based Safety Survey that is a continuation of a multi-year research study initiated in Spring 2014. This **Enhancing Pubic Safety Survey** is designed to better understand perceptions, fear, and actual experiences of crime on or near campus, along with awareness of Safety Initiatives. ...

I do not know if the chance to participate in a "pubic" safety survey attracted students, faculty, and staff. However, I hope that the letter writer was the first to participate.

Coping with the mess of your drunken, irresponsible first draft can be tedious or comforting, depending on your attitude. It's a technical process requiring rule following and precision. If you enjoyed the creative debauchery of banging out the first draft, editing may not be fun. If you suffered writer's block, worried about how to express your ideas, and found your creative

DOI: 10.4324/9781003167532-21

efforts demeaning and uncomfortable, then sober editing may be a joy; you have suffered through the hard parts and now you can just follow the rules. Brew some coffee or tea and find a pen of the color you like best.

Here is what lies ahead in this brief chapter. Next, I describe a four-sweep process for editing your work. I follow this with a brief discussion of automated tools you should use for editing your work. Then I discuss the pros and cons of asking a friend or two to look over your work. I conclude this chapter with a checklist to help you decide whether your draft is good enough to send to a reviewer.

Editing Your Own Work

You are juggling several tasks while revising. First, you are testing your first draft's logic and order of ideas. Do your ideas make sense or do they need reordering? Second, you are looking for gaps and redundancies. Have you missed ideas whose absence confuses or misleads readers? Have you repeated yourself and risk boring your readers? Third, you are checking spelling, punctuation, and grammar. You may have been doing this while compiling your first draft. Maybe you used a spelling or grammar checker. But even the best checker is not perfect. Recall that e-mail above? A spell checker will not flag "pubic." Finally, you are using your intuition to tell you if something is not quite right. Do I have an uncomfortable feeling about a passage; something not right? Pay attention to such feelings.

I used to do all levels of editing in one sweep. This was a mistake. Here is how a typical editing session would go. For example, I start by moving a paragraph from the end to the front. Just as I pasted it, I notice a spelling error, so I correct it. Then I decide I dislike the passive sentence containing the word. So I change it to active voice and delete several adjectives. This leads me to discover that I am using two different names for a concept, one in the beginning and the other at the end. As this will confuse readers, I launch a search-and-replace mission. At the end of the mission, my cursor alights far from where I began editing. And here I find more problems. I continue this way for hours. Eventually, I recall my original aim; deal with the disordered ideas. But now I have forgotten if I had moved that paragraph from the end to the beginning, and if I had, what was the other thing I wanted to do? Frustrated, I stop editing for the day. The next day, I start over because I have lost track of where I was.

Now I use a four-sweep process for anything longer than two pages.

Sweep 1: Order

In my first editing sweep, I give priority to checking order. I find it difficult to address order and attend to other problems. So, put off the other problems for other sweeps.

I review sections to determine if they are where they belong. Then I move sections around and reexamine the manuscript. Is it better? If not, I either go back to the original or keep moving things. As I do this, I create many smaller problems I will need to correct. I have a choice: fix them now or deal with them later.

I am a "deal with them later" kind of guy. So I flag these items with highlights or comments boxes. If a correction is obvious, easy, and fast, I make the correction immediately. But mostly I just mark non-order problems for later.

The first sweep is a good time to make sure that all headings, subheadings, and sub-subheadings are in the same format. This may seem trivial for the first sweep, but as headings mark your document's organization, checking their consistency helps you check the order of your ideas.

I also look for passages I can delete. My story is like planning a trip from Cincinnati to Chicago. I know my beginning and ending points. I find the highways that efficiently connect these points. I locate stops to buy gas, stretch, eat, or relieve myself. These are important to my plan. A side trip to the world's largest ball of paint in Alexandria, Indiana is not. As fascinating as balls of paint are, I remove them from my plan. If I really want to discuss the world's largest ball of paint, I put this stuff in a file I can use later. I am always surprised by the number of balls of paint I discover in my draft during the first sweep.

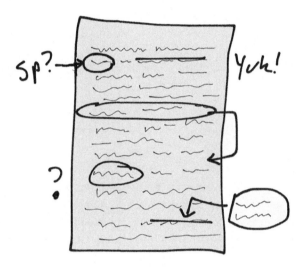

When creating my first draft, I often leave holes to fill in later. These are parts where I could not figure out what to say. I flag these holes and make notes. In the first sweep, I reexamine the holes. I ask, "Can I avoid this topic with no harm to the reader?" Sometimes I can. So I delete the hole. Sometimes I cannot. Occasionally, with luck and the passage of time, I realize what belongs in the hole. Usually, I am still perplexed, but I can no longer postpone hole filling. So, I fill it in and complete my first sweep.

Sweep 2: Gaps and Redundancies

With the manuscript better organized, my second sweep gives priority to the gaps and redundancies. The holes were intentional, but the gaps are oversights. In the rush to bang out my first draft, I always skip something that some readers will need. Now I find these stumbling places and repair them.

In my first draft, I repeat myself often: accidentally explaining the same idea in different sections or using the same example in multiple places. So I remove the redundant stuff that does not aid the reader.

Another thing I tackle in this sweep is consistency in the names of concepts. I might start off using the word "guardianship" but change to using "surveillance" later in the document. If a concept is central to my argument, I do not want to confuse readers with multiple terms. So I pick the word I want and remove the terms I do not want to use.

Sweep 3: Sentences, Words, and Proofreading

In my third sweep, I give priority to sentences and words. So I start by calculating the Flesch-Kincaid Grade Level and the percent passive voice. If it's a long document, I check grade level and passive voice section-by-section, or even paragraph-by-paragraph.

Using information from these checks, I chop apart sentences that wind from line to line. I kill off all the passive voice sentences, leaving only those that carry more weight than their active versions. I discard adjectives and adverbs. I continue with my pursuit of consistency in terms.

Since sentences are connected, after any major change in a sentence, I look at the sentences before and after. Can readers step from one sentence to the next without tripping? If not, I rewrite the group of sentences. And then I check to see if this group connects with its adjacent groups.

Sweep 3 also is where I give priority to proofreading. I check for spelling, punctuation, and grammar errors, as well as missing or extra words. I use automated tools and my own eyes. At the end of this sweep, I check the reading level and the percent of passive voice sentences one last time.

Sweep 4: Last Check

If possible, I wait several days between my third sweep and my fourth. Waiting for several weeks is even better. My goal is to have a manuscript I can share when I am done. So, this fourth sweep is my last examination before seeking outside help. But it is more than that. In my fourth sweep, I am looking for the flow of ideas through the document. I am using my gut to tell me if something is amiss. How does this manuscript feel? I look for passages that make me feel uncomfortable. I then examine them looking for what word or phrase is wrong. When I find it, I change it.

Reading passages aloud is very helpful. Often I can hear problems better than I can see them. I do not read my earliest drafts aloud; it's too disturbing. The other thing I do in sweep 4 is to look again for spelling and grammar errors I missed and formatting consistency.

When I have completed the fourth sweep, I am ready to share the manuscript with others: perhaps. This is a gut-wrenching decision because I know that my reviewer, no matter how nice, will find something wrong. Then I will have my thin ego bruised. That sucks.

My division of editing in four sweeps is too simple. In reality, I am doing all four types of editing in each sweep. I just give priority to different tasks in each. Although I have described four editing sweeps, I often go over documents several more times. Finally, if my document is very long, like this book, I will sweep through sections at different times. I may write the first draft of a later section and get bogged down. So I will go back and edit an earlier section. Still, I go through the entire document, front to back, at least twice.

People vary in their abilities to edit their own work. I am terrible at detecting spelling errors. While writing is a creative process and requires some looseness, editing is not creative and must be tight. The dubious Hemingway quote, at the beginning of this chapter, is useful if interpreted in this light. Do not write drunk, but definitely edit sober.

Murdering Your Darlings

Most of my first drafts are bloated, besides being out of order, containing gaps, and partially coherent. Of these, bloat is the principal problem. It is not only a problem in itself, it hides the other problems. Bloat must be common to most writers, because many writing books give the advice, "Murder your darlings." Arthur Quiller-Couch seems to have stated it first in 1916 (Wickman, 2013). We all fall in love with a word, phrase, sentence, paragraph, or section of our writing. But we have to kill many. It's hard and necessary.

To encourage my editorial executions I deceive myself. I create a document, a discard file, for pasting all the lovely passages I must delete. I tell myself, "I am not deleting these passages, I am putting them in a nice place, from which I can fetch them when I know where they belong." Sometimes I retrieve them. Mostly, they stay in the dungeon. When I complete my final version, I empty the dungeon: delete my discard file. It's an effective deception that I routinely commit against myself. After many years of deceiving myself, I am learning to do without it. My new metaphor is action movie assassin: I terminate the passages without remorse when I see them.

Here is another metaphor I use. I set myself a page or word budget. I set it low. When I create an over-budget draft, I edit the document to bring it within budget. It is even better when someone else sets the budget. When Ronald V. Clarke invited me to co-author a problem analysis manual for British crime analysts, he set a size limit for each chapter: about 1000 words. I created my first draft of a chapter and then killed off words, phrases, sentences, and paragraphs to bring it under budget. The manual has 55 chapters, and I wrote almost half (Clarke & Eck, 2003). I have loved word budgets ever since; only good comes from removing surplus text.

Exercise 16.1

Take something you have recently written. Commit yourself to making it 25 percent shorter (by word count). Then rewrite it. Now, make it 10 percent shorter still.

Practice this exercise several times.

Editing Tools

A friend sent me this sentence from a student paper she was grading. Her student was explaining how offenders were selected for participation in a drunk driving program.

"288 offenders were edible and all except 3 were in ..."

My suspicion is that the student was a victim of two things. First, an aggressive spell checker. Second, a failure to proofread. The student probably misspelled "eligible" in such a way that the spell checker provided the wrong word. If the student allowed the automatic replacement of the old word with the recommended word and then did not check the checker, this sentence would have been the result.

I never allow a spell checker to replace words without my approval. But I am of a generation that grew up without this software so I mistrust their judgment. For those of you who text and tweet on tiny screens, automatic replacement may seem reasonable. Maybe it is for texts and tweets. But not for serious writing. J.K. Rowling gave good advice on this subject in one of her

Harry Potter books, "Never trust anything that can think for itself if you can't see where it keeps its brain."

Even with these misgivings, I believe automated tools are terrific aids. Use a spell checker. Use a grammar checker. Use a passive voice detector. Use any tool that comes your way. But do not just accept the tool's recommendation. Look at the word or phrase the tool flagged. Do you see the problem? Look at the recommendation? Does it make sense? If it is a spelling correction, and you are unsure, look it up. If it is a phrase, read your original phrase out loud then read the tool's recommendation. If these do not work, rewrite it, fine tuning for sweet clarity.

Why am I telling you to check automated recommendations manually? First, they can be wrong. Consider the advice of Ronald Reagan: "Trust, but verify" (if Wikipedia is correct, this is from a Russian proverb). Second, checking turns a labor-saving tool into an educational tool. When you verify you become more attentive to your work. Later, you will catch the error first. And even later, you will not make the error. The same advice applies to human editors' comments. Do not accept them automatically; check the checker.

Here is a personal example. For decades, people and books have told me to not split infinitives. I could never get the hang of what this infinitive thing was. Then, after decades of castigating myself for being an infinity splitter and worrying that someone would discover my secret, I found that it is fine to split infinitives. Famous authors split infinitives before Abraham Lincoln split rails. Sometimes a split infinitive is useful, or even necessary. I still had no idea what an infinitive looks like. Grammar check helped with that. I set it to tag these splits. When it did, I looked at the recommendation and my original. After doing this many times I got the hang of it. Now, I split fewer, but those I split I split with intention.

If you want to write clearly and rapidly, then make every writing project an opportunity to learn to write better. Learn to turn your "ear" to the sound of sweet clarity. Writing tools can help. And the best part is, you can make mistakes in private, without your friends catching you.

Friends

However, you cannot avoid your friends forever. Someone needs to look at your fourth draft. You need someone to catch things you may have overlooked. Exactly what you want them to catch depends on what you are writing and your friend's skills. Although I would love to have a friend who will read everything I write, make a comprehensive check from organization to spelling, and provide me with a brilliant set of suggestions, my friends are too busy with their own work.

When I ask a friend to review my draft, I ask him to tell me whether my draft makes sense, whether I have left something out, and whether there are parts that they did not understand. If they detect spelling and grammar errors, that is great. But I do not ask them to do this proofreading.

Should you ask more than one friend? Yes, ask as many as you can. But quality is more important than quantity.

The major limitation of having friends review your work is that they may be too kind. I want someone who can tell me I am making a mistake. Then I can correct something. If they just say, "It's great," or "I like it," or any superficial positive review, I benefit little. So do not ask friends who have trouble providing critical feedback. It's unfair to them and it wastes time, yours and theirs.

When you ask a friend who can provide critical advice, explicitly assure them you want critical advice. And regardless of what advice they provide, thank them from the bottom of your heart.

One last word on this topic. Treat all your friends' comments seriously. You may not like the comments. You might not understand them. Still, your friend provided you with your first glimpse of your readers' reactions. Such comments suggest you need to make some alterations. Ask yourself, "Why?" Why did I receive this negative comment? Why can't I understand the comment? Why did my friend misunderstand my writing? Let the answers to these questions guide your revisions.

Concluding Editing

You are now ready to send your work out to people who may not be your friends. These are the gatekeepers I mentioned in the chapter "Getting Started." They can be supervisors who need to review your work before passing it on to their supervisors. They can be grant or contract managers who want to see your work before their agency endorses your work. They could be journal editors, and their appointed reviewers, who must approve your paper before the journal will publish it. I discuss these reviewers in the next chapter.

Before you send your manuscript to those who must give it a thumbs up or down, go over this checklist. The last item is a gut check. When I conduct a gut check I ask myself, am I confident I have done all I could do? That is my gut check. I am not asking myself, "Am I anxious about whether others will like what I wrote?" The answer to that question is always, "yes." No amount of effort eliminates my anxiety. If I say "yes" to the gut check question, I am saying I cannot think of any specific changes I can make, now. My "yes" is not a statement that there is nothing wrong, that my draft is perfect. It is a statement that it's time to send my precious work out and into the cold cruel world.

Is It Ready? A Checklist

- ✓ Are your thoughts in order?
- ✓ Have you eliminated gaps in your arguments or evidence?
- ✓ Have you eliminated unintentional repetitions?
- ✓ Have you consistently followed the same format?
  - Font style and size
  - Headings and subheadings
  - References and notes
- ✓ Did you conduct an automated grammar check?
- ✓ Did you proofread your draft out loud and make corrections?
- ✓ Did you check spelling? Automated and with your eyes?
- ✓ Is your Flesch-Kincaid score less than or equal to 12?
- ✓ Are fewer than 10 percent of your sentences passive voice?
- ✓ Did you have someone read your draft?
  - Did you receive comments?
  - Did you address the comments?
- ✓ Did the manuscript pass the gut check?

Remember: The perfect is the enemy of the done.

---

17 Reviews and Reviewers

Outside Examiners

You may feel you are done, but often there is a gatekeeper between you and publication. Someone must examine your writing and give it a thumbs up, thumbs down, or thumbs sideways. Usually, reviewers' judgments are neither heartfelt endorsements nor cruel rejections, but tepid orders for revisions. You must wrestle with their comments, demands, and offhand remarks. Reviewers are the subject of this chapter.

Useful dealings with reviewers require the right attitude, so I discuss these general points first. Then I will discuss reviews by your boss, supervisor, mentor, or other powerfully placed people in your organization. The third section applies to those readers who plan to submit papers to journals or write books. Skim or skip that section if you are not an aspiring academic. After dispensing with academic matters, I conclude the chapter with a template for keeping track of your reviewers' comments.

General Points about Reviews

If you are serious about writing, you will invest much of yourself in your work. You will want others to recognize your effort. You will take criticism personally. Should you?

Yes, take it personally. You should care. So cuddle your crushed ego, but do not think you are unique. Scream, cry, moan, swear, then look carefully at what the awful reviewer had to say. Save other emotional outbursts until after working hours. If you cannot make something useful from criticism, then you are in the wrong business. You cannot learn to write without getting criticism.

One of my former students sent me this in an email (I have changed the names).

Do you remember when I told you about Charlie, who didn't know how I handled the edits that you and Leslie would give us on our co-authored manuscripts? Charlie admired how

DOI: 10.4324/9781003167532-22

we would open a heavily edited document and see the comments as a chance to improve our work. In contrast, Charlie assumed mark-ups from faculty meant his work was terrible. I told this story to my writing-intensive class last fall and showed my students an example of a document you and I had gone over several times. I showed them a particularly marked-up page and said: "This is my life, every day. So when you see comments from me, it's not me being mean. I'm trying to give you things to think about and ways to improve." I think some of them felt better.

I will make five points about reviewers and their comments. First, useful criticism highlights deficiencies in your writing. It tells you that at least one reader is perplexed, unhappy, bored, or angry. Your job is to discover why and then devise a solution. Rarely is the answer to ignore the criticism. Most solutions are apparent, but for some, you will have to work hard.

My second point is to treat all reviewers as honest and their comments as useful, even when the reviewer's remarks reveal he is a jerk in need of professional therapy. You gain nothing from ignoring the jerk or replying with a retaliatory response. Instead, assume there are readers who could feel the same way. You need to prevent them from reacting like your reviewer. If the reviewer has misinterpreted your work, take this as a sign that you need to be clearer. If you have a disagreement that facts cannot resolve, then stand your ground. But try to understand the reviewer's point of view. Typically, you can address the dispute with additional thought and careful writing.

Shannon Linning and I submitted a paper to a journal and received reviews Goldilocks could appreciate. One reviewer loved the piece. Another thought it was useless. And the third's comments were somewhere in between. Our paper took a concept from pesticide testing and applied it to crime prevention. The negative reviewer seemed upset that we compared criminals to insects. That was not our intent. My initial reaction was that the reviewer was an oversensitive idiot. Shannon, being more sensible, found a way of preventing a repeat of this misinterpretation by adding a footnote in the final version.

My third point is that you should bend to the reviewers' criticism, up to where doing this runs afoul of *writing a true story, crediting your sources, and doing both clearly* (see Chapter 2 on Ethics). The reviewer might have a particular "fact" she feels you should include. Include it if it's true *and* relevant. If the reviewer wants you to cite some more sources, do so if they are relevant. Make sure you read them first. When I revise my work, I try to ensure my story stays clear. Sometimes addressing a simple comment requires massive changes to avoid muddling.

My fourth point is that even negative or strange comments can have unexpected value. Years ago, I received comments on a paper that I could not interpret. After wrestling with the vague suggestion, I guessed the reviewer's intent and revised the paper. In retrospect, that revision introduced one of the paper's most valuable insights. I have no idea if this is what the reviewer had in mind, but the reviewer's comments were useful.

My fifth point is to warn you about the downside of sweet clarity. If you write clearly, your reviewers can see more holes in your argument than if you wrote obscurely. You might conclude a reviewer has used your clarity against you. Still, do not take the careerist's solution: write gobbledygook to blunt critics. Instead, anticipate these criticisms and address them before sending your paper for review.

My last point is you should demonstrate to reviewers that you read, considered, and tried to respond to their comments. Often reviewers get a second crack at your work. They will be more accepting of your revisions if you show that you took their concerns seriously. Most reviewers try hard to help, so be gracious (even if you do not feel gracious).

These comments apply to addressing any remarks by gatekeepers. In the next two sections, I examine two specific types of reviews.

Reviews from Supervisors

Who are supervisors? For this section, they are anyone you report to and who has control over what you do at work. It's your boss and the boss's boss, and so forth. If you are in graduate school, it means your mentor, the head of your research team, or anyone for whom you are doing work.

I have been very fortunate to have worked for some brilliant, insightful, funny, and caring bosses. But some supervisors are stupid or worse. As the cliché goes, you can't cure stupid. So, in this section, I will assume you have a reasonably competent supervisor who takes you and your work seriously.

Start at the beginning. Someone in your chain of command came up with the idea that resulted in you getting a writing assignment. Before you started on this task, you and your supervisor should have agreed on several things:

- The content of your product. You need to understand the purpose of the document and the questions the document addresses.
- The deadlines for completing a reviewable draft and final product. Get clarity on this matter early. Meet the deadlines. If you cannot, then warn your supervisors early.
- The person or group who will receive the final product. Try to discover their expectations. Write it with this person or group in mind.
- The people who may read your product. You may have written the document for a committee serving the state commissioner of corrections, but they are not the only ones who might see it. Assume that your document will reach the public. Write it with this expectation.
- The formatting of the document. Organizations have images, and they like to package written products with a particular look. Know what this is early and make sure your review-able draft reflects this style.

If you take these things seriously while you are writing and editing, you will do your supervisors a big favor. You will do yourself one too. You will get less criticism.

It is quite likely, however, that your clear writing gives your supervisors new ideas. In which case, they may ask you to make revisions you did not expect. Although this will cause more work for you, it shows you have done your job well. They would not be asking new questions otherwise.

Sadly, once you finished your reviewable draft, the crisis that caused the demand for your work may have abated. Or a fresh crisis has superseded it. Or the person who wanted your report was transferred, retired, or fired. Your fine piece of work gets a perfunctory review on its way to the archive. You have my sympathies.

Here are five suggestions, based on lessons I learned from my supervisors and from being a supervisor.

Never give your boss a first draft. Never. If your supervisor demands to see the first draft, give her an early draft, but not the very first. The one exception to this is when you and your boss are co-writing the document. Then you can share any drafts (though still try to make your first draft somewhat less crappy before sharing).

You may get the urge to share an incomplete draft hoping your supervisor will fill in some blanks or fix something. Do not do this! If you have a job to write something, do the entire job. Do not ask your boss to do her job and your job. Talk with your boss, or others, about the tricky bits. Look for a solution. Then complete the document yourself. This advice applies to students giving writings to their instructors.

Do not hand over your draft and say, "There are a lot of deficiencies in this." Just say, "Here is my report. I look forward to your comments." As a supervisor, it's annoying. My feeling is that if you know it's deficient, then you should have fixed those deficiencies. Only give your supervisor a product with known defects if you both have agreed that she will review such a draft.

A Parable

Over 30 years ago, I heard a story about former US Secretary of State, Henry Kissinger (see Marsh, 2016). My wife heard a similar story in a different context. So it's probably apocryphal. I will retell it in a policing context.

A police chief asks a lieutenant to write a report on training to reduce racial bias. Before the report is due, the lieutenant returns with a draft. After a week, the police chief calls the lieutenant into his office. The report is on his desk. The chief asks, "Is this your best work?" The lieutenant says, "Chief, it's a good piece of work, but I cannot honestly claim it's my best work." "Then revise it," commands the chief. A week later, the lieutenant gives the chief the revised report, and in another week the chief calls the lieutenant back. The chief, pointing to the open report asks, "Is THIS your best work?" Embarrassed, the lieutenant admits, "Chief, there are some parts I am not happy with." "Revise it," says the chief, shoving the report across his desk. A week later, the lieutenant turns in his third revision. A week later, the chief requests the lieutenant's presence. "Lieutenant, is THIS your BEST work?" "YES, chief, it is," he replies. "Fine," says the chief, "NOW I will read it."

Moral: if it's not your best work, act as if it is. Even better, make it your best work before you hand it in.

Instead of giving some global deprecatory judgment of your work, say something like: "I am particularly interested in your comments on topics A, B, and C." Be specific. You are drawing your supervisor's attention to parts where you had to make judgment calls based on scant or absent evidence or contradictory opinions. They should not be weaknesses in your writing.

Do not expect your supervisor to edit your work. They are not a spell checker or grammar straightener. They should comment on your organization and your logic. They should tell you that passages are unclear, or unnecessarily inflammatory, or too weak. They should be able to tell you whether your product serves the purposes for which they commissioned it.

Thank your supervisors for their comments. And tell them you will attend to their suggestions, criticisms, and demands. Thank them even if you do not have thanks in your heart. At the end of this chapter, I have a template to help you carry out this promise.

Attempt to address all suggestions. All. Often, the changes are simple, even if time-consuming. Sometimes you will disagree with the requests. Have a conversation with your supervisor on the topic. Sometimes what you consider a conflict is not that big a deal to them. Sometimes they have suggestions for resolving the problem. And sometimes you will have to suck it up and follow their orders.

External Reviews

If you are an academic or striving to be one, external reviews are a part of your life. For those of you working in other organizations, this may be of some interest, too.

External reviewers are people, not in your organization, who examine your work and determine if your manuscript will be published. You seldom know who they are, and they seldom know who you are. These people include peer reviewers for journals and reviewers for publishing companies. If you are working for a consulting firm, the agency that contracted with your firm is an outside reviewer.

Exercise 17.1

Reexamine a piece of your writing that an instructor, supervisor, or external reviewer criticized. What parts of the criticism were helpful? What parts were not? Why? What could the reviewer have done differently that would have made the criticism useful? How will you provide advice to authors if you are a reviewer?

Mostly, external reviewers do not care about your feelings or your career. Unlike your supervisor, who is likely to kick your premature draft back to you and demand you rewrite it, journal editors or publishers may just tell you to go away. They do not have the patience of the police chief in the parable. Outside reviewers have not been waiting for your paper. They already have plenty of papers. You must demonstrate the merits of your work.

Therefore, submit your best work and make sure it fits the needs of the journal or publisher. Journals and publishers specialize in topics. They tell you what they are interested in on their websites. Study the publishing outlet carefully. Look at back issues of the journal and look at how the articles are formatted, organized, and written. Talk to authors who have recent experience with the journal, good and bad. All journals demand a specific format; follow it.

Reviewers and editors will not proofread your document. They will focus on your argument. The quality of their reviews is highly variable. Expect to be frustrated by irrelevant comments. You will not be alone, as illustrated by the remarks in the accompanying box.

A Crime Scholar on Peer Reviews

I asked a good friend to look at this chapter and point out gaps and errors. He gave me some great advice. He also said this (and permitted me to quote him).

> I hate reviewers. I find that they do not recognize important ideas. Instead, they focus on technical minutia. They also want you to write the article they want to write. So, my emotional response is to dislike. I externalize all blame. I see them as the enemy and only grudgingly admit that their comments improve what I have written.
>
> (Frank Cullen, PhD, University of Cincinnati. Former President of the American Society of Criminology. Co-winner of the 2022 Stockholm Prize in Criminology)

Academic journals do not make clear writing a priority. Theoretical relevance, completeness of literature discussion, data and analysis methods, and logic of conclusions are more important. So the rejection you receive may not be about writing but other things. Nevertheless, writing matters. Clear writing can help you show reviewers you have addressed their most pressing concerns. Unclear writing, writing filled with grammar and spelling errors, and writing containing numerous mistakes undermine your credibility. Reviewers may not expect perfection, but they do not like sloppiness.

For book publishers, look at books they have recently released. Talk to authors who have experience with the publisher. And talk to an acquisitions editor for the publisher. The editor will send you a set of requirements for submitting a proposal. Follow these instructions.

When you send your article to a journal, an editor will send it to reviewers. The reviewers send reports back to the editor. The editors will give you three types of judgments. Rarely will they tell you your paper or book is perfect and publish it. More frequently, they will give you a "revise and resubmit," or R & R. They will send you recommendations, suggestions, and demands with that judgment. It can be a short or long list. If there are multiple reviewers, their comments may be consistent, on different topics, or contradictory. Some are thoughtful, and some are useless. The last type of judgment is rejection. The reviewers may be unanimous in rejecting your paper or divided in their opinion. It's the editor who makes the decision. Given the number of papers submitted, journal editors are under no pressure to accept your paper. In any case, the editor will send you comments and explanations.

If the editor rejects your paper, you have two options. You can throw the paper away. Or, you can send it to another journal. Your choice will depend on the nature of the reviewers' comments. If you choose to send it to another journal, then revise the paper. Address the comments the reviewers gave you as if you were resubmitting the paper to the same journal. Why? First, there may be useful suggestions hidden in the negative remarks. Second, the pool of reviewers available to editors is small. There is a reasonable chance that the second journal's editor will select one of your original reviewers. Once, I had three different journals ask me to review the same paper, as the journals sequentially rejected it. Sadly, the authors made no changes based on my earlier reviews. My third review was the same as my first. In short, do not expect independent reviewers from different journals.

If you received an R & R, how should you respond to the editor and reviewers? Graciously and on time. Take every suggestion seriously, even those that seem useless. Ask yourself, why did the reviewer respond in this way? Then look for ways of addressing the point. I have had reviewers criticize papers even though I addressed their concerns. I revised my paper to make my original points more clear. Usually, reviewers raise issues I had not considered. Then I have to devise a plan to address their issues within the story I am trying to tell.

Addressing Reviewers' Comments and Commands

If you have a single reviewer and the comments are simple and few, you should have little trouble keeping track of them. If you have multiple reviewers and many comments, keeping track of them can be difficult. Your reviewers may not give you responses in any order. They may give overlapping comments. Their comments may conflict. To make sure you address all comments, use something like Table 17.1. I have invented some reviewer comments and responses to illustrate how I use this type of table.

Table 17.1 Tracking Reviewers' Comments

Page	Reviewer's Comment	Reviewer	How Handled	Explanation and Comments
1	The abstract contradicts the conclusion.	A	We rewrote the abstract to make it consistent with the conclusion.	Thank you.
4	Should cite Snotshotter's (1932) paper.	B	We did not cite Snotshotter, but revised the paragraph to avoid implying we were looking at Snotshotter's topic.	After examining Snotshotter's work we found it does not apply. But we understand why the reviewer thought it was applicable.
5	Third paragraph is extremely unclear.	A & B	We rewrote this paragraph.	Thank you for bringing this mistake to our attention.
10	Reverse the columns and rows in Table 3.	A	Rather than reverse columns and rows, we rewrote the paragraphs explaining the table.	Reviewer B stated that the table was clear, but had trouble with the text (see below).
10	Paragraphs 2 and 3 are poorly written.	B	See above.	See above.
...				
20	The findings can be applied to gerbil ranching.	B	We did not make changes.	Thank you for raising this fascinating implication, which we had not considered. As gerbils are not our topic—we are writing on correctional treatment—we decided not to address this valuable point.
All	Male gender pronouns are used exclusively.	A	We revised passages to be gender neutral. Where we could not, we varied the gender.	Thank you.

The first column shows the page in your manuscript that prompted the comment. In the second column, write an abstract of the comment; just enough to remind yourself of the concern. Identify the reviewer in the third column. In this example, I assume that the reviewers are anonymous, so I gave them labels.

List the comments in page order. Put comments that apply throughout the paper at the top or bottom of the list. When reviewers make similar comments, bundle them in one line. When reviewers give different comments on the same topic, either bundle them or put them on adjacent lines (as in this example).

Complete these three columns first, before you decide how to respond. The table is your master plan for your revisions.

In the fourth column, summarize what you did to address reviewers' comments. In the last column, summarize your reasons or give other remarks. You fill these two columns in as you make your revisions. This assures that you addressed all comments and have a good reason for your actions.

Reviewers may want a summary of how you handled comments, in addition to your revised manuscript. Your table provides a template for preparing the summary. Edit your table so that reviewers can understand it. Add "thank you" to particularly helpful comments. Even reviewers who gave poor reviews did some work that helped. So thank them.

Do not assume you will face only one review round. You may have to go through several review rounds with your gatekeepers, separated by you revising your document. This can be frustrating if gatekeepers bring up new criticisms they could have made in the first round. But your revisions may have raised new concerns. Treat the new set of reviews as you did the first set. Keep doing this until you receive a rejection or acceptance.

If your manuscript is accepted, whoever is publishing it will process it. You may have opportunities to check their editing. Then, one day, you see your writing in print. Take the time to celebrate. Congratulations, you are done with that writing project.

Part VI The End and Beginning

18 Future

The End of the Beginning

All nonfiction writing should tell the truth, have benefits, and possess clarity. I expect you to tell the truth. I assume your writing has use. After reading this book, I hope your writing becomes clear.

I wrote this book to steer you from bad writing and to help you teach yourself to write with sweet clarity so others will understand you. Since you are your first reader, clear writing helps you understand yourself. Clear writing generally reflects clear thought, while murky writing implies fuzzy thinking.

Start by making simple, clear, direct writing your habit. When is clear writing a habit? When you discover your first draft is mostly composed of short words in short active voice sentences. You have included examples and metaphors. That is when you realize sweet clarity has become a habit. Of course, you still want to rewrite, edit, and revise. I do not advise you to obsess over your first drafts. Allow yourself to throw things on the page. Focus on revisions. Dwelling on the beauty of your first draft just makes you anxious. It's the final draft that matters. As you practice revising and editing, you will gain habits of sweet clarity. Gradually your first drafts will improve.

DOI: 10.4324/9781003167532-24

Ten Commandments

As you near this book's end, I hope you have a better idea of how to proceed. In case you forgot, I'll repeat my ten commandments (aka defaults) of sweet clarity I issued in Chapter 1:

1. Write a true story, credit your sources, and do both clearly. These are your ethical obligations.
2. Writing is a craft, not an art. When my teachers first taught me how to write, they suggested writing implies art. Unless you want to write poetry or fiction, abandon this notion now. Get your points across so readers will recall what you meant. Once you master the craft of clear writing, consider art. But never let art obscure clarity.
3. Write for your reader. You're assisting them, not showing off. Consider your readers' range of interests and knowledge, skills, and abilities.
4. Keep things in order. You can order ideas by time, space, process, importance, or by other criteria. If the order is not obvious, you must impose order.
5. Use short common words. Eschew obfuscation in all discourse by applying diminutive vocabulary elements. Or, use short words to avoid muddling your ideas.
6. Use short sentences. Long sentences confuse you and your readers.
7. Use active voice. Passive voice is not to be used. Passive sentences have a role, but their roles are as minor characters, not as stars.
8. Use examples, metaphors, and exhibits. They help you make yourself clear and help readers understand complex ideas.
9. Revise, revise, revise. Keep your first draft to yourself. You will need to rework your drafts several times.
10. Embrace the messiness of writing. Writing oscillates between creativity and tedium, between satisfaction and doubt. Your final draft should be orderly and clear, even if you produce it using a disjointed process.

These commands are straightforward; carrying them out is not. Hence, my last command. Much of what you write will fail. That is my experience and that of most competent writers. You have to rewrite, edit, and revise.

Going Forward?

Once you consistently write with sweet clarity, work on the artsy stuff. I have emphasized the craft of writing rather than the art of writing to this point (see item 2). I have not completely ignored style. Instead, I have given style the cold shoulder. All writing has a style. I have emphasized a barebones style. With sweet clarity a habit, you can depart from maxim 2. You can consider the artful long word. You can create long, lyrical sentences. Give your writing cadence and character. But keep it clear; clarity is one command you must not break. Murky art is of no use to anyone.

Table 18.1 sketches the interaction of sweet clarity and art. If you are unclear and unartful (A), you are in the worst position. If you have something of value to say, you need to work to clarify your writing to move to cell B. But what if your writing falls into cell C? You have an artful style, but readers must spend considerable energy to understand your ideas, and no two readers agree on what you said. If you want to be an ethical writer of nonfiction, you still must progress to cell B. Once you have mastered B, then work toward achieving D. There, your readers will understand you, find your words compelling, and look forward to your next work.

Table 18.1 The Art of Writing with Sweet Clarity

	Unclear	Sweet Clarity
Unartful	**A.** Your writing is wasting everyone's time. Either give up writing, or learn to write with sweet clarity. If you choose the latter, go to cell B.	**B.** This is useful writing. You are socially productive. You can stop here if you choose. However, it would be good if you progressed to cell D.
Artful	**C.** You have become the victim of academic non-sense. Please stop. Either stop writing or learn to write with sweet clarity. If you choose the latter, go to cell B.	**D.** This is your long-term goal, but a goal you never achieve. You work to get better and better and better yet.

You cannot arrive at cell D without going through cell B. My intent, with this book, has been to show you how to get into cell B.

What do I mean by art or style? Consider a passage by the novelist James Baldwin, written in 1962. I clipped it from the middle of a long paragraph. It illustrates unifying clarity and art.

> My friends were now "downtown," busy, as they put it, "fighting the man." They began to care less about the way they looked, the way they dressed, the things they did; presently, one found them in twos and threes and fours, in a hallway, sharing a jug of wine or a bottle of whiskey, talking, cursing, fighting, sometimes weeping: lost, and unable to say what it was that oppressed them, except that they knew it was "the man"—the white man. And there seemed to be no way whatever to remove this cloud that stood between them and the sun, between them and love and life and power, between them and whatever it was that they wanted. One did not have to be very bright to realize how little one could do to change one's situation; one did not have to be abnormally sensitive to be worn down to a cutting edge by the incessant and gratuitous humiliation and danger one encountered every working day, all day long. The humiliation did not apply merely to working days, or workers; I was thirteen and was crossing Fifth Avenue on my way to the Forty-second Street library, and the cop in the middle of the street muttered as I passed him, "Why don't you niggers stay uptown where you belong?" When I was ten, and didn't look, certainly, any older, two policemen amused themselves with me by frisking me, making comic (and terrifying) speculations concerning my ancestry and probable sexual prowess, and, for good measure, leaving me flat on my back in one of Harlem's empty lots.

Using 265 words arranged in six long sentences, Baldwin explains his growing up in Harlem. Baldwin's passage has a Flesch-Kincaid grade level of 12.5 and no passive sentences. He uses concepts, such as "humiliation," with vivid examples. He has force. Most important, Baldwin has a style that is his alone.

You develop a style over time. I suspect style is not something you pick out, like clothing. Instead, style forms around your writing like skin. For example, I doubt you can say, "I want to write like Baldwin," and get a style. Instead, you read Baldwin and many others. You may practice writing like Baldwin. But in time, the style you develop is your style. Your style will be the outcome of your efforts to write clearly and effectively. It results from thousands of tiny experiments you conduct intentionally and intuitively. Most will fail. At the risk of being mystical, style finds you as you work. So just do your work and experiment with different ways to write clearly about truth and what is useful.

That is all very conceptual. What do you need to do in practice? There are five things you can do.

First, *read*. Read nonfiction authors of history, science, philosophy, politics, and anything else. Some of these authors may be historians or scientists, but most of the best will be professional writers. Read widely outside your field. You will see numerous styles and learn much that will help you in your area. As for most academic books and articles, read them for their information. Most will not help you write better (although some provide excellent lessons in how not to write).

Second, *read books on writing*. Read about writing nonfiction and fiction. Read books, articles, and blogs by journalists, columnists, and authors. Pay attention to their quirks, fancies, and peeves. Experiment with their advice. Many are humorous and fun.

Third, *write*. Practice writing whenever you can. Use the automated tools I have mentioned and any new ones that come along. Never treat these tools as if they have access to some holy repository of writing advice. They are just tools: not substitutes for your judgment. Find people who will read your work and will give you their suggestions. Pats on the back are nice but not helpful without challenging comments. If reviewers do not understand what you wrote, treat their comments as a challenge to clarify your work. Do not assume your readers are dumb, lazy, or out to lunch. Even if this assumption is true, you will always have dumb, lazy, and out to lunch readers that you need to reach. Rise to the challenge.

Fourth, *commit yourself to learn to write with sweet clarity*. Writing is not like a high-rise apartment building where you can rest once you reach the penthouse. There is always more to learn, skills to improve, challenges to breach. You can pause along the way to focus on other things or to give yourself a break from writing. But you must resume the climb.

Fifth, *work to improve your writing*. Do not strive for perfection. Strive for improvement. Robert Alexander Watson-Watt's quote at the beginning of this chapter is sound advice.

You are on your own now. Goodbye, and do your best with sweet clarity.

Exercise 18.1

- Create a plan to write something every day, and then follow it.
- Compile a list of well-written nonfiction books on complex topics that you will read this year. Then read them.
- Select at least one book on writing that you will read this year. Then read it.

FURTHER READING

The best way to learn to write with sweet clarity is to practice writing. Reading the works of clear writers is also important. In addition, you should examine what other experts have to say about the craft of writing. To help you start, I've made a list. Of all the books I have read on this subject, these are my favorites. I list the versions of the books I read: for some there are more recent editions. There are many good books on writing so do not restrict yourself to my list.

Read authors with different perspectives. Each of the authors of books listed below defines the writing process differently. Each has a different style of writing. Each emphasizes different features of the writing process. They have different backgrounds: journalism, science, law, humanities, advocacy, politics, and fiction. But they do have something in common. They pay attention to their readers and they are clear. Almost all have produced writing books that are fun to read because I prefer writers with a strong point of view and a sense of humor.

I divided my list into several groups: writing, thinking, reference, and figures.

Writing

With two exceptions, all of these books are about writing nonfiction. Some focus on academic writing and some on communicating with the general public.

Badgett, M.V. Lee. 2015. *The Public Professor: How to Use Your Research to Change the World.* New York: New York University Press.

Badgett's insightful book has a hyperbolic title. It's really about changing an itty-bitty part of the world, which is good enough for me. She covers a number of written and non-written means for getting your ideas to audiences who might act upon them. Rather than a book on writing specifically, Badgett is educating you on how to market your ideas.

Becker, Howard. 1986. *Writing for Social Scientists: How to Start and Finish Your Thesis, Book, or Article.* Chicago, IL: University of Chicago Press.

As Becker notes early in this book, the public knows sociologists are bad writers. Despite being a sociologist, Becker is both funny, clear, and full of insight. The most recent edition is similar to the original. Read whatever edition is most handy or least expensive.

Dean, Cornelia. 2009. *Am I Making Myself Clear? A Scientist's Guide to Talking to the Public.* Chicago, IL: University of Chicago Press.

This compact useful book makes a strong case for scientists talking to the public. It covers all sorts of writing and speaking, including radio, television, blogs, press interviews, editorial writing, and testifying as an expert. As a side benefit, it gives a nice description of how the news media works.

Dryer, Benjamin. 2020. *Dryer's English: An Utterly Correct Guide to Clarity and Style*. New York: Random House.

Dryer is vice president and executive managing editor and copy chief at Random House. He has produced a no-nonsense and witty book on grammar and syntax. If there is a replacement for Strunk and White's classic (below), this is it.

Eco, Umberto. 2015. *How to Write a Thesis*. Cambridge, MA: MIT Press.

Eco was an international literary scholar and writer of some great popular fiction, including *The Name of the Rose*. There are some limits to this book—it was written long before writers used computers, Eco wrote it for Italian graduate students, and his students studied literature. You can ignore all that and focus on the guidance Eco provides that applies to any academic writer. See if your library has a copy.

Farnsworth, Ward.
2012. *Farnsworth's Classical English Rhetoric*. Boston, MA: David R. Godine.
2016. *Farnsworth's Classical English Metaphor*. Boston, MA: David R. Godine.
2020. *Farnsworth's Classical English Style*. Boston, MA: David R. Godine.

These are the best books on the *art* of writing I have come across. In each, Farnsworth provides example after example of how writers have expressed their ideas with interesting sentences and paragraphs. Rather than tell you what not to do (as I have done often), Farnsworth provides examples to show you what you might be able to achieve. His examples show how you can violate the defaults I have prescribed to produce clear and memorable works. You can read these books in any order.

Flesch, Rudolf. 1979. *How to Write Plain English: A Book for Lawyers and Consumers*. New York: HarperCollins.

This is one of the first writing books I read and it may have had the biggest influence on how I write. It's out of print but worth finding. Flesch uses many examples of governmental regulations and shows how writers in agencies can write so that citizens can understand them. It also contains his formula for assessing the readability of your work that is useful. The Flesch-Kincaid Scale came from this. Flesch has several other great books.

Hall, Trish. 2019. *Writing to Persuade*. New York: Liveright.

Hall ran the *New York Times* op-ed page for years and is a journalist. This is a great book if you are interested in reaching readers outside your everyday circle of friends and coworkers.

Hart, Jack. 2011. *Storycraft: The Complete Guide to Writing Narrative Nonfiction*. Chicago, IL: University of Chicago Press.

The author is a former news editor and writing coach. His book focuses more on the structure of telling great nonfiction stories than any other book I have come across. His examples and advice will give you ideas for improving the structure of your work.

King, Stephen. 2000. *On Writing: A Memoir of the Craft*. New York: Scribner.

This is a book on fiction writing and memoir. It is useful and fun to read. I was surprised to see so many connections between fiction and nonfiction writing.

Lamott, Anne 1994. *Bird by Bird: Some Instructions on Writing and Life*. New York: Anchor.

Even if you never plan to write, you should read this if you like reading. Lamott is a brilliant writer and wickedly funny. Though she is discussing the writing of fiction and memoir, like Stephen King's book, much of her advice applies to nonfiction writing on non-personal topics.

McPhee, John. 2017. *Draft No. 4: On the Writing Process*. New York: Farrar, Straus and Giroux.

McPhee wrote for the *New Yorker*, often about geology, natural environments, and the people who study these things. His book is witty and demonstrates how a writer can handle complex topics eloquently. I particularly like his discussion of diagramming order.

Meyer, Herbert E. and Jill M. Meyer. 1986. *How to Write*. Washington, DC: Storm King Press.

I like this book for two reasons: it is very, very short and it is devoid of any pretensions that writing is some mysterious art project. On page 3, they say, "In fact, writing is less of an art than a process. And like any process, this one involves a series of decisions and steps that, when done in the correct order and with reasonable attention to detail, just about guarantees a decent and acceptable result." The first author is a business executive, and the other an English professor.

Olson, Randy. 2010. *Don't be Such a Scientist: Talking Substance in an Age of Style*. Washington, DC: Island Press.

Olson is a filmmaker and marine biologist. Olson argues that most academics do not know how to communicate to the public and much of their efforts are not just wasted, but counterproductive. He gives advice on how academics can continue to be true to the facts but market their ideas.

Pinker, Steven. 2014. *The Sense of Style: The Thinking Person's Guide to Writing in the 21st Century*. New York: Viking.

This is an advanced book on academic writing by a well-known psychologist and linguist. Much of it deals with the rules of grammar, many of which Pinker shows are not rules at all. It is a very good book if you want to dig into the linguistics of writing and understand many of the quirks of English.

Strunk, William and E.B. White. 2019. *The Elements of Style*, 4th edition. New York: Pearson.

This classic book on writing has influenced several generations of writers. Strunk was a professor of English and White was his student, *New Yorker* writer, and author of *Charlotte's Web* and other stories. Despite its age, it has excellent advice. Publishers have reissued it numerous times and almost all books on writing mention it.

Sword, Helen.
2012. *Stylish Academic Writing*. Cambridge, MA: Harvard University Press.

If you are a budding academic, then you must read this. She deflates the numerous myths that academic writing must be ponderous, stodgy, laden with heavy words, and dense with platitudes. She conducted research on academic writing across numerous disciplines to show that you can find vibrant and clear writing everywhere, if you look. In short, she proves academic writing can be lively, swift, direct, and compelling. If an academic asserts you must write heavy, viscous prose, whack them with Sword.

2016. *The Writer's Diet*, 2nd edition. Chicago, IL: University of Chicago Press.

The best book on academic writing available. Sword's book is short, practical, and fun. I assign it to my students. And her website is terrific.

Zerbubavel, Eviatar. 1999. *The Clockwork Muse: A Practical Guide to Writing Theses, Dissertations, and Books*. Cambridge, MA: Harvard University Press.

If you are undertaking a long writing project, something that will look like a dissertation or book, then follow Zerbubavel's advice about organizing your schedule and topic. This slim, useful book will help you make the daunting task in front of you appear less daunting.

Zinsser, William. 2016. *On Writing Well: The Classic Guide to Writing Nonfiction*. New York: Harper.

This *is* a real classic. I read an earlier version when I first became serious about writing. I reread Zinsser while preparing this book and his advice continues to be exceptional. His name may come at the end of the alphabet, but it is among the first writing books you should read.

Thinking

The core of professional writing is developing a useful argument, that is, thinking. Long before you write your first shitty draft, you have to be thinking about your topic. These books help you think. They are not just thought-provoking, they provide exercises for your mind and techniques to help you to see your topic from multiple angles.

Dennett, Daniel C. 2013. *Intuition Pumps and Other Tools for Thinking*. New York: W.W. Norton.

Dennett is a masterful thinker and philosopher who also writes well. The title of his book explains its content. There is so much here you should read it in chunks, not all in one gulp.

Jones, Morgan D. 1998. *The Thinker's Toolkit: 14 Powerful Techniques for Problem Solving*. New York: Three Rivers Press.

The author is a former CIA analyst and he draws on his experiences to help you investigate difficult problems involving incomplete information.

Roam, Dan. 2008. *The Back of the Napkin: Solving Problems and Selling Ideas with Pictures*. New York: Portfolio.

I bought this book on a whim in an airport. It's the only book I have ever bought in an airport that was worth much. Get a crayon, chalk, sharpie, or stick. Then apply it to napkins, scraps of paper, cardboard ripped from a box, or dirt. Draw a picture of your ideas. When you are done drawing, you will be closer to writing.

Weston, Anthony. 2009. *A Rulebook for Arguments*, 4th edition. Indianapolis, IN: Hackett.

This is another short gem. Making a good argument is how you tell stories with facts. Rather than focusing on the writing, Weston focuses on the structure of your argument.

Reference

There are numerous references books for writers such as dictionaries, thesauruses, grammars, and the like. The ones I have listed here are some I found to be useful and mostly delightful. None of these are a substitute for a good dictionary (not an online dictionary, but a real one that is so big you could drop it on a mouse with deadly consequences).

Freeman, Jan. 2009. *Ambrose Bierce's Write it Right: The Celebrated Language Peeves Deciphered, Appraised, and Annotated for 21st-Century Readers*. New York: Walker.

Like other books in this list, I discovered this one in a used book store. Bierce was a well-known satirist and writer of the late 19th century. This is one of his later books: a list of words he loathed and their approved substitutes. His commentaries are witty, mostly. Bierce makes you think more precisely about the correct use of words, even if you disagree with his opinion. The fact that Freeman resuscitated it about 100 years after its first publication points to the durability of Bierce's advice.

Garner, Bryan A. 2016. *Garner's Modern American Usage*, 4th edition. New York: Oxford University Press.

Several colleagues recommended it to me. I now have it within arm's reach and use it like a dictionary (which is also within arm's reach).

Gordon, Karen Elizabeth.

1983. *The Well-Tempered Sentence: A Punctuation Handbook for the Innocent, the Eager, and the Doomed*. New York: Ticknor & Fields.

Like her grammar book, *The Deluxe Transitive Vampire*, this concise reference book is fun and useful. Whenever I forget the purpose of a semi-colon or ellipses, I reach for this book.

1993. *The Deluxe Transitive Vampire: The Ultimate Handbook of Grammar for the Innocent, the Eager, and the Doomed*. New York: Pantheon.

A small enjoyable grammar book filled with good advice and very effective quirky examples. The illustrations are delightful. Who knew grammar could be so funny? I found it in a used book store.

Holder, R.W. 2007. *How Not to Say What You Mean: A Dictionary of Euphemisms*, 4th edition. New York: Oxford University Press.

Do you want to say something mean or insulting, but do not want to be direct? Do you want to refer to something embarrassing or cringe-worthy, but do not have the courage to say it plain? Well, this is the book for you. From addictions, to crime, to death, to sex, Holder has all manner of words to paper over plain and direct words. It is enjoyable to read, particularly if you do not want to use euphemisms.

Figures

The proliferation of web-based graphics and big data has resulted in the publication of many books on the topic. But there are good books on visual depiction of data that precede the internet. Here are several authors I particularly like.

Evergreen, Stephanie. 2020. *Effective Data Visualization: The Right Chart for the Right Data*, 2nd edition. Los Angeles, CA: Sage.

The beauty of this book is that Evergreen shows you how to make effective graphs using Excel. If your writing explains quantitative data, then this is a fantastic book. It pairs well with Knaflic's *Story Telling with Data*, 2015.

Healy, Kieran. 2019. *Data Visualization: A Practical Introduction*. Princeton, NJ: Princeton University Press.

This well-crafted book explains both the "why" of data visualization and the "how" of producing effective figures using the programing language, R.

Knaflic, Cole Nussbaumer.
2015. *Story Telling with Data: A Data Visualization Guide for Business Professionals*. Hoboken, NJ: Wiley.

I wish this book had been available when I first began writing with data. Knaflic has a flair for designing and explaining elegant graphs.

2020. *Story Telling with Data: Let's Practice!* Hoboken, NJ: Wiley.

In this book, Knaflic provides additional explanations and tutorials. I am not sure I would have liked it as much if I had not read her earlier book first.

Monmonier, Mark. 1996. *How to Lie with Maps*. Chicago, IL: University of Chicago Press.

This short book provides the basics for making your maps clear and useful. It contains many examples. For an expanded treatment of how to write with maps, read his *Mapping It Out: Expository Cartography for the Humanities and Social Sciences* (1993, University of Chicago Press).

Tufte, Edward.
1983. *Visual Display of Quantitative Information*. Cheshire, CT: Graphics Press.
1990. *Envisioning Information*. Cheshire, CT: Graphics Press.
1997. *Visual Explanations: Images and Quantities, Evidence and Narratives*. Cheshire, CT: Graphics Press.
2006. *Beautiful Evidence*. Cheshire, CT: Graphics Press.

Tufte is the master of how to use images to convey information and stories. His first book, *Visual Display*, opened my eyes to what could be done, and what should never be done, with graphics. The books are beautiful and a joy to hold, read, and ponder. If you can read only one of Tufte's elegant volumes, select *Visual Display*.

REFERENCES

Agnew, Robert. 2001. Building on the Foundation of General Strain Theory: Specifying the Types of Strain Most Likely to Lead to Crime and Delinquency. *Journal of Research in Crime and Delinquency*. 38(4): 319–361.

Anderson, Craig A. & Nicholas L. Carnagey. 2009. Causal Effects of Violent Sports Video Games on Aggression: Is It Competitiveness or Violent Content? *Journal of Experimental Social Psychology*. 45(4): 731–739.

Baldwin, James. 1962. Letter from a Region in My Mind. *New Yorker*. November 10. www.newyorker.com/magazine/1962/11/17/letter-from-a-region-in-my-mind. Accessed June 22, 2020.

Barak, Rich. 2020. Update: Shooting Suspect Killed at Naval Air Station Corpus. Atlanta Journal Constitution. May 22. www.ajc.com/news/breaking-active-shooter-prompts-lockdown-naval-air-station-corpus-christi/7E2fcvcRfOGFBF7maVVJ2L/. Accessed November 3, 2021.

Braga, Anthony A., Andrew A. Papachristos, & David M. Hureau. 2014. The Effects of Hot Spots Policing on Crime: An Updated Systematic Review and Meta-Analysis. *Justice Quarterly*. 31(4): 633–663.

Brantingham, Patricia L. & Paul J. Brantingham. 1981. Notes on the Geometry of Crime. In Paul J. Brantingham & Patricia L. Brantingham, eds. *Environmental Criminology*. Pp. 27–54. Prospect Heights, CA: Waveland.

Broutman, Larry. 2018. Chicago Gangsters: Enemies in Life, Neighbors in Death. *AGS Quarterly*. 42(2): 15–20.

Carr, Patrick J. 2003. The New Parochialism: The Implications of the Beltway Case for Arguments Concerning Informal Social Control. *American Journal of Sociology*. 108(6): 1249–1291.

Chesney-Lind, Meda. 1989. Girls' Crime and Woman's Place: Toward a Feminist Model of Female Delinquency. *Crime & Delinquency*. 35(1): 5–29.

Claessona, Andreas, Jonny Lindqvist, & Johan Herlitz. 2014. Cardiac Arrest Due to Drowning: Changes over Time and Factors of Importance for Survival. *Resuscitation*. 85(5): 644–648.

Clarke, Ronald V. 1999. *Hot Products: Understanding, Anticipating and Reducing Demand for Stolen Goods*. London: Home Office, Policing and Reducing Crime Unit.

Clarke, Ronald V. & John E. Eck. 2003. *Becoming a Problem-Solving Crime Analyst: In 55 Small Steps*. London: Jill Dando Institute of Crime Science.

Clarke, Ronald V. & John E. Eck. 2016. *Crime Analysis for Problem Solvers in 60 Small Steps*. Step 15. Washington, DC: U.S. Department of Justice, Office of Community Oriented Policing Services.

Clear, Todd R. 2011. A Private-Sector, Incentives-Based Model for Justice Reinvestment. *Criminology & Public Policy*. 10(3): 585–608.

Cleveland, William & Robert McGill. 1984. Graphical Perception: Theory, Experimentation, and Application to the Development of Graphical Methods. *Journal of the American Statistical Association*. 79(387): 531–554.

Coates, Ta-Nehisi. 2015. *Between the World and Me*. New York: Spiegel and Grau.

Cohen, G.A. 2002. Deeper into Bullshit. In Sarah Buss & Lee Overton, eds. *Contours of Agency: Essays on Themes from Harry Frankfurt*. Pp. 321–344. Cambridge, MA: MIT Press.

Cohen, Lawrence E. & Marcus Felson. 1979. Social Change and Crime Rate Trends: A Routine Activity Approach. *American Sociological Review*. 44(4): 588–608.

Corsaro, Nicholas, Daniel W. Gerard, Robin S. Engel, & John E. Eck. 2012. Not by Accident: An Analytical Approach to Traffic Crash Harm Reduction. *Journal of Criminal Justice*. 40(6): 502–514.

DeVries, Henry. 2018. Ernest Hemingway's "Write Drunk, Edit Sober" Great Marketing Advice. *Forbes*. December 11. www.forbes.com/sites/henrydevries/2018/12/11/ernest-hemingways-write-drunk-edit-sober-great-marketing-advice/#4ba40f396bb3. Accessed February 8, 2021.

Donovan, Joan. 2019. How Memes Got Weaponized: A Short History. *MIT Technology Review*. October 24. www.technologyreview.com/s/614572/political-war-memes-disinformation/ Accessed August 25, 2020.

Dreyer, Benjamin. 2020. *Dreyer's English: An Utterly Correct Guide to Clarity and Style*. New York: Random House.

Du Bois, William Edward Burghardt. 1903. *The Souls of Black Folk: Essays and Sketches*. Chicago, IL: A.C. McClurg & Co.

Duneier, Mitchell. 2016. *Ghetto: The Invention of a Place, the History of an Idea*. New York: Farrar, Straus and Giroux.

Eck, John E. 1979. *Managing Case Assignments: The Burglary Investigation Decision Model Replication*. Washington, DC: Police Executive Research Forum.

Eck, John E. 1984. *Using Research: A Primer for Law Enforcement Managers*. Washington, DC: Police Executive Research Forum.

Eck, John E. 2006. When Is a Bologna Sandwich Better Than Sex? A Defense of Small-N Case Study Evaluations. *Journal of Experimental Criminology*. 2(3): 345–362.

Eck, John E. 2014. *The Status of Collaborative Problem Solving and Community Problem-Oriented Policing in Cincinnati*. Cincinnati, OH: School of Criminal Justice, University of Cincinnati.

Eck, John E. & Ronald V. Clarke. 2003. Classifying Common Police Problems: A Routine Activity Approach. In M.J. Smith & D.B. Cornish, eds. *Theory for Practice in Situational Crime Prevention*. Vol. 16. Pp. 7–39. Monsey, NY: Criminal Justice Press.

Eck, John E. & William Spelman. 1987. *Problem-Solving: Problem-Oriented Policing in Newport News*. Washington, DC: Police Executive Research Forum.

Ellis, Andrew W. 2016. *Reading, Writing, and Dyslexia: A Cognitive Analysis*. New York: Routledge.

Espinosa, Erin. 2020. Research Points to Gender Inequities for Justice-Involved Youth. *Evident Change*. March 5. www.evidentchange.org/blog/research-points-gender-inequities-justice-involved-youth. Accessed February 5, 2021.

Felson, Marcus. 1986. Linking Criminal Choices, Routine Activities, Informal Control, and Criminal Outcomes. In Derek B. Cornish & Ronald V. Clarke, eds. *The Reasoning Criminal: Rational Choice Perspectives on Offending*. Pp. 119–128. New York: Springer-Verlag.

Felson, Marcus. 1995. Those Who Discourage Crime. In John E. Eck & David Weisburd, eds. *Crime and Place*. Pp. 53–66. Monsey, NY: Criminal Justice Press.

Flesch, Rudolf. 1948. A New Readability Yardstick. *Journal of Applied Psychology*. 32(3): 221–233.

Flesch, Rudolf. 1979. *How to Write Plain English: A Book for Lawyers and Consumers*. New York: Harper and Row.

Frankfurt, Harry. 2005. *On Bullshit*. Princeton, NJ: Princeton University Press.

Garland, David. 1996. The Limits of the Sovereign State: Strategies of Crime Control in Contemporary Society. *British Journal of Criminology*. 36(4): 445–471.

Government Accountability Office. 2018. Criminal Alien Statistics: Information on Incarcerations, Arrests, Convictions, Costs, and Removals. August 16. www.gao.gov/products/GAO-18-433. Accessed February 7, 2021.

Gray, Geoff. 2014. Weaponizing Psychology. *Counter Punch*. December 24. www.counterpunch.org/2014/12/24/weaponizing-psychology/. Accessed August 26, 2020.

Greenblatt, Stephen. 2011. *The Swerve: How the World Became Modern*. New York: Norton.

Greene, Jack R. & Ralph B. Taylor. 1988. Community-Based Policing and Foot Patrol: Issues of Theory and Evaluation. In Jack R. Greene & Stephen D. Mastrofski, eds. *Community Policing: Rhetoric or Reality*. Pp. 195-223. New York: Praeger.

Hadden, Kristie B., Latrina Y. Prince, Tina D. Moore, Laura P. James, Jennifer R. Holland, & Christopher R. Trudeau. 2017. Improving Readability of Informed Consents for Research at an Academic Medical Institution. *Journal of Clinical and Translational Science*. 1(6): 361-365.

Hall, Trish. 2019. *Writing to Persuade*. New York: Liveright.

Hassan, Carma, Dakin Andone, & Barbara Starr. 2020. Active Shooter at Naval Air Station Corpus Christi Has Been "Neutralized." *CNN*. May 21. www.cnn.com/2020/05/21/us/naval-air-station-corpus-christi-lockdown/index.html. Accessed May 21, 2020.

Hawley, Amos. 1986. *Human Ecology: A Theoretical Essay*. Chicago, IL: University of Chicago Press.

Heineman, Ben W. Jr. 2012. The Gallant Idealism of George McGovern. *The Atlantic*. October 21. www.theatlantic.com/politics/archive/2012/10/the-gallant-idealism-of-george-mcgovern/263909/. Accessed June 17, 2019.

Heritage Foundation. 2019. Crimes by Illegal Immigrants Widespread across U.S.–Sanctuaries Shouldn't Shield Them. April 3. www.heritage.org/crime-and-justice/commentary/crimes-illegal-immigrants-widespread-across-us-sanctuaries-shouldnt. Accessed February 7, 2021.

Higgins, George V. 1982. The *Rat on Fire*. New York: Random House.

Holborn, P.G., P.F. Nolana, & J. Golt. 2004. An Analysis of Fire Sizes, Fire Growth Rates and Times between Events Using Data from Fire Investigations. *Fire Safety Journal*. 39(6): 481-524.

Holder, R.W. 2007. *How Not to Say What You Mean: A Dictionary of Euphemisms*, 4th edition. New York: Oxford University Press.

Hyönä, Jukka & Richard K. Olsen. 1995. Eye Fixation Patterns among Dyslexic and Normal Readers: Effects of Word Length and Word Frequency. *Journal of Experimental Psychology: Learning, Memory, and Cognition*. 21(6): 1430-1440.

Jacobs, Jane. 1958. Downtown Is for People. *Fortune Magazine*. April. http://fortune.com/2011/09/18/downtown-is-for-people-fortune-classic-1958/ Accessed February 7, 2021.

Jacobs, Jane. 1961. *The Death and Life of Great American Cities*. New York: Vintage.

Jonson, Cheryl Lero, John E. Eck, & Francis T. Cullen. 2015. Putting a Price on Justice: How to Incentivize the Downsizing of Prison Populations. *Victims & Offenders*. 10(4): 452-476.

Kane, Thomas S. 2000. *The Oxford Essential Guide to Writing*. New York: Berkley.

Kelling, George. 2015. An Author's Brief History of an Idea. *Journal of Research in Crime and Delinquency*. 52(4): 626-629.

Kilpatrick, James J. 1984. *The Writer's Art*. New York: Andrew, McMeel, & Parker.

Kincaid, J. Peter, Robert P. Fishburne, Richard L. Rogers, & Brad S. Chissom. 1975. *Derivation of New Readability Formulas (Automated Readability Index, Fog Count, and Flesch Reading Ease Formula) for Navy Enlisted Personnel*. Research Branch Report 8-75. Chief of Naval Technical Training: Naval Air Station Memphis. https://apps.dtic.mil/dtic/tr/fulltext/u2/a006655.pdf

King, Stephen. 2000. *On Writing: A Memoir of the Craft*. New York: Scribner.

King, Stephen. 2017. *The Gunslinger*. New York: Scribner.

Kochel, Tammy R., David B. Wilson, & Stephen D. Mastrofski. 2011. Effect of Suspect Race on Officers' Arrest Decisions. *Criminology*. 49(2): 473-512.

Kulig, Teressa C. & Francis T. Cullen. 2017. Where Is Latisha's Law? Black Invisibility in the Social Construction of Victimhood. *Justice Quarterly*. 34(6): 978-1013.

Lakoff, George & Mark Johnson. 1980. *Metaphors We Live By*. Chicago, IL: University of Chicago Press.

Lamott, Anne. 1995. *Bird by Bird: Some Instructions on Writing and Life*. New York: Anchor.

Learning Network, The. 2011. Nov. 17, 1973. Nixon Declares "I Am Not a Crook." *The New York Times*. November 17. https://learning.blogs.nytimes.com/2011/11/17/nov-17-1973-nixon-decla res-i-am-not-a-crook/. Accessed June 17, 2019.

Ledwidge, Frank. 2011. *Losing Small Wars: British Military Failure in Iraq and Afghanistan*. New Haven, CT: Yale University Press.

Lee, YongJei, John E. Eck, & Nicolas Corsaro. 2016. Conclusions from the History of Research into the Effects of Police Force Size on Crime–1968 through 2013: An Historical Systematic Review. *Journal of Experimental Criminology*. 12(3): 431–451.

Lendrem, Ben Alexander Daniel, Dennis William Lendrem, Andy Gray, & John Dudley Isaacs. 2014. The Darwin Awards: Sex Differences in Idiotic Behaviour. *British Medical Journal*. 349(Dec): g7094.

Leslie, W.S., A. Urie, J. Hooper, & C.E. Morrison. 2000. Delay in Calling for Help during Myocardial Infarction: Reasons for the Delay and Subsequent Pattern of Accessing Care. *Heart*. 84(2): 137–141.

Light, Jennifer. 2009. *The Nature of Cities: Ecological Visions and the American Urban Professions, 1920–1960*. Baltimore, MD: Johns Hopkins University Press.

Lydon, Christopher. 1972. McGovern Impugns Nixon, Defends His Own Veracity. *New York Times*. October 3. www.nytimes.com/1972/10/03/archives/mcgovern-impugns-nixon-defends-his-own-veracity-mcgovern-defends.html. Accessed June 17, 2019.

Madensen, Tamara D. & John E. Eck. 2006. *Student Party Disturbances on College Campuses*. Problem-Oriented Guides for Police Series. No. 39. Washington, DC: Office of Community Oriented Policing Services, US Department of Justice.

Madensen, Tamara D. & John E. Eck. 2013. Crime Place and Place Management. In Pamela Wilcox & Francis Cullen, eds. *The Oxford Handbook of Crime Theory*. Pp. 554–578. New York: Oxford University Press.

Markay, Lachlan, Asawin Suebsaeng, & Lachlan Cartwright. 2020. MAGA Fan Peter Thiel Has Had It with Trump's COVID Response. *Daily Beast*. May 17. www.thedailybeast.com/billionaire-maga-fan-peter-thiel-has-had-it-with-trumps-covid-19-response. Accessed May 17, 2020.

Marsh, Rob. 2016. Your First Draft Isn't Good Enough. Neither Is Mine. *Brandstory*. January 14. www.brandstoryonline.com/your-first-draft-isnt-good-enough-neither-is-mine/. Accessed February 8, 2021.

McPhail, Clark. 1991. *The Myth of the Madding Crowd*. New York: Aldine.

Mohamed, A. Rafik & Erick D. Fritsvold. 2010. *Dorm Room Dealers: Drugs and the Privileges of Race and Class*. Boulder, CO: Lynne Rienner.

Montana Department of Transportation. n.d. Proactive Traffic Safety: Empowering Behaviors to Reach Our Shared Vision of Zero Deaths and Serious Injuries. www.mdt.mt.gov/research/projects/trafficsafety-cc-tools.shtml. Accessed October 29, 2019.

Nagin, Daniel & Raymond Paternoster. 2000. Population Heterogeneity and State Dependence: Future Research. *Journal of Quantitative Criminology*. 16(2): 117–144.

Oppenheimer, Daniel. 2006. Consequences of Erudite Vernacular Utilized Irrespective of Necessity: Problems with Using Long Words Needlessly. *Applied Cognitive Psychology*. 20(2): 139–156.

Pinker, Steven. 2011. *The Better Angels of Our Nature: Why Violence Has Declined*. New York: Penguin.

Pinker, Steven. 2014. *The Sense of Style: The Thinking Person's Guide to Writing in the 21st Century* . New York: Viking.

Rabin, Yale. 1989. Expulsive Zoning: The Inequitable Legacy of Euclid. In Charles M. Haar & Jerold S. Kayden, eds. *Zoning and the American Dream: Promises Still to Keep*. Pp. 101–121. Chicago, IL: Planners Press, American Planning Association.

Radford, Tim. 2011. A Manifesto for a Simple Scribe–My 25 Commandments for Journalists. *Guardian*. January 19. www.theguardian.com/science/blog/2011/jan/19/manifesto-simple-scribe-commandments-journalists. Accessed May 25, 2020.

Rayner, Keith & Susan A. Duffy. 1986. Lexical Complexity and Fixation Times in Reading: Effects of Word Frequency, Verb Complexity, and Lexical Ambiguity. *Memory and Cognition.* 14(3): 191-201.

Rello L., R. Baeza-Yates, & H. Saggion. 2013. The Impact of Lexical Simplification by Verbal Paraphrases for People with and without Dyslexia. In A. Gelbukh, ed. *Computational Linguistics and Intelligent Text Processing. CICLing 2013.* Pp. 501-512. Lecture Notes in Computer Science, vol. 7817. Heidelberg: Springer.

Russell, Emma K. & Bree Carlton. 2020. Counter-Carceral Acoustemologies: Sound, Permeability and Feminist Protest at the Prison Boundary. *Theoretical Criminology.* 24(2): 296-313.

Sampson, Rana, John E. Eck, & Jessica Dunham. 2009. Super Controllers and Crime Prevention: A Routine Activity Explanation of Crime Prevention Success and Failure. *Security Journal.* 23(1): 37-51.

Sampson, Robert J. 2012. *Great American City: Chicago and the Enduring Neighborhood Effect.* Chicago, IL: University of Chicago Press.

Scott, Michael S. 2005. Shifting and Sharing Police Responsibility to Address Public Safety Problems. In Nick Tilley, ed. *Handbook of Crime Prevention and Community Safety.* Pp. 385-409. New York: Routledge.

Shabazz, Rashad. 2015. *Spatializing Blackness: Architectures of Confinement and Black Masculinity.* Urbana, IL: University of Illinois Press.

Shannon, Claude E. & Warren Weaver. 1949. *The Mathematical Theory of Communication.* Urbana, IL: University of Illinois Press.

Shaw, Clifford R. & Henry D. McKay. 1967. *Juvenile Delinquency and Urban Areas: A Study of Rates of Delinquents in Relation to Differential Characteristics of Local Communities in American Cities.* Chicago, IL: University of Chicago Press.

Sherman, Lawrence W. 1990. Police Crackdowns: Initial and Residual Deterrence. In Michael Tonry & Norval Morris, eds. *Crime and Justice: A Review of Research.* Pp. 1-48. Chicago, IL: University of Chicago Press.

Shipman, Matt. 2013. *Four Ways to Open a Science Story.* March 9. www.scilogs.com/communication_breakdown/four-ways-to-open-a-story/. Accessed March 10, 2013.

Southern Poverty Law Center. 2017. Trump Is Lying about Immigrant Crime—and the Research Proves It. May 17. www.splcenter.org/news/2019/05/17/trump-lying-about-immigrant-crime-and-research-proves-it. Accessed February 7, 2021.

Spelman, William. 2013. Prisons and Crime, Backwards in High Heels. *Journal of Quantitative Criminology.* 29(4): 643-674.

Stephens, Martha. 2002. *The Treatment: The Story of Those Who Died in the Cincinnati Radiation Tests.* Durham, NC: Duke University Press Books.

Stolzenberg, Lisa & Stewart J. D'Alessio. 2008. Co-Offending and the Age-Crime Curve. *Journal of Research in Crime and Delinquency.* 45(1): 65-86.

Tilley, Elizabeth, Christoph Lüthi, Antoine Morel, Chris Zurbrügg, & Roland Schertenleib. 2008. *Compendium of Sanitation Systems and Technologies.* Dübendorf, Switzerland: Swiss Federal Institute of Aquatic Science and Technology.

Trounstine, Jessica. 2019. *Segregation by Design: Local Politics and Inequality in American Cities.* New York: Cambridge University Press.

Tufte, Edward R. 1983. *The Visual Display of Quantitative Information.* Cheshire, CT: Graphics Press.

Van Gelder, Jean-Louis. 2018. Hot Criminology or What Homer's Odyssea Can Teach Criminologists about Decision-Making. In Danielle M. Reynald & Benoit Leclerc, eds. *The Future of Rational Choice for Crime Prevention.* Pp. 31-49. New York: Routledge.

Wadsworth, Tim. 2010. Is Immigration Responsible for the Crime Drop? An Assessment of the Influence of Immigration on Changes in Violent Crime between 1990 and 2000. *Social Science Quarterly.* 99(2): 531-553.

Weisburd, David, Joshua C. Hinkle, Anthony A. Braga, & Alese Wooditch. 2015. Understanding the Mechanisms Underlying Broken Windows Policing: The Need for Evaluation Evidence. *Journal of Research in Crime and Delinquency.* 52(4): 589-608.

Wickman, Forrest. 2013. Who Really Said You Should "Kill Your Darlings?" *Slate*. October 18. https://slate.com/culture/2013/10/kill-your-darlings-writing-advice-what-writer-really-said-to-murder-your-babies.html. Accessed June 18, 2020.

Wilcox, Pamela & John E. Eck. 2011. Criminology of the Unpopular: Implications for Policy Aimed at Payday Lending Facilities. *Criminology & Public Policy*. 10(2): 473–482.

Wilson, James Q. & George L. Kelling. 1982. Broken Windows: The Police and Neighborhood Safety. *The Atlantic Monthly*. 249(3): 29-38.

Worden, S. Pete. 1992. On Self-Licking Ice Cream Cones. In Mark S. Giampapa & Jay A. Bookbinder, eds. Seventh Cambridge Workshop on Cool Stars, Stellar Systems, and the Sun. ASP Conference Series, Vol. 26. Pp. 599-603. San Francisco, CA: Astronomical Society of the Pacific.

INDEX

Note: Page numbers in *italic* refer to figures; page numbers in **bold** refer to tables.

80-20 rule 11

Abbey, Edward 33
abstract 128, 138
acronym 54, 56, 59
active voice 5, 12-13, 28, 46, 85, 91-96, 130, 202,
    219-220; *see also* passive voice
Adams, Douglas 39
adjectives 67, 78-80, 84, 202, 204; order of 79;
    see also word choice
adverbs 67, 78-80, 84, 204; *see also* word choice
Aiken, Howard 14
analogies 9, 13, 99-101, 108-111, 117-119, 121-122, 126
Association for Gravestone Studies 131
Ayivor, Israelmore 123

Badgett, M.V. Lee 224
bar charts *see* graphs
Becker, Howard 224
beginnings 13, 124-124, 132, 139; four ways
    to begin 135; parts of 138; *see also* endings;
    openings
Brady, Tom 7, 116
Brantingham, Patricia 118, 196
Brantingham, Paul 118, 196
Broken Windows theory 119, 121, 188, *189*
Buddha 123
Burgess, Ernest 118
Burnham, Daniel 184

Capone, Al 131, 135
Callahan, Harry *see* Dirty Harry
Chandler, Raymond 110

charts *see* graphs
CHEERS 111, 113, 115
cigar smoke 3, 7; *see also* Brady, T.
Clapton, Eric 91
Clarke, Ronald V. 59, 111-112, 161-162, 205
Clash 91
Clear, Todd 134-136
cliché 111, 120-121, 210
co-author 33-35, 37-38, 41, 46, 145, 154, 205, 208;
    consistent voice 36; final word 37; first author
    34-36; resolve differences 37; tasks 36
Coates, Ta-Nehisi 147
Cohen, G.A. 4
Cohen, Lawrence 188
Collins, Charles Allston. 3
Corey, Professor Irwin 49
Corgi 60, 91-92, 100, 109; *see also* passive voice
    detector
Corsaro, Nick 145
Covey, Stephen R. 138
crime triangle 187-188, 195
Cullen, Frank 213

Darwin, Charles 33, 127-128
Dean, Cornelia 225
defaults 10-11, 164, 220, 225
Dennett, Daniel C. 227
Devries, Henry 208
diagrams 50, 65, 166, 175, 184-191, 194-196, 198;
    drawing 61, 184-187, 189; flow charts 61, 185,
    190-191; coordination with text 196; layering 185,
    195-196; organization charts 192; path 188-189,
    191; simple 185, 187-188.

dimensions, fake *see* graphs
Dirty Harry 92
drop test 79, 83-84; *see also* tests for word usage
Dryer, Benjamin 225
Du Bois, W.E.B 131-132, 135
Duneier, Mitchell 132, 135
dyslexia 20

Eck, Emily *197*
Eco, Umberto 225
editing 28-29, 175, 201-207, 219; checklist 202,
    207; final word 37; four-sweep process 28, 202;
    helpers 45; tools for 206
elites 20
Ellison, Ralph 219
endings 123-124, 138-140, 143-148, 160; elements
    of 139-140, 143, 145-146, 148; looping 146-149;
    RADAR 140, 143, 148; three types of 143; *see also*
    beginnings
ethics 14, 17, 21-22, 70, 75, 209; credit sources 14,
    17-19, 22, 209, 220; tell the truth 17-18, 22, 219;
    three principles of 14; unclear writing 19-22
Evergreen, Stephanie 229
examples: anti- 111-112, 115, 121; counter 114-115, 121;
    hypothetical 13, 82, 111, 115-116; *see also* stories
executive summary 130

Farnsworth, Ward 225
Federal Trade Commission 86
Felson, Marcus 187
Few, Stephen 153
five questions 39; audience 20, 24-25, 39, 42-43,
    161; gatekeepers 28, 39, 43, 45, 207, 210, 215;
    purpose 39-41, 45-46, 53, 137, 161, 212; resources
    39, 43, 45; usefulness 41-42, 45-46
Flesch, Rudolph 7, 8, 19, 85-87, 225
Flesch's readability formulas 7-8, 19, 85-87, 89,
    225; compared **87**; Flesch-Kincaid Grade Level
    85-90, 100, 102, 129-130, 207, 225; Flesch
    Reading Ease 86-87
flow charts *see* diagrams
Frankfurt, Harry 4
Freeman, Jan 228

Garland, David 77, 78
Garner, Bryan 228
Gasset, Jose Ortega y 108
gatekeepers *see* five questions
Ginsburg, Ruth Bader 85

Gordon, Karen Elizabeth 228
Government Accountability Office (GAO) 125
graphs 13, 29, 83, 153, 165-170, 173, 175, 177, 181,
    183-190, 193, 196, 229; bad, ugly, and good 170;
    bar charts 166, 171, 177; fake dimensions 173, 175;
    how to select 169; hypothetical 185, 193; layers of
    167-168, 173; lumpy data 169-170; pie charts
    170-171, 173; smooth data 169, 177; time series
    179-181.

Hall, Trish 146, 225
Hart, Jack 50, 108, 225
Hartley, Marsden 72
Hawley, Amos 99-102, 118, 131
Healy, Kieran 229
Heller, Joseph 51
Hemmingway, Ernest 3, 201, 204
Herbert, Frank 138
Heritage Foundation 126
Herold, Tamara 191, 192
Higgins, George V. 119, 121
Holder, R.W. 228
Hooks 99, 123
human ecology 99, 101, 131; *see also* Hawley,
    Amos

Institutional Review Board (IRB) 21, 95

Jacobs, Jane 111, 132, 134, 135, 142
Jones, Morgan D. 227

Kelling, George 119
Kerouac, Jack 3, 67
Kilpatrick, James J. 80
Kincaid, J. Peter 19, 87
King, Stephen 9, 33, 67, 120, 130, 219, 226
Kissinger, Henry 211
Knaflic, Cole Nussbaumer 229
Knopfler, Mark 110

Lady Gaga 201
Lamott, Anne 9, 33, 226
Larson, Erik 97
layering *see* diagrams
layers *see* graphs
learning disabilities 70; *see also* dyslexia
Lee, YongJei 145
Light, Jennifer 118
Linning, Shannon 209

Márquez, Gabriel Garcia 65
McGovern, George 69
McKay, Henry D. *see* Shaw and McKay
McPhail, Clark 191
McPhee, John 33, 50, 226
metaphors 108-111, 119-123, 132, 134, 148, 205,
    219-220, 225; mixed 120-121; *see also* examples
Meyer, Herbert E. 226
Meyer, Jill M. 226
mission statement 39, 45-46, 136, 139-141
Moltke, General Helmuth von 66
Monmonier, Mark 229
Munger, Charlie 166

Nightingale, Florence 184
Nixon, Richard 69, 76

Olson, Randy 226
opening 123, 125, 130-131, 133, 135, 137-138, 147; first
    sentences 97-98, 100, 103-104, 123, 130, 132, 134;
    four ways to begin 135; overview 137-138, 140;
    problems and promises 136; stories 124, 132-133;
    titles 123, 125-127; *see also* beginnings
Oppenheimer, Daniel 68, 189
opposite test 80, 84; *see also* tests for word usage
order: adjectives 79; creating 63-64; difficulties of
    51-54; for readers 64-65; types of 54-63

paragraphs: connections 98-99; exclude irrelevant
    105-106; one idea 98-102; order within 102-104;
    structure 97; see *also* hooks
Park, Robert 99, 101, 118
passive voice 12-13, 28, 74, 85, 91-98, 204, 207,
    220; detector 91, 96, 206; examples of 91-92;
    see also active voice
picture test *see* tests for word usage
pie charts *see* graphs
Pinker, Steven 82, 142, 226
plagiarism 12, 17-19
Playfair, William 170
Princess Bride Disorder (PBD) 72, 83
problem-solving flow chart *61, 192; see also* SARA
    process

quagmire of confusion 113, 117-118
Quiller-Couch, Arthur 205

Rabin, Yale 136
RADAR *see* endings

Radford, Tim 123
readability *see* Flesch's readability formulas
reviewers 13, 29, 33, 43, 55, 207-210, 212-215, 222;
    addressing comments 209-210, 214-215; external
    13, 43, 212-214; five points 209-210; keeping
    track of comments 214-215; peer 13, 212-213;
    supervisors 13, 210-212; *see also* gatekeepers
Roam, Dan 227
Routine Activity Theory 187, *188*
Rowling, J.K. 205-206
RULE test *see* tests for word usage
Ryan, Meg 97

Sampson, Rana 112, 196
Sampson, Robert 132
SARA process 190-191
Saramago, Jose 49
Scaramucci, Anthony 121
Schweitzer, Albert 108
self-licking 118-119
Shane, Jon 5
Shannon, Claude 3, 9
Shaw and McKay 92-95
Sherman, Lawrence 193, 194
Shipman, Matt 135
similes 13, 110, 119-121
Southern Poverty Law Center 125
Spelman, Bill 134, 136, 187, 190
stages of writing 23-24; discover
    problem 24-25; draft 27-28; organize
    thoughts 26-27; prepare 25-26;
    revise and edit 28; stop 28-29
stories 113-115, 132-133, 225; in graphs 166, 229;
    see also examples
Strayed, Cheryl 166
Strunk, William 225, 226
substitution test *see* tests for word usage
sweet clarity: art 4, 8-12, 220-221, 225-226;
    ten commandments of 11-12, 220
Sword, Helen 226-227

tables: connecting to text 163-164; definition
    153-154; removing lines 155-157, 159; titles
    160-161; without numbers 161-163
tests for word usage: drop 79-80, 83-84; opposite
    80, 84; picture 84; RULE 77-78, 84; substitution
    84; VOTE 77, 84
time series chart *see* graphs
titles *see* openings and beginnings

Trillin, Calvin 130
Trounstine, Jessica 147
Truman, President Harry 110
Tufte, Edward 229
Tukey, John W. 184
Tversky, Amos 23, 25, 108

University of Cincinnati 88
University of Michigan 4

Van Gelder, Jean-Louis 133
VOTE test *see* tests for word usage

Warren, Elizabeth 153
Watson-Watt, Robert Alexander 219, 223
Weston, Anthony 227
Whistler, James McNeill 208
White, E.B. 225, 226

Wilde, Oscar 14, 67, 115
Wilson, August 85
Wilson, James Q. 71, 119
Wittgenstein, Ludwig 14
word choice: adjectives *see* adjectives; adverbs *see*
    adverbs; common 12, 67, 72-73, 77-78, 83-85,
    101, 124, 130, 220; euphemisms 67, 69, 76, 80-82,
    228; fad words 67, 73-75, 77, 84; gender 67,
    82-83, 116-117, 183; jargon 67, 73-77, 83-84, 156;
    precise words 67, 73-77, 79, 83; short words 8,
    12-13, 67-70, 96-97, 101, 219-220; silly words 67,
    77-78
Worden, Simon 118
Wright, Frank Lloyd 14

Zerbubavel, Eviatar 227
Zinsser, William 227
zombies *see* passive voice detector

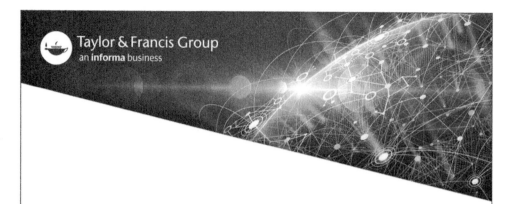

Printed in Great Britain
by Amazon

77244472R00147